GOVERNING

THE

UNIVERSITY

The Campus and the Public Interest

Leon D. Epstein

GOVERNING
THE
UNIVERSITY

Jossey-Bass Publishers
San Francisco · Washington · London · 1974

GOVERNING THE UNIVERSITY
The Campus and the Public Interest
by Leon D. Epstein

Copyright © 1974 by: Jossey-Bass, Inc., Publishers
615 Montgomery Street
San Francisco, California 94111
&
Jossey-Bass Limited
3 Henrietta Street
London WC2E 8LU

Library of Congress Catalogue Card Number LC 73-20967

International Standard Book Number ISBN 0-87589-215-9

Manufactured in the United States of America

JACKET DESIGN BY WILLI BAUM

FIRST EDITION

Code 7408

The Jossey-Bass
Series in Higher Education

Preface

I have been slow enough in completing this work so that a response originally to the campus crisis of the late 1960s has become a study of the persistent problems of governing universities. With the passage of time, my sense of detachment has increased. Although I draw upon experience as a college dean (from 1965 to 1969), as well as on longer faculty experience, I have tried to approach university government as a political scientist would any governmental subject. Other political scientists may be interested in this effort, explicitly noted in Chapter One, to treat the university as an institution within our sphere of inquiry. I hope, however, more generally to address the larger educational community, in and out of universities, that is actively engaged in governing universities or in thinking about governing them.

My principal subject matter is the state-supported multiversity, to use the term popularized by Clark Kerr, and I often cite the University of Wisconsin–Madison for illustrative purposes. In order to clarify the relevance of this knowledge base for the political conceptions of the remainder of the book, I devote Chapter Two to a description of those large, long-established state institutions that combine nationally prestigious research and graduate training with mass undergraduate teaching and many applied and service functions. At least two dozen campuses, among them Berkeley, Ann Arbor, Madison, and Urbana, clearly fit the type, and many more fit if *prestigious* is not defined too narrowly. Except for lesser national visibility and smaller-scale research and graduate training, one or two institutions in almost every state can be called multiversities. Nor is this kind of institution entirely different from many other public educational institutions; four-year colleges and newly developing universities have similar if not precisely the same relationships to state governmental authority. Historical differences are diminishing as many four-year colleges achieve university status and as state governments increasingly standardize their treatment of public institutions of higher education. The prestige state university is often a model, despite its complexity, for other state collegiate institutions. Indeed, the case can be made that the prestige state university is *the* American model of higher education in the late twentieth century. How it is governed, especially in relation to public authority, may well influence the pattern even for private colleges and universities as they seek more and more governmental financial support. The line between the public and private sectors of higher education is perishable.

Readers familiar with private institutions, as well as those familiar with public institutions different in kind from my primary subject matter, will know best how well or how badly my observations fit their situations. Similar judgments may also be made by readers at prestige state universities significantly distinguishable from the Madison campus of the University of Wisconsin. I draw many examples and judgments from this one institution, which I have known over three decades as a student, teacher, and administrator. But I do so in order to generalize about university government and not for the purpose of discussing Wisconsin in particular. Accordingly, where I cite any distinctive Wisconsin conditions, I try to say so. More often, I believe, the Wisconsin experience applies to other institutions. On straightforward matters like enrollment statistics or legal relations with state governments, it is usually plain, from various institutional studies, what is typical or general in the universe of higher education. In more intimate affairs, such as the actual departmental power of faculty members, I compare mainly less systematically gathered information with what I know about Wisconsin. I have read national surveys and several institutional reports, talked with participants at other places, and collected diverse impressions from visiting various colleges and universities. Altogether I have some confidence about the extent to which the Madison campus, itself a multiversity of 35,000 students within a larger state system, provides generalizable experience for the development of a conceptual framework for governing a university.

Many acknowledgments are in order. In addition to the debt I owe generally to the University of Wisconsin and particularly to its Graduate Research Committee for salary subsidy, I am also grateful for financial support from the Rockefeller Foundation, which enabled me to begin my study in 1969, and from the Center for Advanced Study in the Behavioral Sciences, whose fellowship in 1970–71 provided ideal circumstances for detached research, thinking, and writing. The staff of the Center more than fulfilled its well-deserved reputation for helpfulness. So did the Wisconsin Survey Research Laboratory and other Madison staff members. Among many academic colleagues for whose critical counsel I am thankful, David Adamany, Bernard Cohen, Austin Ranney, Ira Sharkansky, and JB Lon Hefferlin read and commented upon the entire first draft of the book. I am doubly thankful to Shirley Galewitz Epstein for reading and criticizing both the first and the revised drafts. In addition, I had the benefit of comments on particular chapters by David Fellman, Jack Barbash, and Erwin Steinberg. I should also thank, although anonymously, the numerous colleagues who reacted to my earlier efforts to treat the same subject, in "State Authority and State Universities" (*Daedalus,* Summer 1970, *99,* 700–712)` and more fully in "The State University: Who Governs?" a paper presented at the 1970 annual meeting of the American Political Science Association. Finally, I acknowledge the stimulation of students in two undergraduate seminars on university government.

Madison, Wisconsin LEON D. EPSTEIN
January 1974

Contents

xiii

GOVERNING

THE

UNIVERSITY

The Campus and the Public Interest

ONE

~~~~~~~~~~~~~~~~~~~~~~~~~~~~~~~~

Political Inquiry and the University

~~~~~~~~~~~~~~~~~~~~~~~~~~~~~~~~

Adding to the already substantial literature on universities may require an explanation. Mine rests on the hope that a political scientist's mode of inquiry, applied against a background of recent experience, will raise new questions or at least state old questions in new ways. While an effort of this kind is not unique, it belongs to a fairly limited body of literature within the much larger field of higher education. Moreover, my frame of reference differs from that in many studies in that I have tried to join internal and external university government as subjects of analysis. They have commonly been separated. Intrainstitutional authority has been studied by one set of specialists, and state authority by another set. But at what point is a multicampus government an external rather than an internal authority as far as a given campus is concerned? Is a board of regents, whether for a single

1

campus or a multicampus university, intrainstitutional in character, or is it primarily an agency of the external state government? The analytical difficulty is only one reason for discarding the concept of separate internal and external subject matter. Neither kind of authority can sensibly be treated apart from the other. Whatever powers are held by external agencies must relate to those held within the university, and so must internal authority relate to outside powers. "Relating" means impinging, influencing, limiting, affecting, allowing, and perhaps determining. The state university is not an island entirely cut off from the political mainland of state affairs. Nor is it at all likely to be cut off. Even "faculty government" in a state university is really state government in the sense that its authority derives from the state.

Defined in this way, so as to bring together the external and internal authorities, the problem of governing the university began to demand scholarly analysis during the last decade, when universities emerged as major arenas of public controversy (Kammerer, 1969). Before that time, studies were confined mainly to the public administration subfield of political science; concern tended to be focused (often usefully) on either internal management problems or external authorities (Corson, 1960; Millett, 1962; Moos and Rourke, 1959). Otherwise, political scientists usually left the study of universities to educational specialists—as though the subject, especially in its internal aspects, were not political at all. Only recently has the university itself become the subject for much consciously political inquiry. Among the several works along this line, the best known is Baldridge's *Power and Conflict in the University* (1971), where a political-process model is used to study a particular university's decision making. Significantly, Baldridge writes as a sociologist rather than as a political scientist, and he draws on his discipline's considerable theorizing for models and concepts. The same or similar theorizing is certainly available to political scientists, and some have in fact made use of it. Yet most of us remain more comfortable with a conventional political science whose concepts derive almost exclusively from the study of formal governmental institutions. These are the concepts that I attempt to adapt to the study of university government. I do so in the belief that the university is as properly a governmental subject as are the more obviously political agencies, and that therefore the customary vocabulary of political science, no less than that of sociology, provides useful tools for analysis.

The earlier scholarly neglect deserves examination; but since the reasons for it tell us more about the field of political science than about universities, this is not the place for extensive comment. It is enough to note that political scientists did not find the subject dramatically compelling (before the protest years) or publicly "governmental" in the manner of the usually studied legislatures, executives, courts, and civil service bureaucracies. Nor did political scientists perceive universities as they did parties and major interest groups directly impinging on the formal government agencies. Tacitly, it was assumed that the university, like the business corporation, was private—as indeed it had been predominantly during most of American history—and that internal university affairs, even in a state institution, were private matters to be sharply separated from whatever was political about state control.

Probably professors in general, not just political scientists, are reluctant to conceive faculty decision making as a properly political subject. In seeking, not without good reason, to maintain the academic character of such decision making, they may overlook the fact that power is being exercised. Studying one's own power is no more natural in universities than anywhere else. To emphasize that all university decision making, in and out of the institution itself, should be treated as a subject of ordinary political inquiry, I use the plain word *government* instead of *governance,* favored by the best-known contemporary studies (Assembly on University Goals and Governance, 1971; Carnegie Commission, 1973). Probably those who speak of "university governance" are not trying to depoliticize the subject, but only to emphasize their concern with a method or system of government. While sharing that concern, I remain attached to government as the term for the exercise of power in any political unit.

A more important terminological matter is the treatment of the university as public rather than private government. It is true that private associations—trade unions and business corporations no less than colleges—can properly and usefully be regarded as subjects of political inquiry (McConnell, 1958; Bachrach, 1967, pp. 95–103; Lakoff, 1973). On that basis, much of my method of study

might apply even to educational institutions completely supported
by private citizens, if any such institutions now exist. But I should
not be able, in those cases, to assume a public interest in their policy
making. Precisely this point is at the heart of my analysis. For the
state university, the public interest is or should be plain. It is not a
purely voluntary association, although its students attend more or
less voluntarily. Its taxpayer support is decidedly unvoluntary, and
its rules and regulations represent state authority. In these respects,
no doubt, the state university differs from the conventionally private
university, even one that receives substantial government funds. But
the status of the private university may not persist in the face of an
increasing need for regular tax subsidies. Because I thus expect the
public stake and so the public interest to become more extensive in
American higher education, it seems reasonable to regard the subject
as essentially nonprivate in character. This approach is also con-
sonant with the general tendency, in our large and power-holding
institutions, for the distinction between public and private to break
down. It is hard to perceive General Motors, American Telephone
and Telegraph, and the Ford Foundation as very private affairs,
just as it is hard so to perceive Harvard, Stanford, or MIT (Waldo,
1970).

Recognizing the university's public character, at least when
it becomes largely tax-supported, is threatening not only to the private institutions that seek government funds but also to the established state institutions whose faculties, in particular, often regard
themselves as quasi-private associations after the older models of
Harvard and Yale. To admit the public nature of academic policy
making seems to remove a barrier against ill-intentioned external
control. The possibility of such unwelcome control certainly exists,
but it is doubtful whether the claimed private association would
ever deter a governmental authority representing citizens whose
taxes support the association. In a public institution, or in an institution becoming public, the much more tenable argument against external interference with academic policy making is that the subject
matter requires specialized professional judgment. In this argument,
the internal policy making, however specialized and professional,
remains accountable to public authority in a way that the idea of
private association excludes.

This accountability anticipates a principal theme of the book: the need to reconcile the claims of academic self-government with the demands of a public service. If these claims and demands seemed almost irreconcilable in certain recent years, it is well to recall that the American state university was governed with evident success over a century or so of its massive development. "Success" then meant stability, the usual standard for measuring the success of any political regime, and the absence of any serious challenge to the legitimacy of authority. Without consciously spelling out the bases for its authority, the established university regime endured while its structure was only modified from time to time to serve new purposes and enormous growth. Different authorities came to exercise responsibility for different functions, but no general pattern of dividing and fixing responsibility was set forth. Thus, when its authority was finally challenged in the late 1960s, the university did not appear as a whole to be governed at all. In most respects that still seems to be the case. There are overlapping spheres of authority—those of the legislature, the governor, the higher education council, the regents, the administrators, the faculty, and the students. And some functions fall between the cracks. There may be a hierarchy, or more than one, but its authority is far from being coextensive with government of the institution. Faculty authority, partly collegial and partly individual, is clearly nonhierarchical and independent in many areas of responsibility. Certain university functions, notably in institutes, are virtually autonomous except for strictly physical management.

So presented, university government is bound to remind the political science student of the late Morton Grodzins' brilliantly apt description of American federalism: "the marble cake of American government" (1963, pp. 1–3). In Grodzins' view, national, state, and local governments are not three distinct and separate levels of authority, as in a layer cake, but rather mixed and intertwined, as in the unstratified marble cake. University government, however, may not be structured even to the extent suggested by the Grodzins metaphor. To pursue the culinary image, the likelier product is a thousand-island dressing. The university has many islands of authority, of different shape and size, scattered through a fluid substance without precise boundaries of its own or of any areas within it. It is truly diverse and confusing. Yet with this structure American higher education achieved the combination of quality and quantity represented by the prestige state university.

An ill-defined arrangement, no matter how chaotic and confused in its distribution of authority, apparently served the university well enough until the middle and late 1960s. Earlier significant disputes between state and internal university authorities had ordinarily involved neither sustained nor fundamental challenges to the consensual basis for the multiplicity of spheres and of authorities. In the middle and late 1960s, however, the liberal and laissez-faire character of the university was attacked as illegitimate, by the political left and the political right, from inside and outside the university community. Previously inactive participants, particularly but not only students, challenged the legitimacy of whatever authorities were once taken for granted. Newly controversial issues, like defense-related research, raised questions about what university policy should be and about who should make the policy—some authority representing the institution as a whole (including students), an external public authority, or (as had usually been the case) individual professors directly concerned with the subject? In other matters, too, the old laissez-faire order came to be questioned. Representatives of the general public as well as students asked, and surely continue to ask, whether professorial drives toward specialized research should not be limited by some authority devoted to undergraduate teaching.

The university is peculiarly vulnerable to an erosion of the legitimacy of its authority once erosion begins. Observance of order and compliance with norms, by staff as by students, is largely voluntary, habitual, and individual. Once the tacit consensus of de facto pluralism is shattered, there turns out to be no concept of authority on which the university community, not to mention its external public, can agree. Instead, sharply conflicting theories are advanced for state university government. The circumstances suggest that we are in a transitional period, between an old set of authorities and a still unsettled future. That future is unlikely to be cast wholly in terms of any one of the now conflicting conceptions, but an analysis of the several conceptual possibilities helps in understanding the choices and the difficulties of achieving a new consensus. Accordingly, after the next descriptive chapter, I devote successive chapters to each of the following governing conceptions: state agency, trusteeship, managerialism, professorialism, collective bargaining, individual consumer sovereignty, and organized student power. Finally, having in mind each set of assertions, I conclude by restating a pluralist conception that seems appropriate for the kind of university that we have and that, I believe, we should maintain.

The conceptions, including the pluralist conclusion, are ways of thinking about university government in theoretical terms. They may serve as analytical models, and I use them in this way insofar as I describe and question existing processes. But the conceptions are also treated as ideas about how governing power should be structured. To this extent, they are normative propositions. Each conception has a philosophical or an ideological support, which I shall try to clarify and criticize. The ideology may be populist or elitist, hierarchical or collegial, representational or participatory, collectivist or individual. At the same time, organized or unorganized interests are always involved, and these need to be identified and understood. The validity of each conception has a good deal to do with the nature of these interests. Examining each conception should tell us something, in the language of political science, about the legitimacy of the various claims to governing power in university affairs.

Organizing the work along the lines of the several conceptions of government fits only partially the several constituencies or sets of interests with claims to university policy-making power. Each conception does have its champions mainly in a given constituency —for example, the state-agency conception among elected and appointed state officials, professorialism in the established faculty, and organized student power among students. And, to a large extent, each conception reflects the interests of a constituency and the ways in which its members pursue their interests within the university. But a conception may be identified with more than one constituency; for example, state agency or trusteeship serves students and the general public. In other words, constituencies may form alliances in pursuit of their interests. Or, looked at from another angle, a constituency may find it useful to adopt more than one conception, perhaps even at the same time but for different purposes. Professorial use of faculty government and of collective bargaining will appear a case in point.

This kind of overlapping means that there would be at least as much difficulty about an analytical organization around constituencies or interest groups. At any rate, the presentation under conceptual headings implies no neglect of the various claimants or of their various purposes. They surely produce the conflicting conceptions of university government. When they do so in such a way as to be irreconcilable with other claimants and their purposes, I shall try to make this clear. It follows from my assumptions that there are many legitimate claimants and purposes, and that the task of governing a university is to provide a means for their effective expression.

The most difficult part of this task, as this introductory chapter suggests, is to allow public input without destroying the advantages of academic self-government. Throughout the book, I shall stress both the reality and the significance of the public interest in the state university. I do so in spite of all the good reasons there are for doubting the wisdom of many arrangements, existing and proposed, for expressing that interest through state governing devices. Whatever the doubt, those of us in the university community must come to grips with the right as well as the power of citizen representatives to insist on a general role in determining the use of tax resources for higher education. The university does not belong only to the faculty, or even to the faculty and students together. We can admit this much without subscribing to the view that the state should manage the university exactly as it does any of its other services. Higher education is a very special public service. But it is public enough so that its government ought to be contemplated as a political problem.

TWO

The Academic Situation

I n pursuing the political scientist's custom of describing what is to be governed before analyzing governmental problems themselves, I concentrate here on the academic situation of the prestige state university. Because I am concerned not just with its distinctiveness but also with its similarities to other educational institutions, I first relate the prestige state university to the larger universe of American higher education. Second, I describe internal university development. Finally, I summarize by emphasizing the governmental problems posed by a university's multiplicity of functions.

The Universe of Higher Education

The magnitude of the total American enterprise in higher education is familiar. It is enough to be reminded that in 1972, according to the U.S. Office of Education, there were more than nine million college and university students—an enrollment of about 35 to 40 percent of the nation's eighteen to twenty-one year olds. Despite a decline in the proportion of this age cohort, from a peak in the 1960s (U.S. Bureau of the Census, 1973), the absolute numbers attending colleges and universities were continuing to increase during the 1970s. Even the most conservative projections, based on recent cohort percentage data and declining birth rates, leave American higher education with roughly its present massive enrollments for the next generation. This scale of the enterprise is very much a product of the 1960s, when total college and university enrollments more than doubled and when graduate enrollments increased even faster, reaching 850,000 by 1970. At the end of the 1960s there were about 500,000 college and university teachers, not including part-time teaching assistants (Trow, 1972, p. 2). These figures pertain only to higher education as usually defined: approximately 2500 colleges and universities, including community or junior colleges but excluding private trade and technical schools, apprenticeship programs, and correspondence schools.

Equally familiar and important is that the new massive enrollment is mainly in the public sector of higher education. Private institutions also increased their enrollments, in fact tripling their total from 1940 to 1970. But public institutions have grown so much faster that—instead of enrolling only half of all college and university students, as they had in 1940—they now enroll about three quarters (or over two thirds even when the proportion is of a total excluding two-year college students). There is every indication that the trend will continue, although at a more modest rate. Private institutions still lead one race in the numbers game. There are more of them. Of the total of 2500 institutions, about 58 percent, compared to 66 percent twenty years earlier, are private (West and Andersen, 1970; Berdahl, 1970). There are many small private colleges—some very small. Most of them, while often expanding generously by their own traditional standards, retain their characteristic smallness relative to state institutions.

Of greater concern here is what happened in the public sector. It has grown only partly by adding new institutions, chiefly two-year colleges. More striking is the growth through increasing the size of existing public institutions, often at existing campuses as well as at geographically removed branches. This is a more notable characteristic of the last two decades of American higher educational expansion than the simultaneous creation of new institutions, important though they may be for the future. What happened chiefly in the 1960s was that certain state universities, often already at the 10,000 to 15,000 level, quickly doubled in size; and others, a little smaller at the takeoff point, more than doubled their enrollments in about fifteen years. Overall limits were set for some individual campuses, but rarely below the 25,000 to 30,000 level, and they were often accompanied by expansion of the university as a multicampus entity. In contrast, the British rigorously limited enrollment at established institutions but doubled the number of universities (Ashby and Anderson, 1970, p. 91). Similarly, in the elite portion of the American private sector—the Ivy League and its academic peers among private institutions west of the Alleghenies—the barriers to massive numbers were maintained in practice, since the occasional 10 to 20 percent increase in undergraduate enrollment usually meant only several hundred more students.

This large and rapid growth of particular institutions within the public sector was not, of course, forced upon unwilling universities. Individual faculty members had doubts, and so occasionally did alumni, students, and other citizens who saw virtues in the older, less crowded order of things. But, to be candid, most of us in administrative or faculty leadership roles during the 1960s favored considerable growth on a given campus. We would have liked it slower and steadier, tapering off eventually at a level fixed by sheer physical planning limits. And ideally we wished that we could add facilities and staff faster than we were adding students, but we well understood the budgetary necessity for the students if we were to have the facilities and staff for research and graduate training as well as for undergraduate teaching. Enrollment growth, at all levels, was one of the main means for achieving educational progress: new programs and new younger staff with new training and new ideas. There were advantages as well as disadvantages to growth and to the scale that came with it. Having 30,000 to 40,000 students need not be viewed as inherently unfortunate, even though the fact of such mass enrollment is one of the problems in governing the state university.

Mass enrollment distinguishes this kind of institution most

sharply from any private university of high prestige in research and graduate training, and in fact from almost all the leading private institutions famous for any kind of quality. They simply are not large by the standards of the great state universities. The most prestigious have fairly small enrollments, especially at the undergraduate level. Harvard has but 5000 undergraduates in a total of 14,000 students; Yale has 4000 of 8500; Stanford has 6000 of 12,000; Chicago has 2500 of 8000; Princeton has 3200 of 4700; and Columbia has 6000 of 17,000. In comparison, Minnesota has 37,000 undergraduates in a total of 44,000; Michigan has 20,000 of 33,000; Berkeley has 17,000 of 27,000; UCLA has 17,000 of 27,000; and Illinois has 21,000 of 29,000 (1966 data from Singletary, 1968). The graduate numbers, constituting most of the remainder in each case, are not so radically different, although even here the state university's numbers are generally higher. The undergraduate enrollments are simply on a different scale. Prestige private universities, like prestige private liberal arts colleges (Swarthmore, Amherst, Oberlin, Reed, and the rest), retain their traditionally small and selective undergraduate programs and are basically untouched by the thrust toward universal higher education. Only a small number of private institutions, especially those whose urban setting is associated with different traditions and reputations, have responded to the massive expansion of the 1960s on a scale approximating that of the major state universities.

Much more similar in their growth to the state universities are the institutions that began as state colleges or as state teachers' colleges. Formerly small and limited in the scope of their educational missions, many expanded even more rapidly than did the major state institutions, and they often achieved university status themselves. In each state they now take large shares of the undergraduates who cannot be absorbed even by the great expansion of the older university. Whether these colleges are brand-new campuses or remade teachers' colleges, whether independent units or branches of an old institution, and whether destined to remain almost entirely four-year colleges or to develop graduate and professional programs, there can be no doubt about their present and prospective significance in providing mass undergraduate higher education so as to resemble both the scale and the variety of the older state universities

(Sagen and Harcleroad, 1970; Woodring, 1968, chap. 4; Chambers, 1968, chap. 3). Even the two-year community colleges, insofar as they concentrate on liberal arts programs, are not entirely different in their missions. The similarities, at least among four-year institutions, are now so striking in the minds of government officials that they often seek to assimilate all of a state's higher educational institutions in a single system whose undergraduate programs can be treated according to common standards. But the adoption of common standards could—instead of converting new colleges to the older established pattern—threaten to make the prestige state university campus more like the newer institutions.

In resisting such leveling down, the prestige state university is formidable not only because of its quality but because of its size and accompanying political influence. In a medium-sized state the single older university campus may have one quarter of the total public school enrollment, and two such campuses in a larger state may be in approximately the same position. Taking the nation as a whole and counting only thirty in the select category, the prestige institutions have about 800,000 students of the 4,500,000 attending public four-year colleges and universities. The proportion is considerably larger if all of the old established university campuses of each state are added to those that are also prestigious in national rankings. Even this might understate the relative numbers, since it would exclude branches or new campuses that the older universities have developed in their own structures. Altogether, then, it must be evident that the state university, as we customarily understand it, is a most salient model even when it is part of a broader state system of higher education.

Its experience in trying to combine quality with quantity in undergraduate programs is a pattern that developing state institutions also seek to establish. With some exceptions, the prestige state universities have historically accepted high school graduates (from their respective states) without imposing a rigorous academic admission standard. Many students of limited intellectual ability, interest, and motivation have attended and often graduated. At the same time, a substantial minority of gifted undergraduate students have always been present. The university sought to serve them too, occasionally in separate programs but more usually through ad-

vanced learning accessible to all even if chosen by the few. It continued to try to do so during the rapid growth of the 1960s. The
large and rapid enrollment increases complicated the task, although
the increases seem to have been accompanied by a rise in the average ability of those attending the prestige state universities—partly
because these universities were able to raise their admission standards while the newer or developing state institutions absorbed
many of the enlarged numbers seeking higher education. There are
indications of better high school records and higher test scores for
the entering freshmen at prestige state universities during the 1960s,
but I doubt whether this change gave us a basically different undergraduate student body. At Madison, for instance, the academic ability of students of the 1960s seemed only a little higher, on the average, than that of the previous generation. The problem of teaching
masses of relatively unselected undergraduates along with a minority
of highly talented students remains much as it has always been.

Although its undergraduate situation resembles that of other
public institutions, the established state university has a special mission in research and graduate work. If other four-year colleges were
to emulate it on any large scale, such colleges would in effect be
transformed into major universities. To be sure, some have thus
transformed themselves; but now that the pressure to expand graduate training has given way to an apparent need to contract, there
can be few additional transformations. Even during the rapid expansion years, much of the growth in graduate training and research
took place at long-established universities, many of which had had
only limited graduate programs, often of high quality but so small
as to be almost peripheral in relation to large undergraduate programs. Their great development in the 1960s put an end to the nu-
merical dominance of private universities in producing Ph.D.s
(Hodgkinson, 1970, pp. 10–11). Nearly two thirds of American
Ph.Ds now come from public institutions.

Qualitatively, private institutions maintain their traditional
leadership at the graduate level. The nature of the competition is
clear from a recent survey of graduate faculty ratings by professors
in thirty-six academic disciplines (Roose and Andersen, 1970, pp.
10–11). Departments in private institutions, led by Harvard, held
most of the first-place rankings in their respective disciplines, and

they also held a majority of the first five rankings in most fields. Below this very high level but still in the category of "distinguished" or "strong," private university departments, it is true, had a much less striking lead. More to the point, however, is that especially since World War II, the leading state universities (Berkeley and Michigan most successfully, but increasing numbers in the 1960s) have competed with the highest-quality standards of the great private university faculties—matching high salaries, special professorial chairs, generally low teaching loads, quasi-autonomous research institutes, graduate student fellowships, and all the rest of the enormously expensive features of the best graduate and research programs. In the 1950s and 1960s financing such programs may have seemed no different in the two kinds of universities, since each had become heavily dependent on the federal government to support research, especially in the sciences. But the state universities, unlike their private competitors, also had the increasing responsibilities of an enlarged mass higher education. Budgetarily, although there is no inevitable conflict between the quality thrust in research and the maintenance of undergraduate teaching programs, some competition for funds occurred in fields lacking large-scale federal financing of research. Even without that difficulty, state universities were bound to suffer from a sheer physical shortage of staff and facilities to meet the double burden.

Combining quality at the most advanced levels with quantity at all levels is plainly a special challenge flowing from the otherwise unprecedented American effort to extend higher education to almost everyone. This double purpose, while not new in the 1960s for several of the older major institutions, became both more characteristic and more complicated as the scale of each task increased.

What else is distinctive about the state university? Compared again with the private institution, the prestige public institution, not to mention the less famous state college or university, charges its own state resident students a much lower tuition than they would pay at any even slightly prestigious private university or college and substantially less than they would pay at most nonprestigious private institutions. By the end of the 1960s the average yearly private tuition charge was nearly four and one half times as high as the average public tuition charge for state residents (Cartter, 1969, p. 162;

Mushkin, 1972, p. 169). A few 1973 examples will make the point in a different way. Berkeley was charging California residents $640 per year, and Ann Arbor was charging Michigan residents $696; Harvard's tuition was $3000 and Yale's was $3400. Or compare the University of Colorado's $600 with Denver's $2550, and the University of South Dakota's $500 with Augustana College's $2175. Only the nonresident tuition charges of some state universities were reaching the $2000 level, close to the range of many private colleges but not of the most prestigious private universities.

It is plain that state universities, if not as inexpensive as they once were, remain economically accessible for large numbers of students who would find private education, especially of similar status, out of reach without special scholarship subsidies. There are large additional costs for room and board everywhere; and so students, even at public institutions in their own states, ordinarily need financial help from their families, from loans and grants, or from their own earnings. Typically, therefore, state university students are neither disadvantaged nor affluent. Their education is subsidized only in substantial part, but not wholly, by the taxpayers.

For many of these students, as well as for the taxpaying community that helps support their education, the state university, like the state college, continues to emphasize career preparation. Administrators and faculty members, at both public and private universities, accept this as a difference between the two kinds of institutions (Gross, 1968, pp. 533–535). At a state university any desire from leisure-class students for more humanistic, nonutilitarian teaching programs must compete with the established demand for pragmatic studies. The result may be a belief that public institutions cannot be as experimental as private institutions, or even an argument that without private colleges and universities "certain major goads to innovation and differentiation would disappear" (Assembly on University Goals and Governance, 1971, p. 9).

It is hard in a democratic age to justify private institutions just because they are smaller, more selective, and more expensive per student. Only a few private colleges have experimented educationally in ways beyond the capacity of a state university, and these experiments have been expensive (Cremin, 1962, pp. 308–318). Many other private institutions have had sectarian religious environments, but these are becoming both less numerous and less rigorous in their distinctiveness. Increasingly the small colleges, often poorly financed, have to rest their case on the superiority of their limited size, contending that their sense of community provides educational as well as social advantages. They may be correct, but they are unpersuasive unless they are in the elite group of famous pace-setting institutions that maintain themselves in style and quality, including scholarship support for economically disadvantaged students. This requires a combination of large endowments, federal funds for special programs, and high tuition charges for their largely paying student clientele.

Altogether it is hard to generalize about private institutions. In many ways, as their champions have told us, they suffer from the competition of increasingly available public colleges and universities. Without greatly increased endowment income to match inflationary rises in cost and without more general government subsidy, they fear that they are being forced to raise tuition charges so as to price themselves out of the market. Yet by some measures the private sector has been thriving while meeting a smaller share of the demand for higher education. For example, between 1959–60 and 1965–66 private institutions increased their income per student twice as fast as did public institutions, and even increased their share of federal nonresearch aid more rapidly (Bolton, 1969, pp. 20–21). Similarly, for the whole decade of the 1960s Kerr compares private schools with public: "Their faculty salaries have risen faster, their expenditures per student are greater and have risen more rapidly, and their square footage of space per student is also larger and has increased more rapidly" (1970, p. 142). Finally, there is evidence of higher instructional costs per credit hour in private than in public colleges and universities; this evidence, however, is qualified by doubts about the comparability of private and public costs, especially because of a higher student-retention rate in private institutions (Carnegie Commission, 1971, pp. 66–67).

There is nothing, of course, inherently wrong with relative expensiveness, even of the kind that certainly exists in elite institutions. As long as private sources, be they generous benefactors or students and their wealthy parents, support these educational programs, no substantial public question seems to arise. We can overlook the indirect government subsidy implied by the tax advantages allowed to private educational institutions and to their contributors. But lately the privateness of financing private institutions has become much less completely characteristic. In this crucial area the private-public difference may be breaking down. Conventionally it was government support as well as government control, in some degree, that defined public as opposed to private institutions. There existed only a scattering of mixed cases, mainly residual from pre-public days. Now federal dollars have become available to private as well as state institutions, and in many forms for many purposes. Certain great private research universities have been largely converted into federal-grant institutions; Stanford, an extreme example, has received just under 65 percent of its annual income from the United States government (Cheit, 1971, p. 114). Moreover, the educational community, private and public, has been expecting more and broader federal financing in the future, although that future looks less promising now than a few years ago (Carnegie Commission, 1968, pp. 7–8).

A more significant although less massive blurring of the public-private financial distinction is the increased funding of private schools by state governments. These governments, accustomed not only to financing public colleges and universities but also to controlling them, would seem likelier than the federal government to assume an active policy-making role in what have been private institutional matters. Historically, it is true, there has been some state funding at private institutions. But—apart from very early days, when there was virtually no identifiably separate public institutions —such funding was ordinarily exceptional and partial, in the manner of New York's support for particular programs at Cornell (Becker, 1943, pp. 91–93). Now that pattern is becoming more widespread, as are other methods of state financing of private higher education (Carnegie Commission, 1971, pp. 87–91). New York itself, going beyond a now widely adopted state scholarship program for private as well as public college students, provides direct financial aid to private institutions (Palola, Lehmann, and Blischke, 1970, pp. 478–481). This aid for 1973–74 was estimated to be as high as $48,000,000 (*New York Times,* Feb. 27, 1973, p. 33)'. Voucher plans would similarly provide state financial support for general educational programs. Pennsylvania provides state funds in still other ways, some of which are accompanied by state controls. It has designated the formerly private Temple University and the University of Pittsburgh, along with the previously state-supported Pennsylvania State University, as "state-related" institutions; and the state plays a major role in their government. Drexel and the University of Pennsylvania, however, are financially aided by the state but still retain their almost completely private status (Berdahl, 1970). Even Wisconsin, with much stronger and well-defined traditions of publicly supported higher education, is financing a medical school that severed itself from a Catholic institution, Marquette University, in order to become constitutionally eligible for state aid. The medical school retains a largely private board with state representatives.

These mixtures of state and private financing, as observed, have not always resulted in shifts to the direct state control characteristic of the established public universities or of the once private universities (Kansas City, Houston, and Buffalo, for example) now converted to state institutions. Perhaps the voucher method, or another form of state support of private institutions through their students, will work to limit the case for the exercise of state power. But as any direct or virtually direct state funding of a private college or university begins to approach the level of state funding for a state institution, it would seem hard to resist a state interest in the management of the one as of the other. Indeed, it would be hard to justify such resistance. Private universities, if no longer actually private, might be forced to admit many more undergraduate students, change their faculty teaching loads, lower their per-student expenditures, and otherwise come to resemble the state institutions that I have been describing. For most of the private sector this outcome is hardly imminent. But it is not unimaginable.

Internal Development

The internal educational structure of the state university does not seem uniquely different from that of a major private university. To know one large university is to know the basic pattern in which any other is organized. And to have known any such university at any time since 1910 is to know most of its present pattern (Veysey, 1965, p. 338). Since then, it has been nearly uniform with respect to administrative officers, departments, faculty ranks, registration, transcripts, and so forth. Even the structure for big-time collegiate athletics was established at the beginning of the century (Curti and Carstensen, 1949, Vol. I, p. 710; Vol. II, pp. 536–537, 543–545)'. Generally, then, it is a fairly old structural pattern into which the university has sought to accommodate its enormous growth in size and functions.

The one important organizational novelty since 1910 is the "appearance of the semiautonomous research institute" (Veysey, 1965, p. 338). It was not unknown early in the century, notably in the form of the federally financed agricultural experiment station at the land-grant college, but the type was not numerous on any one campus and it did not constitute a significant element in the general university pattern until the decades following World War II. It began in the natural sciences, reaching there its fullest but not sole development in response to the need for large-scale, organized, and directed research. The institute now coexists with the teaching department in the basic structure of every large university. An individual is a member of one or the other or both. An institute (sometimes called a center or a laboratory) is any unit organized around an academic subject matter at roughly the same administrative echelon as the department but separate from it and from its teaching functions. Its usual purpose is to organize research within a university and yet remain apart from departmental teaching and from strictly departmental subject-matter limits. It shares a university's facilities, status, and presumably other benefits, while its own structure resembles that of a research organization functioning outside the university.

The importance of the institute, apart from its organizational impact, is that it represents the growth of large-scale research within major universities. Even the critics who perceive the growth of institutes as too hasty and unsystematic are ready to concede the need for them if universities are to undertake the modern research whose subject matter and organization cannot be confined by discipline-oriented departments (Dressel, Johnson, and Marcus, 1970, p. 131). The quasi-autonomy that the institute provides some professors would have followed in one way or another as the new tasks were undertaken. Whether universities should ever have undertaken these tasks is another question altogether. Large-scale modern research, we can assume, would have been carried out somewhere in American society. But the strictly federal agencies, business corporations, and various independent nonprofit research organizations, already doing a good deal of such research, might have undertaken much more. Universities would then have limited themselves to the traditional individual research and scholarship that still dominates the humanities and is not completely discarded in other fields. Such work could no doubt have been contained within the departmental organization, where—in the United States at least—it has thrived (Ben-David and Zloczower, 1962, p. 76). By avoiding altogether the new large-scale research, American universities would also have avoided the development of most of their now characteristic institutes.

Moreover, the universities would not then have developed the broader institutelike organization that has come to dominate most of their major research effort. I refer to any team research, in or out of the departmental context; to all collegial projects managed by committees; and generally to grants and contracts requiring more than one investigator. Along with the institute itself, they contribute to the establishment of decision-making units at roughly the same level as the teaching departments. Not only are there such units in the natural sciences, but many social scientists and some humanists have established similar mechanisms—partly to compete with natural scientists and partly for better reasons. Their usefulness for research can be assumed. But the creation of many additional decision-making units, some very large, has complicated the problems of university government. They mean dual loyalties for many professors. Often, with federal, foundation, or corporate funding, these units are quasi-independent authorities apart from the conventionally funded departments and colleges.

Less direct in governmental impact than the creation of such authorities is the sheer increase in the university's professional staff that flows from its new research undertakings. This increase is well beyond that which comes from the addition of new faculty in response to increased enrollments. The scale is apparent from the massiveness of federal research funds in many university budgets, and the large amounts that come from research-supporting foundations, corporations, and various other private and state sources. For example, the Madison campus, even with its 35,000 students, spends more for research than for instruction. Another measure is the size of the research staff. Using Madison again as the example, not only do most of its two thousand professors spend large portions of their time on research (often being paid from research funds), but there are about three thousand other professional staff members, predoctoral and postdoctoral, who are employed to engage in research. Only about half of them are part-time assistants. In addition, the university's various research projects employ at least their share of administrators, secretaries, and other helpers. Altogether, the research staff seems to be nearly as large as the whole of the instructional staff, even when graduate teaching assistants are counted along with professors as part of that instructional staff. Madison, in this respect, is hardly unique. Research workers are unquestionably numerous at every major university; their rapid increase since 1945 has transformed the noninstructional professional staff from auxiliary to equal if not dominant status.

By the late 1960s the university's large-scale research programs became the target for critics, who went beyond ideological objections to particular projects. They argued that universities, acting for their greater financial and organizational glory, assumed tasks of a kind unrelated to and perhaps incompatible with truly educational purposes. Probably the argument can be neither proved nor disproved in any fully convincing way, but anyone who accepts the argument should realize that the administrators and the professors (chiefly the professors) who assumed the new research tasks did so on the assumption that what they were doing was related to, compatible with, and usefully contributory to the established educational mission of the university. Exceptions among professors and projects probably exist, but I know of none and I doubt that there are many. It is true that the definition of "educational mission" here is broader than the most conventional view allows; research scientists are unlikely to think primarily of classroom contact hours with undergraduates, or of many graduate students except those helping with their work. But even in the extreme instances, when professors build separately financed research programs at the expense of their own teaching time, the justification is that the research itself is educational, producing rather than dispensing knowledge, and that it contributes indirectly to the university's teaching program by attracting the ablest young staff members, who become at least part-time instructors. This, it will be recognized, is a statement in behalf of the virtue of the multipurpose nature of the large prestige university. I want to emphasize it and not only the problems that go with it.

The problems, however, are unquestionably oppressive when one contemplates the impact of the increasing research emphasis on the state university's undergraduate teaching. No matter how correct it is to believe that more and better research can produce qualitative improvements in teaching, there remains only a finite amount of professorial time and talent. Its availability for undergraduate teaching is reduced by increased devotion to research and perhaps graduate teaching. Of course, when professors shift from state teaching budgets to federal or foundation-funded research projects, their salaries are freed for faculty replacements. With equally able replacements, more readily available in the 1970s than in the 1960s, the damage to undergraduate teaching is limited to a kind of general devaluation flowing from the higher status associated with research on a given campus (Orlans, 1962, pp. 53–67). But this has not been the major difficulty.

Rather, what happened in the 1950s and especially in the 1960s, following a longer-term trend, is that teaching loads—number of classroom hours and number of courses taught—were generally reduced, though less sharply, even for professors who lacked external financial support. No one was expected to do less work, and many probably do more. The work, however, is much more heavily research (or scholarship, as humanists prefer to call it) and graduate teaching, plus the many professorial tasks accompanying the research. By 1970, in all prestige state universities and in many other places, professors in almost all fields were teaching fewer undergraduate classroom hours (and fewer classroom hours generally) than they did fifteen or twenty years earlier. The counterpressure in the 1970s, reflecting a new professorial supply-demand relationship, is unlikely to do much more than hold the line against further teaching-load reductions.

If anyone still wonders how the reductions were made, it is sufficient to note that the desire and capacity for research and graduate training increased rapidly just when the tremendous expansion of total college enrollment gave professors, particularly the most talented, sufficient bargaining power to gain lower teaching loads along with higher salaries. The bargaining power was enhanced by the competition of the leading private universities, where teaching loads had always been lighter and now were lighter still. No doubt, this kind of competition led to individual reductions that are hard to defend by any reasonable standard of the teaching-research mix, but exceptions of this kind should not lead to the conclusion that the reductions generally were bad for education. Most of the new teaching loads familiar to me are closer to the best allocation of professorial time consistent with quality teaching and to the research conducive to such teaching. Almost all American professors always taught too many hours, and many outside the leading universities still do, if we think of college teaching as rightly requiring scholarly preparation, creative ideas, and attention to individual students.

It is the way of achieving the lower loads that should cause concern for undergraduate teaching. Here and there, the achievement, even without external funding, might have been fully supported by the additional state money needed to pay new faculty to teach the classroom hours being vacated by current staff members—appointing, for example, about half again as many professors in a department when its teaching load dropped from nine to six hours. With so happily generous a financial arrangement, universities would eventually have been able, after the 1960s, to find enough additional professors. No such straightforward arrangement, however, has been usual or entirely feasible. A state university administration could hardly be comfortable in citing reduced teaching loads as a basis for asking a governor and legislature for vast sums to appoint new faculty members. The very idea is politically ridiculous and close to suicidal. Therefore, the relevant new funding was ordinarily obtained indirectly, on the basis of other justifications, if obtained at all. To some extent, an increased state funding for the instruction of a larger number of graduate students served the purpose honestly enough, since the effect was to add salary money to the university's budget. Some professors were supervising more individual graduate research students and could be compensated accordingly, while additional professors were appointed on the basis of the continued undergraduate teaching needs. Costs to the state rose accordingly, even more than larger total enrollments themselves required, because teaching graduate students is more expensive. Yet the budgetary requests to meet these costs could at least be presented, and often successfully, during the good years of the 1960s. This is very different from a request for funds for new staff to compensate for wholesale or piecemeal reductions of professorial classroom teaching loads when such reductions could be explained only as means to provide professors with more time for research and for preparation for teaching. But without the presumably unobtainable earmarked funds for this purpose, the state university would, by cutting an individual professor's teaching, also reduce effectively the total professorial time potentially available for teaching.

Determining how many and widespread such reductions have been in any period of time is hard and complex even for a single institution. The process does not usually occur in any public, across-the-board manner in a given university or college, and only occasionally is there a flat reduction at any one time for all professors in a group of departments or even in a single department. At Wisconsin and, I believe, at several similar universities, the nature of the field, including its competitiveness as well as its subject matter, creates distinctions. So does seniority and, to a greater extent, research productivity and scholarly eminence, measured most saliently by competitive offers (Caplow and McGee, 1958, pp. 145–146). Individual reductions, although justified originally on their competitive merits, tend to become universalized within a department once there are several cases. Similarly, a reduction for one department spreads, certainly to departments whose work is closely related. And finally, the lowered teaching load of the most favored group of departments, in the natural sciences, is sought, although not yet fully obtained, by the less advantaged humanities and social sciences. The remaining disparities, as well as the piecemeal process of changing teaching loads, make it risky to rely on calculating averages. Anyway, they are hard to calculate meaningfully because of considerable doubt about actual classroom hours as the definition of total teaching time. For good reasons, educational as well as political, neither administrations nor faculties like to present teaching loads purely in terms of classroom hours. Yet a report of classroom hours can tell us something useful about one period as compared with another. An unusually candid report of this kind was made by President Hitch for the University of California. He showed that between 1960 and 1968, although the regular faculty increased its time given to graduate instruction from 11.6 to 14 hours a week, there was a net decrease in its average instructional time for all students (undergraduate and graduate) of four hours a week; this decrease resulted from declines in the undergraduate categories, from seven to four hours a week in lower-division instruction and from 12.8 to 9.3 hours in upper-division work (McConnell, 1971b, p. 28).

The magnitude of California's decrease in faculty instruction seems unusually great, reflecting that university's leadership among state universities in emphasizing research; but at least a considerable change in the same direction took place at almost every state university in the 1960s. Administrators and professors know that this happened. College and university presidents so reported in a large-scale survey in 1968 (Hodgkinson, 1970, p. 133). This reduction in professorial teaching load was not offset by any comparable improvement in faculty-student ratio. At most, in the 1960s there might have been a slight gain in the number of teaching faculty in relation to the number of students on some campuses. No one suggests that such an improvement, if it occurred at all, was sufficient to reverse the trend toward fewer hours of professor-student contact.

The result became visible on virtually every state university campus: larger lecture classes, since the typical teaching professor is teaching fewer classes and therefore has more students in each class. Whether this is bad educationally, as is usually assumed, may be doubted; no one has yet demonstrated that learning, in a clearly testable sense, is less likely in a large than a small class. Much may depend on how large, or how much larger, a class we are considering, as well the varying capacity of teachers in different fields. For instance, I believe that I can teach political science as effectively in one class of about fifty students as in two classes of twenty-five students each, and that the former is a more efficient use of my time. I would not make the same claim for a class of two hundred or more, but I know some professors who are notably effective as lecturers to hundreds of students. Also many students prefer large classes, not only because of the quality of the lectures but also because they enjoy the anonymity of such situations. They may even choose a large university because it has some large classes. Nevertheless, almost everyone agrees that too many classes became too large in the 1960s. Whatever their merits by objective learning standards, they seemed to lower the quality of undergraduate education in the eyes of students, faculty members, and the public at large.

Large class size is but one source of dissatisfaction with professorial teaching of undergraduates in a state university. Another matter, also associated with the increased research and graduate training, is the greater specialization of professors within their professional disciplines. As a close observer of the curricular impact of this specialization has said, "the dominant trend in course expansion and reform from 1962 to 1967 was away from service and away from the consideration of the significance, function, and utility of the disciplines. For better or for worse, academic fashion and academic respectability pointed instead toward the analysis of disciplinary issues for their own sake and for the sake of knowledge itself" (Hefferlin, 1969, p. 63). Thus, when they do appear in undergraduate classes, professors are increasingly open to criticism from nonspecialized students for the substance of their teaching. Whether we call the professors too serious and specialized, or the students too uncommitted and ill-prepared, clearly a bad fit sometimes occurs in a prestige state university.

The institution brings together, in an inherently uneasy relationship, a specialized research-oriented faculty and a mass of undergraduate students, many of them not obviously ready intellectually or motivationally for the higher learning. Or, to put the problem differently, by some "cruel paradox . . . a superior faculty results in an inferior concern for undergraduate teaching" (Kerr, 1966, p. 65). An old difficulty has only been exacerbated by the trends of the 1960s. As early as 1914, when the University of Wisconsin was starting to become both large and research-minded, there was public concern that professors were devoting too much of their time and attention to research rather than to undergraduate classroom teaching (Curti and Carstensen, 1949, Vol. II, pp. 270, 311–312). Among the public criticisms reported by a state investigating body were these: "That the university is in politics. That the members of the faculty are sacrificing instructional work to write books, to lecture and do other work for outside pay. That, under the cloak of research, faculty members are shirking classroom work and devoting much time to other pursuits. That students are deprived of personal contact with the strong men of the faculty, and that instruction is left to men of less experience" (Board of Public Affairs, 1914, pp. 6–7). I cite the historical record not to minimize the criticism as an old refrain but rather to stress the continuity of the tension existing between the two major functions of a state university.

Coexistent with this tension, now more evident than ever, is a link between the two functions that can be said to be as characteristic as the two functions themselves. The link is the graduate teaching assistantship. On its assumed usefulness rests much of the case for the intramural compatibility of mass undergraduate education and advanced graduate training and research. In fact, the case involves more than mere compatibility. The graduate teaching assistantship is supposed to establish the complementary nature of the two functions. Large numbers of qualified graduate students, attracted by the university's quality of research and advanced training, are supported by modest salaries for part-time teaching of the undergraduate masses. The convention is that the graduate students benefit—because the teaching salaries support their graduate studies and because they gain teaching experience under professional supervision—and that the university's undergraduate education benefits from the availability of inexpensive teaching talent, without which the large numbers of undergraduates could not be taught. Professors, it is assumed, cannot be numerous enough, given their higher salaries, to do the teaching now assigned to assistants even if professors could be induced to devote more attention to elementary courses. Thus, teaching assistantships seem useful for everyone: the taxpayers, the professors, the graduate students themselves, and even the undergraduates.

There are four broad categories of graduate assistants (if we consider only assistantships related to teaching and put aside the many kinds of research assistantships held by graduate students). First is the assistant who in the literal sense helps a professor by grading papers and examinations and by performing a number of clerical and other chores, but without any regular classroom presentations of his own. Second is the laboratory assistant, ordinarily in a natural science course. He conducts particular laboratory class meetings that are a part of a larger course lectured in and supervised by a professor. The third type of assistant is ubiquitous; he is a discussion-section teacher, meeting usually once a week with each of several classes of about twenty students who also attend a large lecture class taught by the professor in charge of the course. This pattern of breaking down a course into discussion as well as lecture sessions, so that a student has in effect two teachers for one course, is used in almost every large undergraduate teaching department. The fourth category consists of graduate students who are really much more than mere assistants and who sometimes carry other elevated titles more appropriate to their work. They are largely independent teachers of the tool subjects of English composition, elementary foreign languages, introductory mathematics, and a few other similar courses. Although these teachers may be supervised in a general way, perhaps even helped a good deal by a professor in charge of a given set of classes, the fact remains that students in the course meet, three or four times a week, only with their particular graduate-student teacher. This degree of responsibility seems inconsistent with the notion of an "assistantship" and perhaps also with the role of a graduate student, but the fourth category has always provided a great many graduate appointments and will continue to do so as long as the tool subjects are taught (in small classes) in a state university. Here professors would be especially expensive and unwilling replacements.

Another principal way of displaying the significance of assistants is to note their large numbers. The national total stood near 44,600 as early as 1963–64, the last year for which I know of a summary tabulation, and it no doubt rose greatly in the later 1960s before any decline in the 1970s. The 1963–64 tabulation remains useful, since it includes important comparative data. Of the 44,600 assistants, over 31,000 were in public universities, relative to almost 86,000 regular faculty in those same institutions; in comparison, there were nearly 13,600 assistants relative to over 58,000 regular faculty in private institutions. In other words, public universities, while not the exclusive users of assistants, employ not only more of them but also a number that is a much larger proportion of total instructional staff. Moreover, in ten years' time (from 1953–54 to 1963–64) public universities nearly tripled their numbers of assistants, while not quite doubling their regular faculty (Dubin and Beisse, 1970, pp. 272, 275). Even if these calculations seem to overstate because they ignore the part-time character of assistantship appointments in relation to the full-time character of most faculty appointments, they still provide a reasonable indication of the growth and the scale of teaching assistantships in public universities generally.

Visualizing the impact of assistantships on the teaching situation is easiest when one looks at one institution. For this purpose, the Madison campus of the University of Wisconsin is fairly representative, at least of prestige state universities, in general scale and use of assistants. Madison has been unusual, however, in that its assistants unionized, conducted a strike, and obtained a collective bargaining contract. Also it seems unusual in employing over 1800 teaching assistants in the late 1960s and in then reducing the number by about one third in the early 1970s. Near the peak, in the first semester of 1967–68, the chief undergraduate teaching college alone had over 1500 individual teaching assistants (= 620 full-time equivalents), compared to only 900 regular faculty, and these assistants met 69 percent of the classroom and laboratory hours in the college's undergraduate courses. Of course, most of these hours were with small groups while professorial undergraduate classroom hours were often with large lecture groups. Multiplying students by hours would thus reduce the share of teaching in the hands of assistants. The impression of the predominance of assistants might also be softened by observing their concentration in introductory courses. And in any event the 1967–68 proportions ought now to be reduced, since the university has reduced the number of its assistants by one third, largely through increasing the sizes of professorial classes.

Nonetheless, state universities in general, and some other institutions, are maintaining large-scale use of graduate students to teach undergraduates. The pattern has been well established at least since the 1920s and 1930s. It is almost certain to survive the 1970s despite continued pressure to reduce the numbers of assistants as a means of cutting teaching budgets without cutting faculty positions. There remains the counterpressure to support graduate students, who will now have less financial help from research projects. Neither most professors nor their institutions want to eliminate the widespread use of teaching assistants.

This pattern, as I suggested, is crucial in linking the major functions of the prestige state university. The link does not derive solely or mainly from the desire to provide inexpensive undergraduate instruction. There is, it is true, a *belief* that the assistantship system is the only financially feasible way that the state university, and other universities as well, can meet the mass undergraduate teaching obligation. That belief rests on the dubious assumption that there should be many very small classes (with twenty or fewer students), thus requiring a large number of teachers working at a lower per-hour rate than regular faculty. Graduate students, as assistants, do work at a lower rate, although it is not spectacularly lower than that of a full-time instructor or even a new assistant professor. Roughly speaking, for Wisconsin in 1970 one could figure the academic year cost for twelve hours a week of teaching assistantships at about $8500–$9000 (salaries for two half-time graduate students plus estimated amounts covering tuition remissions, substantial for most assistants because of their nonresident status). Instructors, some of whom could also be graduate students just short of degrees, would then have been paid about $10,000 for nine or ten hours a week, and beginning assistant professors about $11,000 for six to nine hours, depending on the department. Similar calculations for California at a different time, were not radically divergent. They showed a full-time instructor receiving about $1400 more than a full-time teaching assistant (Hansen and Weisbrod, 1969, pp. 34–35).

It is plain that assistants are less expensive, but the differences in cost would vanish, on a per-student cost basis, if instructors and assistant professors were assigned slightly larger classes than those customarily taught by assistants. And any substantially larger classes (say, forty instead of twenty students) would make the instructor–assistant professor teaching considerably less expensive. Admittedly, substitutions of this kind are impractical for science laboratories and perhaps for the tool subjects, which, if taught at all, may require very small classes. Also, it would be argued, having thirty or forty students in a discussion class is not as desirable as having only twenty, but that argument rests on the challengeable and untested notion that the small discussion section, led by someone other than the course lecturer, is more valuable educationally than a combined lecture-discussion format in which the professor regularly meets forty, fifty, or even one hundred students. Clearly, then, there is no strictly cost-based necessity for a large part of the teaching assistantship pattern; the cost advantages are there in many instances only because of a conventional instructional method that may or may not be justified on educational grounds.

If an institution were interested *only* in providing the best possible undergraduate education at the least possible cost, it probably would not adopt the teaching assistantship on anything approaching its present scale. Nor would it do so, except temporarily during a period like the 1960s, because of any actual shortage of aspiring full-time teachers. For the very broad use of the assistantship, there are more fundamental and persistent motivations. The principal one is certainly the desire of professors to support graduate students; only briefly in the 1960s, and then chiefly in some science departments, did this motivation diminish because of federal and other funds sufficient to support graduate students on fellowships (Orlans, 1962). The perpetuation of the auditorium-scale lecturer in the modern university furnishes another basis for appointing assistants. There are professors whose time is so valuable, whose dramatic capability is so striking, or whose popularity is so great that they have 300 to 800 students in a lecture class. It then seems desirable to break down the large lecture class, at least once a week, into discussion sections too numerous to be taught by the professor himself. In this circumstance as in others, there is the additional and attractive justification of providing teaching experience for the prospective professor. These motivations do not suggest narrow professorial self-interest or even ego-serving in conflict with educational purposes. Perhaps there is a little of each in a professor's pleasure in securing help in grading examinations, but not enough to account for any large part of the use of assistants. That pattern should be broadly understood as a dynamic element in the combination of large-scale graduate training and research with mass undergraduate education.

Multiplicity and Government

The combination just described is important because both major functions, not just one or the other, are highly developed in the prestige state university. For this kind of institution in particular, but for many other large universities as well, the relationship of these two functions is a persistent problem of government. Each function has its own interested constituencies and participants. Because of the importance of the relationship and also because of its familiarity, I most often use it here as a focus for the analysis of governing arrangements. But it must be understood that a state university performs other functions besides those of graduate training and research and mass undergraduate teaching, and these other functions are part of the multiplicity that complicates the government of such an institution. *Service* is the general term for the many less conventional educational activities that the university undertakes. The term includes the obvious servicing of campus research and teaching, through maintenance and numerous auxiliary agencies, and also many activities reaching beyond the usual boundaries of the campus. There are extension courses for citizens in their home communities and special applied research programs for clientele groups in agriculture, business, labor, and various other pursuits. Add to these functions the service, for a larger community, of a university hospital, art museum, music school, theater program, lecture series, radio and television stations, and athletic teams. The last of these, especially the football team, deserve some emphasis. Not only is intercollegiate competition the most publicized of all the university service activities, but it is also the most explicitly oriented toward off-campus judgments of success or failure. Measurement of performance, on the sports pages, is exact and instantaneous.

Service activities, although employing faculty members with substantial academic credentials, certainly add many para-academic appointees to a university staff. Some of these appointees may be separately organized in an extension division, but others may be located within the regular departmental structure. In any case, they are a numerous category of university participants to put alongside the professional but nonfaculty associates of research institutes, the librarians, the research assistants, and the teaching assistants, all of whom coexist with faculty and students in a campus community. Similarly counted as participants are the hospital staff linked to a medical school, a host of administrators, the secretarial and related office employees, the psychological and academic counselors, the food-service workers, the maintenance staff, business office specialists, the campus police force, and many others in areas too widespread to list here. A campus telephone directory gives a fuller picture of the variety. Total numbers themselves are impressive: nearly 9000 (amounting to about 6200 full-time equivalents) in a 1972 head count of all the academic staff (faculty and all other professional employees) on the Madison campus, plus about 5600 full-time classified civil service employees. Beyond even these numbers are certain part-time student employees in nonacademic positions and nearly 1500 academic and nonacademic staff members employed by the university's extension division, administratively but not geographically separated from the Madison campus.

These large numbers, like large numbers of students, characterize the multifunctionalism of state universities. Size and multiplicity accompany prestige in state institutions but not always among private universities (Lazarsfeld and Thielens, 1958, p. 21). There are, it is true, large and diverse state universities without great prestige. But there are no prestige state universities that are not also large and diverse. It would seem that size and multiplicity are necessary conditions for an American state university to earn a scholarly reputation.

Accepting this situation, as I do, means coping with the governmental consequences of an inevitable complexity. As Amitai Etzioni has written: "All multipurpose structures face a common difficulty—namely, to establish and maintain the desired balance among the various specialized divisions which serve different goals. There is a strong tendency for one of the divisions, and hence one of the goals, to prevail and absorb ever more of the resources and energy of the total organizational pool" (1970, sect. IV, p. 4). I appreciate the difficulty, although I do not share the despair of critics who, like Etzioni, would split the present-day multiversity into three or four separate organizations. My own hope is still to reconcile the diverse functions and purposes that produce the often conflicting conceptions of university government.

A great but presumably not insuperable problem for this reconciliation process emerges from the situation described in this chapter: the reduction of professorial teaching loads and the increase in teaching assistants in the 1960s. In these instances university policy decisions, responding to internal academic drives and competitive conditions, were made piecemeal or incrementally, with only state and high-level administrative acquiescence rather than direction. Yet these decisions established a general public policy determining the nature and the cost of a state service. Specifically, a new mix of research and teaching became state policy without explicit state government enactments. I cite only the leading examples of what has been characteristic of the governing arrangement that I have known. More of such decision making, and the basis on which it rests, will be explored in later chapters, especially in the discussion of the governing roles of professors. For the time being, it is important to observe that this intrauniversity exercise of power rests on sharply different assumptions from those that I am about to describe for the state-agency conception.

THREE

§§§§§§§§§§§§§§§§§§§§§

State Agency

§§§§§§§§§§§§§§§§§§§§§

Like every other conception of university authority to be presented in this book, the state-agency conception involves claims that need not and should not be considered total or monopolistic. Sensibly understood, state authority in higher education hardly excludes the exercise of considerable authority by other claimants. It does, however, affect, limit, and occasionally conflict with internal decision making, as in the general allocation of professorial time to teaching and research. Some conflict is implicit in the very conception of the university as a state agency. The other conceptions of university government assert, in one degree or another, the university's autonomy in relation to the state. At an extreme, claimants within a university may reject state authority altogether, proposing that the state's elected representatives simply deposit the taxpayers' money, preferably in the amount requested, for the university itself to allocate and spend according to self-generated preferences. More moderate than the "leave-it-on-the-stump" philosophy, but still potentially in conflict with many aspects of the state-agency conception, is the very limited acceptance of the legitimacy of the taxpaying public's interest insofar as that interest

36

can be represented and protected by "nonpolitical" bodies rather than by legislators, elected state officials, and their administrative staffs. This "trusteeship" conception, with its board of regents, will be treated separately in the next chapter. Here I confine the discussion to the deliberately direct, external, and popularly based authority over a university.

The legitimacy of state authority rests heavily on the view that a university is itself a kind of state agency, different in many but not in all important respects from the other arms of state government. The state may concede the special mission of higher education, the distinctive nature of its principal employees, and even its nearly unique need for freedom in a very large sphere. In spite of these concessions, the state still may claim that it has a right and a duty to oversee the university—somewhat as it oversees and administers welfare, highways, conservation, and other programs requiring major tax funds. Elected officials, after all, have title to speak for the people. The same popular democratic credentials are not so obvious for the authority of a state government's professional administrators, but of course their claim flows from that of elected political superiors. To question the state's legitimacy altogether in university matters is to question also the legitimacy of elective officials and so the general authority of the state. That there is such questioning tells us a great deal about the special place of higher education, and to some extent of all education, in our theories of government. Surely no other large-scale governmental activity thus challenges the legitimacy of the usual forms of public control.

State authority in higher education has a bad name among academic people. It would be hard to find anyone working for or in a university who does not want to minimize and preferably to eliminate the exercise of that authority (except to appropriate money). Regents want institutional independence, university administrators want autonomy in relation to their administrative counterparts in the state capitol, and faculty members want freedom to pursue their own academic commitments. All assume that their own powers and interests happen to coincide with the welfare of the university, and that the authority of the state threatens that welfare. Understandably, such a threat appears during the usual budgetary controversy when the state gives the university less than it requests; it is reasonable to assume that the university would benefit from the larger amount even if well treated relative to other times or other institutions. So it seems also whenever the state seeks to limit university programs.

But there is another way in which the state appears negatively and unfavorably in the eyes especially of faculty members. This is in highly publicized instances of external pressure against a professor or his program because he or it is politically controversial, or perhaps just eccentric or esoteric. Then the state, by adopting conformist and know-nothing policies, attacks the core values of the educational enterprise. As the likeliest target of these policies, the political left, ranging from liberal to radical, is associated with resistance to state authority in universities. But conservative intellectuals may have the same concern. Russell Kirk, for instance, has said what no one, from Jacksonian democrat to socialist left, likes to say: "The private institutions, in short, have the inestimable advantages of diversity and of appeal to a select body of opinion, as contrasted with the dependence of the state institutions upon an executive and legislative political authority chosen by a mass of citizens inferior in education and discipline to the scholar and teacher" (1955, p. 38)'.

Understandably, most members of the academic community, being committed to democratic ideology, are reluctant to face the elitist implications of an outright rejection of the legitimacy of state authority in university government. They come close to doing so, however, when they argue for institutional autonomy, not just traditional academic freedom, and seek to avoid accountability to the public and its representatives. Such an argument assumes that the university should be treated differently from most state agencies— that, in fact, despite its public funding, it should be governed generally as though it were a private rather than a public institution. There is little in the democratic tradition, or in any tradition of accountability for public money, to justify a large taxpayers' endowment of a privately run enterprise. It could even be said that unrestricted private authority to spend public money is not legitimate. And it is unlikely for large sums over any long period. The apparent exception, a segregated revenue source like the gasoline tax for highway construction, is not a real exception, since it rests on legislative renewal and occasional increase of the tax, not to mention a continued legislative power to determine highway policies.

Historically in the United States, despite colonial exceptions, general funding by the state has distinguished public from private universities. States created public universities as alternatives to established private institutions, even though some private colleges had received state funds along with their charters. William and Mary College in Virginia was thus sufficiently private so that its distinguished alumnus Thomas Jefferson persuaded the state legislature in 1819 to establish the new University of Virginia (Bruce, 1920, Vol. I, pp. 221–226). And in the same year the United States Supreme Court ruled that the state of New Hampshire could not constitutionally alter Dartmouth's earlier charter by substituting state control for the will of the trustees of the college. Most significant in American history for its protection of private corporations and so of private property from state control, the decision had particular relevance for the development of higher education. Not only did it encourage the founding and preservation of privately endowed colleges now that their private government was secured, but it also meant that the states would have to develop their own institutions if they were to exercise public control. The states, especially outside the Northeast, began doing so on a large scale forty or fifty years later (Rudolph, 1962, pp. 210–211). These institutions became distinctively public, in contrast to the private control that Chief Justice John Marshall fully delineated and protected in the Dartmouth College case. In most states the line between public and private institutions was relatively clear-cut for over a century. Not every nation has had a similar experience in maintaining two such distinctive sectors in higher education. Doing so in the United States has meant the development of a legal tradition of state authority for public universities, in contrast to the protected status of private institutions, and this tradition accompanies the democratic theory of popular control.

Popular Expectations

What does the public expect of its university? What does it want its representatives to seek from the university besides a general financial accountability? Customarily the public is assumed to prefer that the university concentrate on educating the state's undergraduates, especially in practical career-oriented fields, and on applied research of benefit to the state's agriculture, industry, and business. And the public is supposed to want the university to limit student exposure to radical ideas. To explore such suppositions about public attitudes toward the university, I have made use of the responses of Wisconsin citizens whose opinions were sampled in several statewide surveys, principally in May to July of 1970, when I had the opportunity to compose questions concerning attitudes toward the university. These surveys, all probability samples conducted by the Survey Research Laboratory of the University of Wisconsin, are described and analyzed more fully in another study (Epstein, 1971). I report here and in the next chapter only the most relevant findings.

The degree of public toleration, or the lack of it, is displayed in Table 1 for three years that surely provided a severe test of such tolerance. Despite the high and increasing frequency of the anti-

Table 1.

OPINION OF POLICY ALLOWING CONTROVERSIAL SPEAKERS
ON CAMPUS

Statewide Sample of Wisconsin Citizens

Opinion[a]	1968	1969	1970
Too lenient	35%	41%	47%
About right	28	30	25
Should encourage more	18	14	15
Depends	5	3	5
Don't know	14	13	8
Total	100%	100%	100%
N	(573)	(574)	(619)

[a] The following question, in each year, was asked: "Student organizations are allowed to bring to the campus speakers of their choice. Occasionally these speakers express views which are considered highly controversial by one or more groups. In this respect, would you say that the University of Wisconsin is too lenient, about right, or should this be encouraged more?"

libertarian view that the university's policy was too lenient, it is doubtful whether the findings substantiate the worst academic fears of popular attitudes. Even in 1970, immediately after the Cambodian-inspired turmoil and following several years of other Madison campus disturbances of high visibility and considerable violence, the antilibertarian view commanded less than a majority of the whole sample. Earlier, it will be noted, this view was less widely held than the more liberal options. These encouraging results were recorded in years when there had already been massive demonstrations and violence on the Madison campus. The context, in each of the three years but especially in 1970, must be taken into account in interpreting the responses. Mistaken or not, citizens were likely to associate "controversial" speakers not just with peaceful dissent and academic discussion of radical ideas but with the revolutionary rhetoric of certain actual speakers whose presentations had seemed to be followed by physically disruptive and destructive acts by students. Therefore, it says much for the public's libertarianism that its opinion in reaction to events was not more heavily repressive. Similarly encouraging, at least for the future, is the finding, in the 1970 survey, that the twenty-one to thirty age group responded much more favorably than the rest of the sample to the tolerant university policy (Epstein, 1971, p. 6).

What about the presumed parochialism of public attitudes? There is some confirmation in the response of Wisconsin citizens in 1970 to limiting out-of-state undergraduates to one quarter of the Madison campus's total undergraduate student body—a policy established a few years earlier. Forty-seven percent thought this policy about right, and 29 percent thought that the proportion should be still lower. But these results should be observed against a background of an already large and crowded campus of 34,000 students; disruptions in which out-of-state students were conspicuous; a long association of radicalism and Jewishness with out-of-state students; and the fact that the one-quarter proportion, while lower than the former figure of nearly one third, was relatively high for any public university, particularly for one supported by a small and unrich state. The parochialism of citizens seems decidedly limited, since not only did 47 percent think the one-quarter proportion about right but another 7 percent thought it should be higher. Thus, over half of the entire sample (and a slightly higher proportion of those respondents registering preferences) supported at least the one-quarter figure. This suggests no overwhelming popular pressure for drastic cutbacks. I am aware that many citizens were being asked for opinions on a subject about which they previously had no information or thoughts. They might, in that circumstance, have been tempted to accept whatever policy was established, including one subsequently inaugurated to lower the out-of-state proportion below one quarter.

A similar difficulty arises in evaluating the expression of public preferences about various kinds of university programs. Hence, I shall be especially cautious in generalizing from Table 2. There appears to be substantial majority support for each listed activity,

Table 2.

OPINION OF EMPHASIS THAT SHOULD BE GIVEN TO VARIOUS UNIVERSITY ACTIVITIES
Statewide Sample of Wisconsin Citizens

$(N = 619)$

| | EMPHASIS | | | | |
Activity*	Great	Some	Not at all	Don't know	Total
Research and training in practical subjects which could help Wisconsin farmers, business, and industry	68%	25%	2%	5%	100%
Teaching which will help undergraduate students prepare for particular jobs and professions	64	29	2	5	100
Teaching of undergraduate students	62	27	1	9	100
Research and training in subjects which could help in solving problems such as poverty, injustice, and other social ills	57	31	6	6	100

Table 2. cont.

Basic scientific research	51	41	2	7	100
The teaching received by graduate students	47	41	2	10	100
Teaching and providing conferences and workshops for adults throughout the state who are not regular students	29	54	11	6	100
Teaching subjects—like literature and philosophy— that are valuable in many ways but do not help undergraduate students prepare for particular jobs and professions	12	62	16	10	100

[a] List of activities was presented to respondents in a different order from that shown in the table's descending order of positive percentages. Respondents were asked the following question: "I'll read a list of things the University of Wisconsin at Madison does. For each one, please tell me if you think it should be emphasized a great deal, it should be emphasized to some extent, or it should be emphasized at all."

since the total of the "great" and "some" emphases is never below 73 percent. Even the lowest-ranked activity, humanities teaching, is completely rejected by only a small minority, and the wording chosen for that listing is almost certainly pejorative for many citizens. Having chosen the words in the realization that they would not be as popularly appealing as humanities teaching can be when presented without the negative clause, I am impressed that the public response is still so generally favorable. It is true, however, that activities of a practical and applied kind receive more favorable responses, as long suspected by educational politicians in and out of universities. Also, as suspected, undergraduate teaching itself ranks very high, notably above basic scientific research and graduate teaching. If there is an inferential message here, it is that the public expects all these activities to be performed but that it remains especially concerned with the undergraduate program, notably in its job-oriented aspects, and in any academic work closely related to the state's economic needs.

Undoubtedly this message conflicts with the aspirations of many professors, notably in the liberal arts and sciences, who emphasize the pursuit of knowledge for its own sake, assert the claims of basic research, and resist job-oriented training and applied research. State pressures for such programs—utilitarian, vocational, and service-oriented—have long been criticized from an academic standpoint. Early twentieth-century writers as different as Flexner (1930, pp. 248–249) and Veblen (1957, pp. 31–32) have objected to the tendency of state universities to do the wrong (nonacademic) things. Given the opportunity, professors have made their institutions more "academic" in the Flexner and Veblen senses. Although none of my data show that the general public opposes the graduate and basic research programs or even the nonutilitarian undergraduate programs associated with academic developments, there are continued expectations, among state citizens, that their university should emphasize the programs with which it has traditionally been associated.

Financial Basis

A state's expectations for its university are obviously related to its financial support. State tax money, despite greatly increased federal funding, still provides the principal governmental support for higher education and particularly for its mass undergraduate enterprise. In 1968–69 state governments contributed 40 percent, compared to the federal government's 13 percent, of all the money received by American public colleges and universities (Congressional Quarterly, 1972, p. 13). State funds had increased mightily even as federal and private contributions to public institutions also rose. Between 1959 and 1967, the fifty states tripled their appropriations for annual operating expenses of higher education (Chambers, 1968, p. 191). Even most prestige state universities, with large-scale federal research funding, obtained between half again and twice as much of their operating income from state as from federal sources (Cheit, 1971, pp. 129–131). For example, the Madison campus, in 1972–73, received over $92,000,000 from the state of Wisconsin and about $50,000,000 from the federal government. Clearly, the state's own taxpayers were the principal contributors to the salaries of university teachers and to related operating expenses.

The rapid growth in state expenditures for higher education has done more than maintain the financial dependence of colleges and universities on state authority. It also means that higher education has become a very large category in the budget of every state government. Wisconsin, a medium-sized state, spent over one quarter of a billion dollars on its merged college and university system in 1972–73. This amounted to about one fifth of the state's total governmental expenditures, as such expenditures are most often defined. The proportion is not very exact, and it is probably lower in many states traditionally less generous than Wisconsin in supporting higher education. Nevertheless, it gives a rough idea of the financial importance of colleges and universities for a state government.

This actual importance, in size and proportion, has not always made university budget proposals as salient for state officeholders as are the requests of other state services with more openly active constituencies of proponents and opponents. This was the finding from interviews conducted in 1968 among legislators and executives in nine states (Eulau and Quinley, 1970, p. 50). Legislators in particular reported relatively little communication, except of course from university officials. They felt that they had considerable freedom of action with respect to requests for funds. Perhaps this worked in favor of the university as long as legislators had reason to assume fairly broad public approval of the cause of higher education. They are less likely to do so in the 1970s than in the 1960s. Since the 1968 interviews with state officials, there has apparently been a decline in public approval of higher education and also an end to the relatively low salience of university budgets in the minds of state legislators and executives. Now more than ever, university requests are balanced against the general desire for economy and lower taxes (or the avoidance of higher taxes). Higher education funds are tempting targets for economy; in most states they constitute one of the few substantial budgetary segments financed on a discretionary basis from general funds, in contrast to the many segregated, dedicated, or earmarked funds (for example, gasoline taxes going only to build highways)'.

The widespread state economizing efforts to the 1970s probably rest on a shift in popular opinion that is sufficient to encourage political officeholders to identify themselves with restraints on spending for higher education. Even a shift is compatible with the maintenance of considerable public support. Such data as I have indicate a substantial drop from the mid-1960s to 1970 in the percentage of Wisconsin citizens who favored paying more taxes to expand and improve the University of Wisconsin (Epstein, 1971, p. 3). But even in 1970 almost half of the interviewed sample still chose an "expand and improve" option, although the university had already greatly expanded and had just completed the worst of four successive years of campus disturbances. It is reasonable to think that opinion of the university was at a low point in 1970; the near 50 percent support is indeed encouraging even if significantly below the 70 percent mark of the mid-1960s. Nevertheless, the public's commitment seems to have declined enough to create a new political climate, in which state officeholders are more likely to propose economies than expansion in higher education. No one would minimize the import of this change in climate. There are many reasons for it besides the reaction to campus disturbances of a few years ago. The smaller increase in demand for higher education, after an enormous institutional growth, is one factor. A kind of growing disenchantment with a previously oversold college experience is another. And there is also a suspicion, especially among state officeholders but more generally among students and the general public, that the state is being asked to provide funds for institutions whose programs and expenditures have been established by internal drives rather than by public needs.

Much of that suspicion is directed to a state's prestige university and to any other state institution developing a similar pattern of academic research. That kind of institution is likely to have the more expensive specialized programs, and so the appearance of higher per-student costs than state colleges, and to have, in particular, numerous professors heavily engaged in research. The response to this situation was revealed as early as the 1968 survey of state officeholders: "Few legislators or executives considered research to be a necessary part of the academic role. Most thought that faculty should spend some of their time in the classroom, and many equated work load with classroom teaching hours" (Eulau and Quinley, 1970, p. 111). This line of criticism, as observed in the previous chapter, may seem an old refrain to members of the academic community. But the criticism seems both more widespread and of greater significance in the 1970s. There has been a reaction, often a knowledgeable one, to the previously fast growth of professorial research and especially to the corresponding reduction in professorial undergraduate teaching time. Political officeholders and their administrative staffs have learned that state funds ostensibly appropriated for instruction were not going exclusively for instruction, in the classroom sense, when professorial teaching loads were being reduced. They may be incorrect in believing that higher education would be improved by restoring heavier teaching loads, but they surely ought to be understood as acting legitimately in behalf of the state's taxpayers in trying to establish budgetary controls over instructional funds.

National Status and Federal Relations

Should state controls, beyond those related to the expenditure of state funds for state-determined purposes, be extended to general university policy making? Even apart from specifically academic objections, the question arises from the status of a university as a national as well as a state institution. This national status is only partly a matter of federal funding. In addition, the prestige state university in particular serves national and indeed international constituencies. Its service outside its own state is an aspect of the growing academic professionalism that Jencks and Riesman stress in their well-known analysis of American higher education (1968, pp. 161–162, 185–186, 191). Increasingly, professors, like many of their advanced students, are not state-oriented in their work or in their interests. The university that they constitute and mold to their pursuits has less to do with the concerns of the state and its public than with those of a cosmopolitan community that is geographically and politically dispersed. But the constituencies of this broader community cannot and do not directly help the university obtain state support.

Indirectly, the national reputation of a university may perhaps gain state support for the enterprise. Citizens of a state and their political representatives may take such pride in having a great university that they can be persuaded to maintain it on the scale necessary for its national reknown. Or citizens might be convinced that their university's reputation brings additional research payrolls for the institution and so for the community in which it is located, and that it attracts income-producing business enterprises from elsewhere. But such possibilities will not always outweigh the political risks for a university that *seems* to be distracted from state-oriented programs, in particular from teaching undergraduates, by its service to national and international constituencies.

Whether or not the university is in fact distracted from state concerns, there is no doubt that its educational realm extends well beyond the state's boundaries. This brings us back to the large question about the state-agency conception of governing the university. Higher education's inherent claims to a different status from that of other state services are, in a sense, enhanced by a university's national character. That character makes it seem anomalous for a state to have exclusive control. Again, federal funding alone does not make for this anomaly. Other state services—notably welfare and highways and even elementary and secondary education—also receive federal money in large amounts, and they may in some instances be subject to greater federal control than higher education. But they serve the state and its citizens almost solely (allowing for the use of a state's highways by interstate travelers). The state university, on the other hand, often attracts a large nonresident student clientele from other states and other nations. Its graduate student body is recruited nationally and internationally. And its research, apart from some largely residual but locally well-publicized work designed to help state enterprises, is in the national and international market for ideas, discoveries, and scholarly learning. The relevant political constituency, for this purpose, would seem to be represented by the federal government as the custodian of the national interest in scientific accomplishment.

Yet the federal government does not substitute its general direction and control for the state's. There is no sign of such a development even in the 1972 plan for general institutional funding by the federal government. The old link between the states and their universities looks like a durable feature of American higher education. Evidence for its durability, resting on custom as well as on American constitutional law, is surely to be found in the limited policy-making intervention of the federal government during the past twenty-five years of rapidly increasing federal financial support. The limitations on federal policy making seem to follow from the postwar history of the funding. Federal grants, however large, have been designed either to add new programs or to expand existing programs at already existing institutions. Moreover, until the mid-1960s federal funds were almost entirely for academic science (National Science Foundation, 1968, pp. vii, viii, 7). Even in the late 1960s and early 1970s, when the federal government was financing college construction and other activities and when the federal government was granting $3,500,000,000 a year to all public and private colleges and universities, over two thirds of the total was for scientific purposes and most heavily for science research (Wolfle, 1972, p. 149). Salaries for research professors, associates, and assistants, as well as money for buildings and equipment, come from these academic science appropriations. Mostly these funds have gone to the prestige universities, both state and private (Reagen, 1969, p. 237). Most colleges and universities have not been major recipients of the big science money; even at the prestige state universities, as I have noted, federal funding has not generally been as large as state funding.

Apparently, this federal funding has been large enough for many in the academic community to fear federal control. Certainly much of what is disliked about university developments since World War II has been blamed on the federal government. One critic goes so far as to attribute to "federal support and direction" even the supposed increased vocationalism of the public university (Litt, 1969, p. 9). Surely, however, vocationalism is an old characteristic produced more directly by state than by federal pressure. Indeed, the hallmark of the federal contribution to universities—private as well as public—since 1945 has been support for basic science. Even so, private universities might perceive the federal impact as relatively vocational. In any case, they were in a different starting position with respect to external governmental intervention. Unlike state universities, they were not accustomed to any such intervention, state or federal. Thus, one who writes from the standpoint of the private university may well consider that the federal government's role poses a new problem; he is mistaken only insofar as he poses the problem as a new one for institutions generally (Graubard, 1970, p. vi). The fact is that, to date, a state institution is bound to find the federal governing role only occasional as compared with the active power of the state government. To be sure, the occasional role, be it in auditing or in the imposition of affirmative action programs of employment, can be burdensome. But it is not the same in scope as the state's customary direction.

Federal *influence,* of course, does exist. Such influence is obvious when a university receives $50,000,000, one quarter of its total operating budget, and when most of that is for specific research and development projects regarded as important and worthy by federal agencies acting under the authority of Congress. Everyone understands that the chosen fields, mainly the "hard" sciences, and the chosen professorial investigators are given status as well as money; the response of universities is favorable to a relatively rapid growth of programs and salary levels associated with the federally chosen people. On the other hand, universities sometimes can use the federal support of science to free state funds for other programs. This too represents federal influence, albeit of a sort unlikely to arouse humanist complaints. In neither case, however, is there any federal control in the usual sense of that term. Nor is state control decreased except insofar as a university administration, representing state authority, is weakened in relation to professors who obtain the federal research money and use it to achieve a degree of independence from the usual institutional claims.

The way that the federal government distributes most science money helps to explain the absence of much accompanying federal control. In granting funds for professors or groups of professors, although technically to the university for the particular projects of the professors, the federal government deals with university administrators only for legal, accounting, and public relations purposes. The substantive questions about quality of the project and its staff are answered by professors. And they usually give their answers to scientific or professional peers who serve the granting federal agencies. These peers may be regular federal employees, but more often they are consultants or advisors borrowed temporarily by the federal government from the universities where they too are professors (Orlans, 1968, pp. 29–34). Significant changes in this procedure, proposed by the Nixon administration, remain in abeyance. Scientists still decide which scientists, and accordingly which universities, get the funds; and they do so within a decentralized governmental organization. Several federal agencies distribute science grants, and in large agencies there can be several separately administered programs. No wonder that Reagen, in a study of federal financing of science in and out of universities, can conclude that there has been no stifling of free expression, that scientists have not become tools of government, and that "we have in general let the scientific pipers call the tunes, rather than having them called by the government patron" (1969, p. 316). Or if one is convinced of the enslavement of scientists to evil programs under federal sponsorship, the scientists appear to have enslaved themselves. In the process, their universities may have been enslaved as well, but such enslavement looks like a willing submission rather than an imposition of government power (Adams and Murphy, 1967, p. 15).

Since universities have come to perform so many national tasks, nationally financed, it is probably true that "if universities were just being organized now, the federal government and its research arms would undoubtedly play more of a role in university government" (Stinchcombe, 1965, pp. 159–160). No doubt, this would mean federal determination of general policies that are now left to university communities themselves or to state governments. The issue, it seems to me, arises in a different way for a private university; there, any general federal authority, following federal funds, would challenge only a nonpublic authority. But for a state university the challenge would be to the state and so to the American federal system. Nationalizing American higher education, in other words, would involve two kinds of takeover, each radical in its own way. No one, as far as I know, is proposing either. Indeed, there seems a considerable American resistance to a national system of education, despite its prevalence in some other nations without the demise of academic freedom. Even the proponents of greatly increased federal aid accompany their financial proposals with recommendations for the preservation of both state responsibility

and private institutions. It is a common article of faith to state, as
the Carnegie Commission has done in italics: *"We are opposed to
the development of a single national system of higher education"*
(1972, p. 2).

Dissenting from this view is not my intention. I expect state
authority in higher education to remain largely intact, perhaps even
to be strengthened, so long as the prestige state university retains
mass undergraduate teaching along with research and graduate
training. But state authority raises special problems when exercised,
as it is, with respect to a university whose programs and whose
fundings are heavily national. One ready illustration of these problems is the establishment of policy limiting nonresident (out-of-
state) students both by quotas and by much higher tuition than that
charged state residents. Whether that policy is made directly by
state governmental action or by the university's board acting under
state government pressure, the principle justifying it is that a state
can decide to what extent, if at all, its taxpayer-supported education
should be distributed to the offspring of residents of other states.
And in practice both quotas and high nonresident tuition have been
the means that attractive and conveniently located state universities
have used to limit the attendance of students from states spending
relatively little per capita on higher education (Carnegie Commission, 1971, chap. vii). The issue is an old one in several states,
but currently very much alive as enrollment pressures and the
need for income cause state universities to raise their nonresident
tuition charges to high levels, both in absolute terms and in relation to resident charges. Even if the nonresident charges had
not risen so greatly, they would now be perceived more critically,
since state boundaries are culturally less meaningful and since
state universities are supported by substantial federal funds. Also
the perception becomes more critical as students increasingly regard themselves as establishing residence independently from their
parents, and insist that they be treated as residents of the community and state in which they have chosen to attend a university. When these students register to vote, now at age eighteen,
and otherwise signify (as by renting property or by part-time
employment) a nearly continuous residence of more than a year
or so, states meet legal as well as political objections to high non-

resident tuition fees (Carbone, 1970, p. 9). At this writing, it is uncertain that all of the usual distinctions between nonresident and resident students will survive constitutional challenges in the federal courts.

The conventional basis for maintaining the nonresident classification is that the student comes to the state for an educational purpose, as evidenced by the absence of previously established residency for any other purpose by the student or his parents. States vary greatly and confusingly in their requirements for residency, but all maintain a substantial discrimination against nonresidents. Without this discrimination, it is fair to assume that many more students would cross state lines to attend institutions of their choice. Large numbers do so anyway. In the fall of 1968 (before the largest increases in the already high nonresident tuition barriers), over 444,000 American students (at all levels) migrated to public institutions outside their own states (while over 682,000 migrated interstate to attend private institutions). Perhaps the 444,000 figure is more significantly related to the nearly 4,236,000 nonmigrating students at public institutions in their own states (Carbone, 1970, pp. 7–8). Although the effect of this comparison is to stress the limited proportion of students who migrate, it should be remembered that the migration pressure is directed especially to the twenty or thirty prestige state universities. And these are the universities whose state authorities, therefore, most definitely respond with quotas (for undergraduates) and with high fees for nonresident students generally.

How well justified are these responses by institutions with national programs and national funding? Not justified at all, it can be answered, with respect to admission to any programs funded wholly or largely by the national government. For example, I doubt whether a state should charge a nonresident student more than a state resident entering a graduate program in physics supported almost entirely by the Atomic Energy Commission. At the other extreme, however, is general undergraduate education (or legal training), whose federal support is ancillary now and unlikely to be more than partial in the foreseeable future. Here, it has always been taken for granted, the state is justified in reserving its subsidized service for its own taxpayers and their children. Yet this distinction is also open to objection. Even without national funding, the state university's undergraduate education—not to mention its more advanced work—constitutes a national program. Its faculty comes largely from outside the state. Its graduates are not assumed to remain in the state despite their original residence there. No matter where they settle, their contributions are to the larger economic, social, and political order of which the state is but a part. It can be argued that a state itself gains in the long run by subsidizing the education of students who will later contribute to national progress and so to people in all states. I derive the argument from an innovative economic analysis of the advantages for a nation that exports its educated talent to other nations (Johnson, 1965). The famous brain drain may help rather than hurt a state as well as a nation that "loses" its trained manpower.

However appealing this line of reasoning—and I find it very appealing—it is incapable of undermining the basis for the exercise of state authority. The states are identified with their universities, and they will remain so at least as long as they, rather than the federal government, subsidize most of the teaching programs. If forced by the federal courts to charge nonresidents no more than residents, a state may well meet this challenge to the legitimacy of its authority by asserting the authority in another way: by excluding nonresident undergraduate students almost altogether, or by taking in only as many nonresident students from another state as that state takes from it. Hence, the nonresident issue, while a useful illustration of the problems of state authority in dealing with an institution of national status, is not likely to be settled by dissolving state power. To reiterate, that power remains substantial, in principle and in practice, despite the national character of many state universities.

Instruments of State Power

The means for the exercise of state authority over universities are so many and varied that they provide more than enough material for a large separate volume. Here it will be enough to indicate the general nature of the state's principal instruments: budget making, creating the structure of higher education, providing for the selection of board members, and imposing administrative controls.

Even the strongest proponent of university autonomy acknowledges the legitimacy of the authority of the legislature and the governor to decide the state's appropriations for higher education. The debatable question about this annual or biennial process is over the scope of policy decisions to be made by state officials when they are enacting the university budget. As part of the state's total budget, the university budget follows the standard procedure of submission through a governor and his staff, who review requests before they run the legislative gauntlet of hearings and debates. State officials have the opportunity to modify university requests when they are submitted, and they can also influence the development of the requests by imposing overall budgetary guidelines or by letting it be known what they will favor and what they will disapprove. With larger and increasingly sophisticated administrative staffs, governors and legislators tend more confidently to use their budgetary power to affect substantive policies. Doing so, however, is an old practice. The most notorious method has been the line-item budget. Its legally fixed amounts for particular programs, purposes, or even individual positions are the bane of university administrators. In states employing this budgeting method, the effect is to deprive universities of the flexibility that they cherish and regard as especially important in managing higher education.

In one way or another, the state's acknowledged budget-making authority is intertwined with policy-making power. Simply to appropriate generously or ungenerously over a period of years itself amounts to a policy of developing a certain kind of university, quantitatively or qualitatively. Salary increases, new staff positions, and new programs all require legislative and gubernatorial action. The need for this state authorization allows the possibility of attached conditions—for instance, that faculty members teach a certain number of hours a week in order to be paid from appropriated funds. Even without such conditions or the restrictions of a detailed line budget, state officials can use their power over appropriations to influence university policies. The always threatening possibility that they will cut requests for funds, either generally or for particular programs, is a powerful force that university administrators must take into account. Moos and Rourke describe it as "the implied threat of legislators to reduce funds unless there is university compliance with particular conditions" (1959, p. 269). The threat seemed to materialize in California in 1970, when the legislature denied faculty members the cost-of-living salary increase legislated for other state employees (Cheit, 1971, p. 17). Ordinarily the retaliation, whether overt or potential, is much less salient for faculty members. In fact, professors often believe that university administrators and regents overreact in trying to avoid unpopular policies for fear of gubernatorial and legislative budget cutting. Perhaps so, assuming that the principle at stake is important enough to risk the loss of funds. But it requires only a little knowledge of a university's relations with a state to realize that the possible loss of funds is no myth. There is no time like legislative budget making for a university's responsible leaders to be conscious of the policy-making authority of state officials.

For many state universities the governor is a more active budget maker than is the legislature. He has a larger professional staff of budget analysts; he probably identifies himself more clearly with higher education policy (either to build it up or to produce economies in it); and he may also exert partisan leadership over a substantial legislative following. Ordinarily a university's financial request has to become part of the governor's executive budget if it is to have much chance of legislative approval. Furthermore, in many states the governor, equipped with the item-veto power, can delete specific appropriation provisions that he finds objectionable without much likelihood of being overridden. This item veto, while significant for the university's budget as for any other, is less influential than the governor's role in determining the nature of the budget in the first place. In addition to an influence over the size of a total university request, there can be hints of gubernatorial favor for a particular program or kind of program. Most university administrators would surely act on such hints by attempting to devise an academically acceptable proposal to obtain the implied funds.

Appropriations are not the only means for policy making by governor and legislature. They are just the most convenient and periodic. And they are the most clearly universal in that the legislative and gubernatorial power of the purse exists for universities with constitutional autonomy much as it does for those without that formal status. For example, the University of Michigan and the University of California, both enjoying special constitutional recognition as quasi-independent agencies, do not thereby escape the state's budgeting authority and its accompanying policy-making potential. Perhaps they are better protected against certain gross legislative interventions unrelated to appropriations (Moos and Rourke, 1959, pp. 32–35). But constitutional autonomy alone may not always provide such protection; furthermore, the protection may, in practice, be obtained by some institutions that lack constitutional autonomy. Budgetary control, through state government, now seems basically similar regardless of constitutional provisions. The very size of a state's appropriation for higher education and its political visibility in the last decade have encouraged state action even where autonomy had been constitutionally established.

A university whose status and governing arrangement are specified in a state constitution does, however, seem protected against an ordinary statute abolishing it or merging it in a larger institution. The state would need a constitutional amendment to accomplish such a purpose. But the legislature might accomplish nearly the same thing by transferring its other institutions of higher education—institutions without constitutional autonomy—to the protected university. At any rate, most state universities are not even to this extent insulated by constitutional status from the legislature's plenary power to organize or reorganize the state's higher education system. The use of this power over the last two decades has been frequent and contentious. It will remain so as state governors and legislatures, more than ever, seek economically to rationalize the relationships of their public colleges and universities.

Usually any rationalizing effort deals with more than one established institutional structure. Most states have at least one state university, often itself with more than one campus, and a group of former state teachers' colleges. Some other states are more complex in their patterns, having two or even several separate state universities plus numbers of separate state colleges. There is also the New York system, which embraces the state's various college and university campuses into one State University of New York (SUNY), apart from the City University (CUNY). But the prevailing arrangement in the early 1970s is still to have two or more separately governed state institutions or sets of institutions. Usually the established state universities have their own boards, and the state colleges or newer state universities have theirs. Each board, it is well to note, is likely to be governing several campuses, be they the campuses of an old state teachers' college grouping or the campuses that a state university developed along with its original site.

These multicampus structures do, in effect, limit the number of separate institutions of higher education under state authority. The structures serving this purpose, however, appear to be products mainly of their particular historical development. To be sure, a state government would have approved any such development when it occurred; California, for example, approved through its legislative process the development of the eight-campus University of California and the expansion of its separate state college and university system. Approval has sometimes been piecemeal and sometimes according to an overall plan. Either way, the multicampus university has often emerged more clearly in response to the internal dynamics of institutional growth, and even in response to institutional initiative, than as a governmental arrangement imposed by external state authority. The use of the pattern is widespread and growing. As of 1968, fifty-four of ninety public universities were multicampus, and they enrolled over three quarters of the students in these public universities. The multicampus proportions in other public four-year colleges and two-year colleges were lower but still substantial (Lee and Bowen, 1971, pp. xviii–xix).

Because it did *not* develop primarily as a state-imposed governing device, a multicampus pattern like that of the University of California deserves attention here. It can be viewed as a way to avoid or limit state control by assembling several campuses under the board formerly governing only the one prestige university campus and, in this new form, maintaining as much of the old autonomy as possible. Thus, a multicampus university organization is an alternative to a total merger, under closer state direction, of all of a state's higher educational institutions. From the prestige university's standpoint, the multicampus alternative seems the more desirable, since it enables the university to extend itself through the establishment of new campuses or the elevation of old ones (especially in urban settings) and yet avoid the greater dilution of quality implicit in a merger with existing state colleges. Not every prestige state university has followed this course. The University of Michigan is an important exception, and there are others as well. But, in addition to California, the list of established state universities that have developed the multicampus pattern at one time or another includes Illinois, Wisconsin, Texas, Indiana, North Carolina, and many others. Despite this widespread use, the pattern may not be stable. Once established, so that the prestige campus is part of a somewhat larger organization, the multicampus university may appear as only a half-way house to total merger with the state colleges, often renamed state universities, whose missions no longer vary greatly from some of the campuses of the multicampus university. And from the standpoint of the prestige campus, there may be less to lose from total merger when autonomy has already been reduced within a multicampus university, and when the prestige, or "flagship," campus can no longer dominate through its command structure as it did in the first stages of organization (Lee and Bowen, 1971, p. 68).

Regardless of the preference of the prestige state university or campus, there is a drive by state authorities to use their legislative authority to organize higher education under a single agency of some kind. A more popular means over the past twenty years than full merger of all institutions in one university system has been a state coordinating council, established in addition to existing college and university governing boards. This council is unmistakably a state instrumentality, external to a given university. Unlike a board of regents associated with a particular university, the coordinating council is supposed to represent the state's interest in higher education generally. By 1970 over half of the states had a coordinating mechanism of this kind (Millett, 1970, p. 102; Glenny, 1959)'. Despite considerable variation in status and power from state to state, the council's common characteristic is an attempt to plan and allocate the state's resources for higher education (Palola, Lehmann, and Blischke, 1970, chap. 1)'. Institutional budget proposals are submitted through the council. And ordinarily the council is given authority to decide which state institution is to have which new program. From the viewpoint of the state, notably the governor and the

legislature, the council is to exert fiscal and general programmatic
control over universities and colleges, and presumably to do so more
effectively and continuously than the governor and the legislature,
even with their staffs, could do themselves (Berdahl, 1971). Universities, however, have not willingly accepted council power in this
regard. Rather, they have preferred to conceive the council as a
transmission belt for their requests—really as another champion in
the state political arena for university needs and interests. To this
end, universities have wanted the councils to consist mainly of members from existing university boards, and to have staffs that would
in one way or another be dependent on university personnel. Genuine independent power for the council and its staff is resisted by
universities insofar as it means the transfer of established institutional autonomy. And somewhat similarly the growth of council
power is resisted by other state administrative staffs insofar as overall
budgetary decision making might be transferred from their offices
in the capitol.

　　These comments obviously indicate doubts about the workability of the coordinating council. It is fair to say that the doubts
arise from observation of the difficulties of Wisconsin's council in
the 1960s and of its abandonment in the 1970s (Kelley, 1972). The
Wisconsin mechanism did not satisfy legislatures and governors
when it was dominated by university board members and university
personnel, and it did not satisfy them when the council was made
into a more genuinely autonomous public body with its own professional staff. In its later stages, the council reduced institutional
requests sufficiently to offend university personnel but insufficiently
to please state officials. It never succeeded in establishing itself as a
body capable of allocating academic resources. In 1971 a new governor insisted on abolishing the council and gaining legislative passage of a measure to merge all of the state's higher education—the
multicampus University of Wisconsin and the state universities
(formerly state colleges)—into one University of Wisconsin system
under a single combined board of regents. Coordination as such
thereby gave way to a plan to try to achieve the same state purpose
under a different name and in a much more direct way. The new
board would presumably coordinate while it governed (Abbott,
1969).

The coordinating council does remain the more commonly used instrument of state control. It seems likely to endure where its powers are strengthened sufficiently, at the expense of institutional autonomy, to satisfy state political leaders. In that case, the council becomes a virtual superboard. Otherwise its popularity might wane as it did in Wisconsin. There is, however, a strong case against complete merger in most large states. The sheer size of each of California's two university systems, for example, makes a single system appear forbiddingly complex. The State University of New York provides a precedent for merger even in a large state, but it falls short of embracing the City University of New York. Within the Wisconsin size range, North Carolina has created a superboard to govern a merged system including its multicampus university and expanding former teachers' colleges. Oregon represents an older partial precedent for merging some but not all of a state's previously separated universities.

Whether states maintain coordinating councils or decide to merge their colleges and universities, there is no question about their continued quest for effective mechanisms of overall educational planning and allocation of budgetary resources. Moreover, the thrust of the entire argument drawn from the state-agency conception supports the quest. With massive public funds appropriated to provide a massive public service, the public's elected representatives naturally seek means for general control over the allocation and expenditure of those funds. By establishing coordinating councils and superboards, the regular state officeholders are acknowledging that they themselves, while responsible to the public for fiscal control, need help from the educational community in exercising this control. If dissatisfied with this help from councils, boards, and their staffs, the state's elective officials could turn to their own staffs. That is, higher education would no longer be treated in the traditional American manner as a special kind of state service requiring its own managerial personnel; instead, there would be much greater and more direct control by a state's general administrative staff or by a particular state department—an expanded department of education or a new unit for higher education.

Establishing in this way the line authority of a governor would differ sharply from authority customarily exercised through councils or boards. Yet the state's authority is already substantially involved with respect to even the conventionally quasi-autonomous membership of governing boards. By providing for the selection of board members, as for coordinating council members, the state uses what I have listed as its third instrument of control. Except for the relatively few states whose constitutions prescribe a board's membership, legislatures are able to specify numbers of members, their terms of appointment, and their manner of selection. Moreover, these legislatures can and do change their specifications from time to time, even abolishing boards and creating new ones without always changing university organizations in other ways at the same time. In most states the legislature authorizes the governor to make the appointments, ordinarily subject to senate confirmation; but it may choose to elect some or all regents itself or to have them elected by the voters. A state may provide for the governor and other state officials, executive or legislative, to sit ex officio on university governing boards. More broadly, without such direct involvement the governor usually has substantial direct influence though the power of appointment. Despite long regent terms that overlap gubernatorial terms, there are always some vacancies and expirations. A two-term governor, or even a one-term four-year governor, is likely to have a chance to appoint several regents who share his general educational outlook. This relationship is discussed in the next chapter. For the present, it need only be stressed that the state's power to determine board appointments is old and established, and that as a means of control it remains in the arsenal along with the more direct instruments.

This leaves only the fourth of the principal instruments of state control that I set out to describe; it is really a large and general category called *administrative controls*—controls that are publicized very little and are left, for the most part, to nonelected members of the state bureaucracy. These controls include the enforcement of procedures for purchasing goods and services (often through a state purchasing bureau), the requirement that new buildings and improvements to old buildings be designed in a state construction bureau by state architects and engineers, the insistence that most nonfaculty positions (and sometimes faculty positions too) be under state civil service or other central personnel arrangements, and the subjection of all university business to the same stringent preaudit and postaudit procedures exacted of other state agencies. This is the chamber of horrors, compounded by the line-item budgeting previously observed, that universities would like to avoid but have often had to learn to live with.

The extent of such controls varies a good deal from state to state, but almost everywhere the controls tend to increase as states seek to rationalize all their governmental activities, not just those of universities, in a pattern of central accountability. As a result of this general "swing toward overhead control of state administration" (Moos and Rourke, 1959, p. 55)', some university administrators who had escaped the most onerous of certain older controls, like line-item budgets or central purchasing, now find that their institutions are subject to the more modern requirements of program budget requests relating specific costs to specific purposes. With such requirements come cost-benefit analysis and productivity measurements. These are the "management tools" of state administrators, whose drive for rationality and efficiency reaches universities as well as other state services. Their impact is painful for university personnel, both because they are unaccustomed to using these tools and because they are convinced, with considerable reason, that the academic enterprise cannot be managed by the same methods used for other enterprises.

Drawing the Line

I share the academic community's objections to having the university treated in many ways as though it were entirely like any state agency. But I realize also that the university is a *kind* of state agency, even if a very special kind. I assume the legitimacy of the public interest in a public institution. I also contend, more controversially, that the pursuit of this public interest implies the exercise of some power by state representatives who are outside the university. Fundamentally, this is a theory or philosophy of government that might stand apart from experience even if there were substantial experience to the contrary. Relevant experience, however, is in accord with the theory. There appears to be an inevitability about the exercise of substantial state power, in one way or another, whenever higher education becomes a large and expensive government service.

Proving the point absolutely is beyond my aspiration, but I can add to the American experience a persuasive reference to British developments. During much of this century British universities served as the model for American academics who believed that they could receive large government funds and at the same time exclude external authority almost entirely from universities. Probably the model was never very applicable to the United States, given Britain's less populist political tradition and the fact that its universities were historically private. Nevertheless, the pattern of the government-university relationship was appealing because for a few decades it approximated the leave-it-on-the-stump formula that American academics could only dream about. There were block grants from Parliament to a university grants committee, which represented the universities. This committee conducted negotiations for funds (annual operating funds and five-year development funds) directly with the chancellor of the exchequer rather than through any government department. The committee then distributed the funds to the several universities in accord with plans developed by the universities and the committee. As late as the 1950s, when over 70 percent of British university income already came from the national government, this procedure remained the dominant one, despite some earmarked grants in the immediate postwar years. The government, through the chancellor, accepted the policies implicit in the committee's submission of fund requests and exerted no control, although perhaps some indirect influence, over universities beyond that of an outer financial limit on overall commitments (Berdahl, 1959)'.

The situation changed markedly in the 1960s, when university opportunities were extended to larger numbers of students, and Britain built new universities and began to raise expenditures for higher education to much higher levels (Halsey and Trow, 1971, pp. 60–61, 84–99)'. The block grant then lost its old significance. The university grants committee was placed under the ministry of education and science, reporting to it rather than directly to the treasury. Higher education thus became much more directly responsible to direction from a parliamentary minister—and from one who, with his staff, is in a position to weigh university missions along with other postsecondary educational programs. A similar tendency is apparent in the parliamentary decision to subject university accounts to the scrutiny of the comptroller and the auditor general (Caine, 1969, pp. 156–157). Altogether, British universities, now almost completely dependent on government funds for operating income, find themselves treated much more like other government agencies than their technically chartered corporate status might indicate. In some respects, they may even be subject to greater governmental direction than American state universities. And, of course, it is a uniformly national direction rather than the several different state government controls with which American universities deal. The British national government, directly or through the grants committee, sets uniform salaries for various faculty ranks, determines the ratio between senior and junior ranks, and establishes student tuition fees (Caine, 1969, pp. 186–188, 201). Furthermore, the British government fixes the number of total university places available for prospective students. It also fixes the number of such places available in each general area of study—as it did by specifying that two thirds of the new places in the expansion of the 1960s be reserved for science students (Bowen, 1964, p. 65). The traditional academic freedom of British faculty members remains inviolate as ever, but the freedom of students to study what they might want is surely curtailed. This particular aspect of British governmental control, however, does not have to be stressed in order to make the point that there is now in Britain little if any of the old university autonomy. American academics no longer have a live British model for drawing the line against virtually all state control of higher education.

Neither this development nor the American experience itself provides any reason for believing that the line between state authority and the university should not be drawn somewhere. On the contrary, it may now be even more urgent to do so. The university has values and purposes which we know have thrived in circumstances allowing considerable autonomy. We do not know of any comparable success for a university established and maintained in the manner of an operating agency of the government. That model is rejected out of hand, just as is the leave-it-on-the-stump model at the other extreme. In between, there are as many possibilities as there are degrees of assimilation of the university to the usual state agency conception. Relatively great assimilation is involved in anything that substitutes management directly responsible to the governor and legislature for management responsible to a board that is at least partially independent. There is only somewhat less assimilation when broad management control is imposed by the capitol on the board's conventional administrators, especially if these administrators are de facto responsive primarily to the governor and his staff. Closer to any autonomy model is the establishment by the state of an accountability body, which would regulate universities as a public utilities commission regulates special kinds of enterprises.

Most of the discussion of where to draw the line is less concerned with such general models than with specific subjects that the state should or should not control. The Carnegie Commission lists eleven broad matters—including general salary levels, accounting practices, general admissions policy, and "effective use of resources" —that it regards as appropriate areas for state influence or control. But it also proposes limitations to prevent interference with the institution's government. The commission would allow state budget control only over the total appropriation, accompanied by a post-audit; and it would preclude any state role in determining salary or other personnel policies beyond the setting of general levels. It also argues against direct gubernatorial involvement in university affairs and against investing coordinating councils with budgetary authority (1971, pp. 20, 28–29, 105). These are all intelligent and well-informed recommendations from a distinguished source, and they do not unreasonably ignore the state's responsibility to represent the public interest.

Much as I appreciate their merits, however, I have to admit that the Carnegie Commission proposals are tipped to the side of a traditionally cherished institutional autonomy that is harder and harder to sustain. I am not thinking here of the commission's disapproval of the fairly widespread extension of state control through personnel systems, purchasing procedures, building plans, and the like. These devices, like line-item budgets, often seem clumsy and unnecessary. For instance, the public interest can be served at least as well, and the university's better, if the university is allowed to have its own classified civil service for its secretarial and maintenance employees. But an important principle is raised when universities resist the authority of the state to determine how higher education funds are to be allocated. There is a substantial public interest in the allocation of funds as among various broad programs and as among campuses.

Drawing the line here is not easy. To have the state decide which programs are to be maintained and where they are to be maintained tends to usurp policy making that the university claims for itself, either in the name of its governing board or of its academic expertise, or in the name of both. I shall explore these claims in succeeding chapters and return to the problem of drawing the line in my conclusion. Generally, as I have indicated, I follow the Carnegie Commission's concern to limit the detailed intervention of state authority. Insofar as I qualify my agreement, it is to emphasize that citizens through their representatives should be able to have some impact on the policy of their university. In making that case, I may too narrowly have stressed the financial or taxpaying basis for the state's role. There is also the broader view that citizens have a genuine stake in higher education because of its service to the whole community and not just to the students and other resident members of the university.

FOUR

Trusteeship

A governing board of externally chosen nonacademic citizens is the conventional method for the American state university to conceive its authority as legitimately public and yet largely autonomous. Legally and politically, this board is supposed to represent the public in university policy making. The university claims that its regents or trustees provide a sufficiently legitimate means for state approval of its academic programs and internal allocation of resources. Such a claim implies that higher education is a distinctive state service requiring a distinctive political status. The board exercises authority in the name of the people of the state, but it is not as directly responsive to the will of the people as are governors and legislators. And it is not, in principle, as directly responsive to governors and legislators as are most state agencies. I call this type of governing *trusteeship* to stress the combination of public authority and quasi-independence. The trustees themselves are more commonly termed *regents*, the word that I shall use as a generic for the various names given board members in the several states. Under one title or another, all states have governing boards of public representatives identified with particular universities or university systems.

Regents are not always popular in the academic community; but their university critics, especially experienced university administrators reconciled to some public authority, almost invariably prefer the trusteeship conception to direct control by elected or appointed state officeholders, whose responsibilities are broader than and more plainly external to the university. Indeed, they often want to reform and fortify regent authority against the power of the state capitol. I respect their reasons, and I shall explore the possibilities after examining the traditional situation. But I raise questions about the basis and prospect for strengthening regent power in our time.

The Tradition

Trusteeship is universal in American private as in public higher education, and its origin is definitely private. Also its form is purer among private institutions. As President Brewster of Yale has said, obviously referring to trusteeship in his kind of university: "It is concerned only that the original understanding which chartered the institution shall be faithfully adhered to, as free as possible from the temptation to conform to the dictates of political or other passing pressures" (1970, p. 22). Consistent with this understanding, private trustees may respond to alumni, benefactors, or other groups, but they do not represent the public interest in any general political sense. Their responsibility is heavily to dead donors and particularly to those whose will is embodied in the charter of the institution. Ordinarily trustees are free to choose most or all of their new and succeeding fellow trustees. This self-perpetuating oligarchical character may help nowadays to diminish a private board's legitimacy on a campus. Unlike a public board, it cannot claim to represent, even indirectly, the people of a well-defined political community. On the other side, the private board does not face the challenge of the broader governmental authority of the state. The trustees of a private college or university are the ultimate legal authority and also the ultimate political authority.

Possibly American state universities would have developed

the trusteeship idea without the private model, but its presence was surely influential when state universities were established. It is important to understand the nature of the early model. There was nothing uniquely American about a chartered trust, for education or other purposes, or about a board of mainly self-perpetuating members empowered as a corporate body to administer the trust. But a distinctive if not quite unique feature of American colonial colleges was that their boards consisted of nonteaching, nonresident members. In contrast, most European universities, reflecting their medieval past, were governed chiefly by corporate bodies of teachers. The only likely European source for the American arrangement was the Calvinist method of controlling schools through clergymen and elders of the church. The earliest and long-predominant American colleges were denominational, and their boards included many church representatives. They were "lay" boards only in the sense of being nonacademic. By the middle of the eighteenth century, whether or not heavily clerical, they were making the major decisions for the colonial colleges, and this system of government was definitely established for American higher education. Harvard, Yale, Princeton, and William and Mary all exemplified the pattern of nonresident, nonfaculty control (Hofstadter, 1964, pp. 114, 121–124, 134–151). The state governments, having chartered the private institutions, could be expected to use a similar mechanism when establishing state universities, especially in the early nineteenth century. Even Thomas Jefferson, whose University of Virginia was innovative in other ways, helped to establish a lay board and served as a member (Bruce, 1920, Vol. I, pp. 141–143, 164–166, 322).

American states, besides their tendency to follow the existing private college pattern, may also have been encouraged to adopt trusteeship by the nineteenth-century prevalence of lay governing boards in governmental affairs generally. Whatever the state activity —turnpikes, prisons, or canals—it was usual to depend on a board of presumably public-spirited citizens, sufficiently well-off to afford to serve as part-time, unsalaried overseers. Despite its old-fashioned origin, a board of this kind has persisted in many areas of state government into our own time. It has been modernized mainly by the addition of professional administrators responsible to it. But in most fields the governing board has not maintained the quasi-independence of university regents, varied though their authority is in the several states (Carnegie Commission, 1971, pp. 100–101). On this score, state arrangements for higher education are more closely paralleled by local governmental structures for elementary and secondary education. At both levels, boards of lay citizens exert a control that is separated from the rest of the governmental apparatus. They conform to the tradition that education generally is a special kind of public enterprise (Millett, 1970) and that it is too important to be left to the politicians—that is, to legislators and executives elected for broader governmental purposes. Whether we have thus effectively insulated public schools from politics, even from partisan politics, is seriously questioned (Ostrom, 1961, pp. 32–33). The same questions may be raised about the effort to secure for higher education both the virtues of private enterprise and the means of remaining somehow responsible to the public.

Responsibility of regents to the public is not like that of legislators or governors. Even when regents themselves are elected by popular vote, they are seldom expected to run on their records of performance. Their terms, whether elective or appointive, are deliberately so long and overlapping as to obviate anything like a popular verdict on them or their policies. Legally, as trustees, they are answerable to the people of the state; but politically, because they are trustees, their answerability is thought to differ sharply from that of popular representatives, who often regard themselves as delegates of their constituencies. State university regents, like private university trustees, are conceived as an independent authority vital to the freedom of a university. The elitist implications are clear enough. Trusteeship generally implies guardianship by superiors of one kind or another. The guardianship of regents, however, is not that of specialized experts—certainly not that claimed by a faculty in academic matters. Rather, the credentials of regents are those of public spiritedness, disinterested civic responsibility, and general wisdom.

In maintaining trusteeship as the mechanism for public authority to be represented in university government, citizens tacitly fill a gap created by their rejection of a direct role for other state officials. The gap is evident in the responses of California citizens to survey questions about higher education. In the respected statewide

California poll by the Field organization (press release, March 16, 1971), more than two thirds of the California citizens sampled in four out of five polls, 1967 to 1971, agreed strongly or somewhat with this statement: "To keep its high standing, the state university and college system must stay independent of political control by the governor or the legislature." Yet, in the same five polls, at least two thirds of the Californians also agreed, strongly or somewhat, with the statement "The taxpaying public should have more to say about the state university and college system." Citizens were not asked, it is true, how they were to have more say if colleges and universities were to be independent of elected officials, and we cannot assume an implicit endorsement of regent power. It is hard to see, however, what else is available to fill the gap.

I have tried to learn more about citizen expectations in these respects from the Wisconsin survey of 1970, cited in the previous chapter. Note the responses to the questions specified in Table 3. Here, because of the nature of the questions, the rejection of gubernatorial and legislative responsibility is explicit. The response strengthens the view, obtained from the California poll, that the public maintains the traditional American view that higher education is not and should not be in the hands of conventional political authorities. Even in the times and places—1970 in California and Wisconsin—when university troubles appeared most salient, citizens did not turn to the full state-agency conception to meet the troubles. On the other hand, the Wisconsin data of Table 3 do not represent an overwhelming commitment to regent authority except in preference to that of governor and legislature. Rather, university administrators received the largest endorsement as the authority that ought to have most responsibility. We cannot infer that citizens always perceive university administrators as agents of the regents, but of course they are appointed by regents and are legally responsible to them. With that perspective, the Wisconsin public might be viewed as assigning policy-making responsibility indirectly to regents when assigning it to administrators. There would then be a very large total percentage to be counted in an endorsement of the traditional trusteeship conception of an autonomous public service.

This calculation may well overinterpret the data so as to bias the findings against ordinary state authority. I cannot be sure how

Table 3.

STATEWIDE CITIZEN PERCEPTIONS OF RESPONSIBILITY
FOR MAKING POLICY FOR THE UNIVERSITY OF WISCONSIN*

Perceived Authority	Now Has the Most Responsibility	Ought to Have the Most Responsibility
Governor	6%	5%
State legislature	7	12
U.W. board of regents	35	30
President of the U.W., chancellors, deans, and other administrators	27	41
Faculty	4	5
Students	7	2
Don't know	15	5
Total	100%	100%
N	(619)	(619)

* Perceptions are reported from responses to a list of groups and individuals (noted in the left-hand column). The list was shown to respondents, who were asked: "Of these, which do you think now has the most responsibility for making policy for the University of Wisconsin?" and subsequently "Which do you think ought to have the most responsibility for making policy for the University of Wisconsin?"

citizens understood "making policy for the University of Wisconsin." Many may have been thinking of essentially internal matters, including student discipline, and so have responded by naming internal authorities although they would not have done so if asked who should decide budgetary allocations. Assuming that the questions thus prompted answers against obvious external authorities, it is significant that, in choosing among the *non*external authorities, citizens overwhelmingly rejected faculty as well as student power. We may hope and believe that they would not have done so if specifically asked who should make policy about course content and instructional methods. But there is every reason to believe that their reported answers do mean a preference for publicly responsible authorities to decide some other policies over which the faculty and occasionally the students claim considerable power. Such policies might well concern the relative size of graduate and undergraduate programs, the establishment of new schools, the maintenance of freedom for controversial speakers, the offering of an ROTC program, or the undertaking of defense research.

Such policies raise broad and general issues for public authority, traditionally a board of regents. However great the reliance on faculty and student advice, the public's trustees provide the public's consent in the absence of policy making by more popularly based state officials. The alternative is to surrender public authority altogether to the professional academic community. Should this community itself decide a question like that of having military research on a campus? As an overall policy matter, that question involves an institutional commitment, which is quite different from decision-making by professors as to their individual participation in particular military research projects to which they have moral, political, or academic objections. A university's collaboration or non-collaboration with the national government is a political act by the institution. Recognition of this point is usual, particularly by critics proposing noncollaboration in military research at a time when many citizens disagree with the national government (Wallerstein, 1969, pp. 28–29). It is probably less usual to perceive that at least in a public university any plainly political act by the institution will have to be agreed to by a public authority. It would be different if a scientific issue were at stake; then professors themselves might legitimately decide that a certain kind of research was academically invalid and therefore excludable from the academic community. But when the grounds for banning research are explicitly political, we should not expect the state to leave to professors, with or without student support, the power to impose institutional limitations on inquiry. To turn the political question around, we would not expect a state committed to pacifism to be willing to have its university staff make the political decision to allow military research. Perhaps no authority, external or internal, ought to prohibit any research on political grounds, thus leaving the political and moral decision making to individual professors as long as their proposed work meets peer-group scientific standards (including openness of findings). But if there is going to be an overtly political decision, citizens will and should look to a public authority to make that decision. Regents, now as in the past, constitute that authority unless governor and legislature intervene.

There are many other matters, often less overtly political, in which regents exercise public authority. The tradition that they should do so is long and tenacious, but it is challenged. The challenge comes partly from state officeholders, for all the reasons explored in the last chapter. It also comes from the academic community—even though most university personnel probably still consider regents a lesser evil than other forms of state authority. Futhermore, faculty, students, and administrators are accustomed to regent decision making and ordinarily accept it as a fact of life. There is nothing to suggest a persistent and active revolt against it. But in crises there are objections both to the particular decisions of regents and to the conception of lay authority on which the decision making rests.

Students, when at odds with regents' decisions, display their restiveness more directly. In a Madison campus poll in December 1970, following a contentious period in which regents had reversed certain internally preferred policies, students perceived regents to be in control but decisively rejected the idea that they should have such control. Table 4 makes this abundantly clear and also shows a dramatic contrast to the Wisconsin citizen preferences of Table 3. When presented with options resembling those of the general citizen poll, students plainly chose some version of internal university policy-making responsibility.

I do not have comparable survey data for faculty members, but my strong impression is that professors also prefer a decidedly limited role for regents in university affairs. In a large national survey at both private and public institutions, 45 percent of all faculty members said that the "trustees' only responsibility should be to raise money and gain community support." The percentage thus responding rose to 62 percent among faculty members age thirty and under (Carnegie Commission, 1973, p. 90), possibly portending even less support in the future for regent governing roles. Apart from the polled opinions, professorial behavior often suggests a drive for dominance by faculty and faculty-oriented administrators. As will be seen in Chapter Six, the drive is at odds with meaningful

Table 4.

STUDENT PERCEPTIONS OF CONTROL OF POLICY MAKING FOR THE UNIVERSITY OF WISCONSIN[a]

Perceived Authority	Now Has the Most Control	Ought to Have the Most Control
State legislature	13%	1%
U.W. regents	61	5
U.W. administrators	17	24
Faculty	4	39
Students	1	12
Combination of above	1	15
Don't know	2	3
Total	100%	100%
N	(505)	(505)

[a] Perceptions are reported from responses in a cross-sectional sample of University of Wisconsin students, Madison Campus (December 1970), to a list of groups and individuals (noted in left-hand column). Note that list does not include "Governor," and that tabulation also differs from the statewide survey in that answers involving more than one group, "all groups," or "other groups" are recorded as "combinations of above." Students were asked: "Which one group on this next card do you feel now has the most control in determining the policies of the University of Wisconsin?" and "Which one of the groups do you feel should have the most control in determining the policies of the University of Wisconsin?"

regent authority. Admittedly, however, most professors and their organizations do not overtly reject all of the traditional governing authority of regents. For example, the moderate American Association of University Professors (1966) is committed, jointly with administrative and board associations, to a balanced "Statement on Government of Colleges and Universities." The statement (p. 377) recognizes a board's "general overview," its task of ensuring "the publication of codified statements that define the overall policies and procedures of the institution," and its "central role in relating the likely needs of the future to predictable resources" (for which it exercises broad fiscal powers). This language, while remaining com-

patible with a board's great legal authority, is also consistent with
the standard AAUP view that policies should develop within the
university community and that boards, in the words of the statement, "should undertake appropriate self-limitation." There is no
easy agreement about the self-limitation that is appropriate, but the
phrase itself implies the well-established faculty view that the actual
exercise by regents of much of their legal authority is not academically legitimate when contrary to faculty policy. For professors, even
more clearly than for the more transient students, the regents are
not *in* the university and so are not suitable policymakers for it.

The academic community, however, does want regents to
champion its institutional interests. This expectation is most explicitly that of administrators, but it is shared implicitly by faculty
and probably by students too. No one in the university community
is at all likely to object when regents, collectively and individually,
defend the university in general and its budget requests in particular. Trusteeship in this sense is happily legitimized within the university. It means, in Clark Kerr's language, that regents represent
the university to the public, rather than the public to the university
(1969, p. 1104). Kerr is in a large company of experienced academic administrators who want just this kind of representation and
are disappointed when regents respond to apparent outside pressure and begin representing that pressure in making university
policy. As a Berkeley faculty-student report has said of California
regents, "What may have been intended as a buffer has become a
conduit" (Study Commission on University Governance, 1968, p.
25)'. The university expectation, when put this way, may seem politically unrealistic. It supposes that regents should absorb public
criticism, perhaps even when they sympathize with it, and do nothing to attempt to soften the blows to their own status and to the
university's. This too is a strand in the tradition of university trusteeship, occasionally accepted by regents themselves, but generally un-
congenial to nonacademic outsiders.

Board Membership

However much authority regents are supposed to exercise, it
will help to understand their problem in exercising it to know more
about their selection, terms of office, and backgrounds. State efforts

to maintain a nonpolitical public authority may seem a contradiction in terms and unrealizable in practice. Yet trusteeship has survived in association with the development of large and qualitatively superior educational institutions. I should not want to contend that American state universities became great in spite of their regents. It is more reasonable to believe that trusteeship, despite inherent contradictions and imperfect institutionalization, has included advantages for universities over a considerable period of time. Like so many other governmental mechanisms, it has worked more effectively than its conceptionalization might lead one to expect.

One explanation for workability is that the states have made regent selection political in almost every sense. The variation in methods from state to state seems less material. Regents may be elected by direct popular vote, even on a partisan ballot as in Michigan (Halperin, 1960), or by the legislature, alumni, the board itself, or combinations of these along with gubernatorial and ex officio appointments. The most common method, gubernatorial appointment, is obviously political; its impact is countered only partially, though sometimes significantly, by provisions for the long tenure of board members. They are, it is true, ordinarily appointed for terms of five years or more—often for as long as nine and even for sixteen years. Appointments are also staggered, so that most of the time only one regent term (or perhaps two), on the usual board of nine to fifteen members, will expire in a given year. Thus, no one governor serving a term or two, nor any one legislature, should have the opportunity to load the board with regents of a given persuasion. Even the public, if electing regents, is not given the chance to choose a majority of members at any one election. But these provisions, on their own, will not make a board nonpolitical or even nonpartisan when there are strong state forces compelling the selection of regents with political associations.

Provisions for long and overlapping terms can, however, produce a board whose politics are different from those of an incumbent governor and legislature. The longer the regents' terms (and the shorter the governor's), the likelier this outcome. It is virtually inevitable when an electoral overturn brings to office a governor belonging to a party that has been out of office during the previous six, eight, or ten years. Then, even with the usual appointive power, a new governor is unable to choose enough new regents to change the board's partisan majority during his first few years of office. At least he cannot do so just by replacing regents as their terms expire. Death or early retirement of regents for other reasons increases gubernatorial opportunities, perhaps enough to tip the political balance within a four-year gubernatorial term. Also a minority of new and vigorous appointees may persuade the more weakly committed partisan holdovers to join in supporting positions closer to those of the governor (insofar as these might be defined as political or ideological). Nevertheless, long and overlapping regent terms mean in fact, as they are intended to mean in principle, that board memberships outlast governors and most other elective office-holders.

This relationship of regents to governor is rather like that of U.S. Supreme Court justices to a newly elected President. With a board of regents as with the court, the executive can seek authorization to change its total membership by adding new positions. In many states he can secure authorization through ordinary legislation, and in these instances legislatures may abolish old boards and substitute new ones. But the political risks of seeming to pack an educational board by changing the rules of the game are as great as those involved in seeming to pack the Supreme Court by creating additional justiceships. Even governors who have the legislative or constitutional majorities needed for restructuring boards are likely to find it wise and expedient to live with the established process of gradual and incomplete replacement of regents. But this is not the same thing as a President's acceptance, since 1937, of a Supreme Court whose members he can replace only slowly. The court, while it surely makes public policy and of a momentous kind, is nonetheless a body whose independence is cherished and protected because of its judicial functions. A university's board of regents, on the other hand, is simply a policy maker whose independence depends on the special nature of its subject matter. Furthermore, regents seldom have the credentials of learning and experience in educational matters that most judges have in the law.

It says a great deal, therefore, about higher education, especially the major state university, that its governing board has generally been secure against *immediate* gubernatorial or legislative packing of its membership. But the board may still be a highly political body even in the partisan sense. A board of Republican regents, for example, is no less political under a new Democratic governor than it was under a Republican governor who appointed most of its members. Of course, it might not have been very political (meaning very partisan) to start with. The Republican governor might have appointed some non-Republicans, perhaps even Democrats, in the absence of any significant university issues dividing regents by party affiliations. In some states this type of nonpartisanship probably has prevailed over a substantial period of time, coinciding with one-party politics or with little ideological conflict between parties or factions. On the other hand, the Wisconsin record of 1940 to 1970 is that Republican governors regularly appointed Republican regents (with only one exception) and Democratic governors regularly appointed Democratic regents. Earlier, without the conventional two-party competition, but with intra-Republican factional contests, conservative Republican governors appointed mainly their fellow conservatives and La Follette progressive governors appointed progressives.

Without the benefit of national studies, we know that there are other states whose partisan pattern of regent appointments resembles Wisconsin's, although state electoral contests, in and of themselves, do not impinge on university affairs. Being a Republican or a Democrat, or in one or another faction of either party, does not inevitably associate a regent or anyone else with a viewpoint toward the policies of an institution of higher education. In general, however, favorable and unfavorable dispositions toward a state university, and toward its particular policies, are often associated with statewide contests for political power. The question of how much to spend on a university, and how to spend it, can divide politicians and their publics. Parties and individual candidates may well represent interests and attitudes that identify with, or oppose, various university programs. In these circumstances, which seem ordinary enough, why should not regents be expected to represent the viewpoints of their selectors?

Political representation of this kind is encouraged by certain practical considerations surrounding the selection of regents. Board membership is an honor, a well-publicized civic responsibility, and a position of apparent power. The fact that regents are unsalaried may even enhance their prestige. Consequently, many citizens with political claims greatly desire and actively seek such appointments from the governor. These citizens may well be important campaign contributors, whether in cash or in organizational effort, and enough of them will seem educationally respectable so as to constitute a sizable roster of eligibles. For a governor to pass over all such aspirants in order to choose a nonpartisan citizen, because of his educational credentials, is more than we usually demand of any elected officeholder. In choosing among his most helpful fellow partisans, however, a governor faces other political considerations. Geographical representation, sometimes mandated by statute, always seems desirable. So does the choice of at least one regent from a state's agricultural constituency, if at all large and important. Similarly, it may be useful to appoint a labor union leader, representatives of ethic minorities, and women.

The university itself has an interest, or a set of interests, in the choice of regents. Its president most plainly has a stake in new appointments and in reappointments. Since the regents hire and fire the president, and more regularly just support or oppose his recommended policies, he would naturally like to help choose them. Influencing a governor as he makes this choice is not always easy for a president. His counterpart in a private university has more convenient access to the selectors of his trustees, since the selectors are usually the current trustees or an alumni group or a similarly university-connected entity. Assuming that the private university president has the confidence of these selectors—who are probably the same body that chose him as president and now retains him in that office—he should be able effectively to suggest new trustees and also to advise effectively against undesirable possibilities. No close observer of a reasonably enduring president of a private university doubts that he and his administration do a great deal to shape their governing board. This is an important reason why he endures.

To do as well by way of influencing board membership, a state university president needs unusual political advantages. Personal rapport with a governor is the most desirable, but hard to carry over from one political regime to the next. A university president known to have been on good terms with the most recent ex-governor does not thereby endear himself to a new governor of a different party or faction. A president suffers a similar limitation when working through present regents to try to influence gubernatorial appointment of new ones. Regents close to one governor may not be close to his successor; and regents who are close to the successor might have become alienated from the president because they identify him with the former governor and his regents. None of these difficulties keep a president from trying to exert influence, or other university personnel from promoting candidacies. In addition to the regents themselves, administrators at various levels—particularly deans associated with client-oriented programs like medicine, agriculture, business, and engineering—often become active. So do faculty leaders with direct or indirect political access. These staff members may have the same concerns as the president, and he then takes advantage of any political access that they are fortunate enough to have. But possibly other administrators, individual professors, and regents, as well as various alumni, have different or even opposing concerns from those of the president. Conceivably they want new and different regents in order to secure a new and different president.

Despite the possibilities for intrauniversity disagreement about regent choices, a consensus probably exists in the educational community about the kind of regent who ought to be appointed or elected. This belief underlies Rauh's perceptive generalization in his study of trusteeship: "In the absence of any formal methods, public boards and their presidents go to great lengths to assure quality appointments. This is most commonly achieved by informal contact between the governor, the president, and the chairman of the board" (1969, p. 120). The key term here is *quality appointments*—meaning, it is fair to assume, regents who appreciate the nature of a university sufficiently to champion its policies and interests, as defined by its administration and faculty. Quality in this sense is sought regardless of which party happens to hold state office. More or less desirable choices always occur within the party whose opportunity is at hand. Rauh goes so far as to say that the existing board presents the governor with a list of recommended candidates, so that by choosing from this list he knows that the new regent has the institution's endorsement. Insofar as this practice is followed—and I doubt its uniformity and even its frequency—it approximates for a public institution the private college board's cooption of its own new members. Still Rauh's description accords the board only a nominating power. Moreover, the power is limited to suggesting several names rather than one; it is probably limited also to names of those who, the board realizes, are not just educationally eligible but politically eligible from the governor's standpoint. A governor, we must assume, is constrained by his own electoral associations and usually by calculations of senatorial willingness to confirm his choice.

Undoubtedly we understand too little about this process of gubernatorial appointment and other processes of regent selection. My statements are strongly conditioned by impressions from a single state, fortified by a few impressions from other states, and I do not know of any systematic study of the subject. So I must qualify the regent-selection process just described by saying that it may not hold in states whose universities are publicly less salient and whose politics are less ideologically partisan than Wisconsin's. And, of course, the relevance of the description is decidedly limited in states whose regents are elected rather than appointed. In such states university personnel, along with their interested educational supporters, must seek to influence the election itself—possibly by influencing the choice of candidates by parties or by nonparty groups of alumni or other education-oriented citizens who publicize their endorsements.

The remaining reasonable generalization is that the selection of regents (though public representatives) is subject to considerable and sometimes successful pressure from the institution that the public representatives are supposed to govern. Certainly those who identify themselves with the university, through their leadership positions or other associations, think that they should exert such pressure. They believe that the interests of the people of the state will best be served by regents who recognize the virtues of the institution's own management. In this respect, they resemble any other interest being governed or supervised by the state; electrical utility officials, for instance, must also believe that state regulating commissioners should be men who appreciate the needs of the business being regulated. What is significantly different about a university in relation to its regents, however, is the open and widely held assumption that board members should indeed be identified with the interests of the institution being governed and that, to this end, the instituition ought to influence the selection. Whatever influence electrical utilities may have in the choice of their regulating commissioners, it is hardly legitimized in principle.

Much easier to learn than the intimacies of the selection process is the nature of the board memberships that have resulted from the process. Several useful tabulations have been made of the socioeconomic characteristics of regents along with private college trustees. Overall, board members are predominantly male, usually over fifty years old, well above average in income and wealth, heavily business and professional in occupation, and mainly college graduates (Rauh, 1969, pp. 89, 150; Hartnett, 1969, p. 19)'. In these respects, public boards differ from private only in being somewhat less completely upper and upper-middle class in character (Beck, 1947, pp. 66–67)'. Their general socioeconomic character is roughly the same. So is the limited membership of educators as such on all these boards; there are, however, more and growing exceptions in the private than in the public sector. Professors are not unknown on the boards of private universities; the only educators on state university boards are almost certain to be those who sit ex officio as superintendents of instruction or as presidents of the institutions being governed (Rauh, 1969, pp. 101–102). In neither case has the predominance of businessmen and closely related professionals, chiefly lawyers, been substantially shaken, at least through the 1960s. That predominance has long been noted and ordinarily deplored by academic critics. The best known of these critics, Thorstein Veblen, stressing the incompatibility of business and academic pursuits, characteristically thought it ironic that educational authority should be entrusted "to men who have proved their capacity for work that has nothing in common with the higher learning" (1957, pp. 50–51).

Whatever the merits of the Veblenite critique, it is not hard to understand how the predominance of business representation has occurred. Partly it reflects the traditional high status of business in the United States, particularly for the purpose of exercising the trusteeship of educational, philanthropic, and similar institutions charged with spending large sums of money. Partly it reflects the

availability of businessmen for unpaid public service; like independent professionals, they can take the time for occasional travel and
meetings. They are also politically available, since their wealth and
income facilitate campaign contributions of money and effort. These
contributions seem to be the state university regents' equivalent of
the private university trustees' direct monetary donations to the relevant educational institution (although state regents may also thus
donate funds).

Predominantly business and related professional board memberships have prompted numerous proposals for change that would
increase the legitimacy of board authority in the eyes of one element
or another in the community. The already adopted practice in many
states of adding labor as well as agricultural representatives is a step
in this direction, as is the addition of women and ethnic-group members; but since these appointees usually constitute fairly small board
minorities, the old predominance is not changed. Moreover, women,
ethnic-group leaders, and agriculturalists may be of the business community in one way or another. Even the labor union representative,
whether a lawyer or an elected union official, often has a good deal
in common with the business outlook. Adding active politicians
would be more likely to change the nature of a board's composition,
but there is hardly any demand from the academic community for
a move in that direction. Indeed, the Carnegie Commission on
Higher Education specifically opposes the inclusion of the governor
on a university board of regents (1971, p. 2). This opposition may
reflect a preoccupation with the problems then posed for the University of California by a particular governor's active participation
as a regent, but the arguments advanced are generally persuasive
against the ex officio appointment of legislative leaders and of
elected executive officers. A conflict of interest arises between their
roles as regents, representing the university's claim for funds, and their
roles as legislative or executive reviewers of budgetary requests from
the university as from other state agencies. Or at least such a conflict arises so long as regents are conceived as of the university and
not as outsiders in every sense. Former elected officeholders, on the
other hand, might well contribute something as experienced public
representatives without raising the conflict-of-interest question.

The more popular proposal in universities is to substitute

educators for businessmen. This proposal does not broaden representation of state interests, as do proposals for women, labor, or ethnic-group members. It really narrows representation by displacing laymen with educational insiders. Membership would become less public as it became more specialized and professional. Internal campus legitimacy would be enhanced, but externally the legitimacy of regent authority might well be seriously eroded as lay members were superseded by those occupationally identified with the interests of educational programs. Legislators would hardly have more confidence in appropriating funds for a board of professional educators than for a board of businessmen. The assumption has always been that safe-and-sound lay citizens add respectability and political influence to the university's case. The advantages of business regents in this respect would not be lost, however, if educators displaced only a minority of the presently more typical regents.

Where should a state university recruit even a few educator-regents? In a national poll of faculty at public and private institutions, 89 percent (26 percent with some reservations) thought that there should be faculty representation on their governing boards (Carnegie Commission, 1973, p. 97). But from the state's standpoint, a university's faculty, even more than its administration, seems to represent the institution itself rather than the public interest. To have faculty regents goes beyond the accepted principle that regents should hear from and be influenced by faculty and administrators—perhaps even through ex officio memberships that are kept to a small minority and probably to a nonvoting minority. What, then, about educators from other institutions? This is easy for private universities, and they have, as already observed, been adding educators to their boards. These trustees are ordinarily professors or administrators who hold their academic appointments at other institutions, although they might previously have been students or teachers at the university on whose board they now serve. A state university, however, is more sharply limited in its range of possibilities. If not by law then by effective political custom, it must have regents who reside in the state that supports the university, and this means that almost all prospective educator-regents will be at rival institutions—at other state institutions that compete for legislative funding or at private institutions whose relative status in attracting students is affected by how well or badly the state provides financial support for the state university. Alternatives from the educational community are readily excluded. Secondary school people do not commend themselves as experienced in dealing with the special problems of a university, and retired university educators suffer the disadvantage of age at a time when younger rather than older people are thought to need more representation.

Lowering the average age of board members is feasible for a state university as it is for a private university. Even if students are excluded as possible voting regents, just as faculty members are excluded as interested parties, it is easy enough to appoint or elect young men and women very near student age and just recently graduated from the university. Having at least a few members in their twenties and thirties does not diminish the political usefulness of trusteeship. A governor can select representatives from an otherwise unrepresented generation and still fulfill his partisan obligations. He is likely to have young as well as old campaign contributors, and some of the older ones may have sons or daughters whose appointments as regents would be welcomed as family honors. But the consequence of youthful appointments is not likely to be dramatic. Aside from being younger, boards would probably remain much as they are with respect to the socioeconomic backgrounds, work experiences, and general educational interests of their members.

On the basis of this probability, it is sometimes suggested that the quality of the lay membership could be improved if a panel of educators would screen possible regent nominees before a governor, or the voting public, exercises a choice. The panel would submit only a few names, from whom the choice would have to be made. A procedure of this kind is familiar in universities where faculty-dominated search-and-screen committees present short lists of administrative nominees to the selecting authorities. A more relevant political model, however, is the Missouri plan for nominating judges; this plan, like the regent-screening proposal, involves a public authority conventionally chosen either by popular vote or by popularly elected officials. The Missouri judicial plan turns over the nominating procedure for a given court vacancy to a commission composed mainly of lawyers elected by the bar association, plus a sitting judge and two other lawyers appointed by the governor. This commission, or panel, presents the governor with three approved candidates, one of whom the governor appoints. Plainly, the Missouri plan, without excluding political influence altogether, attempts to ensure judicial qualifications by reliance on the organized legal profession. Whether the judge will be a Democrat or Republican, the idea is that the bar association ensures professional quality. The idea appears to be fulfilled in the operation of the Missouri plan, according to Watson and Downing (1969). Their careful study, however, does not lead to an overall judgment. Even in the selection of judges, the plan is open to the objection that it gives too much power to a closed-shop professional group. This objection is much stronger, it seems to me, when applied to the screening of regents by a panel of educators. I do not mean that educators would be more self-interested than lawyers, but only that they would be screening and nominating for a policy-making board whose members, by tradition, are lay representatives rather than fellow professionals in the manner of judges administering the law.

Practical as well as principled arguments stand against the proposal to use a counterpart of the Missouri judicial-selection procedure in limiting the governor's choice of regents. Note, for example, Rauh's specific suggestion for "an advisory council composed of educators and citizens of standing which would advise with the governor in the selection process" (1969, p. 121). How would this advisory council be selected? Such a question cannot be settled as conveniently as it can be for the commission nominating potential judges. There the bar association is the obvious constituency to choose the nominators. It contains the relevant group of professional peers, conveniently organized in a quasi-public structure. True, these peers are interested parties—namely, lawyers who appear before judges—but there is no employment relationship as there is for the faculty and administrators of a university with respect to regents. Even if this difference is not as material as it seems, it remains hard to believe that the public and its elected officeholders would readily accept the power of a university's own staff to choose the representatives who would in turn nominate the limiting list of possible regents for the governor to appoint.

Perhaps, however, it would be easier to accept the idea that university personnel (perhaps including students) should select *some* of the nominators while nonuniversity groups selected others. But what nonuniversity groups? Alumni? Public school associations? Legislators? Present or former regents? The state supreme court? These questions are not answered in the Carnegie Commission's proposal for a screening device (1973, pp. 34–35). Yet it is crucially important to secure a base for the advisory nominating council that is legitimate from the state's standpoint in representing the public interest, and not just a base that members of the academy find legitimate. Rauh recognizes the point when he suggests that the council should have "citizens of standing" as well as educators, leaving open their manner of selection. The governor plainly loses his present freedom of choice under any kind of screening arrangement, just as he would with only educators on the advisory council. It is true that he remains the appointing authority, in behalf of the electorate, and he may occasionally welcome the constraints imposed by a panel of screened nominees when he wants to resist political or personal pressure to appoint someone the university regards as unsuitable. But it is highly unlikely that a governor will foster a plan to limit his freedom of choice. Politically effective resistance must be expected.

Regardless of its feasibility in this political sense, the screening device remains questionable as a means for strengthening regent authority. Only faculty and administrators seem to gain through the formalized opportunity to be represented in a council nominating regents, both to suggest sympathetic nominees and to argue against unsympathetic possibilities. Students may not regard the panel-nominated regents as possessing much more legitimacy than the presently selected regents unless students themselves had strong representation on the nominating council. Even if the student problem is put aside and only faculty and academic administrators appear on a nominating council, I doubt the efficacy of the council. Specifically, I doubt whether the university representation could be made large enough to serve the purposes of the academic community without becoming so large and dominant as to make nomination seem strictly the work of educational insiders. Trying to enhance in this way the legitimacy of regents internally while retaining it for the public is a little like squaring the circle. It endangers the essence of trusteeship as traditionally understood—that citizens

representing the public should govern the university in behalf of
the state to which it belongs.

Performance

Just how regents are to govern is a perplexing question. They
simply do not have the time, the experience, or the knowledge to
govern much of the large and complex educational institution for
which they are legally responsible. Nor is there any way, compatible
with the traditional conception of trusteeship, for board members to
acquire the time, experience, or knowledge. They would cease to
fulfill their roles as lay-citizen trustees if they were to become specialized. Therefore, regents continue to meet only a day or two a
month, plus a few days more here and there for committee or other
informal negotiation, while they also carry on their ordinary business or professional pursuits along with other civic and political
activities—often including service as trusteees for other institutions.

Having a substantial and expert staff is a usual answer for
this kind of difficulty. A board of regents, like the almost equally
part-time board of a business corporation, may be thought capable
of evaluating the recommendations of its chosen administrative
officers. Regents, frequently businessmen themselves, probably find
the parallel congenial. But it is deceptive. Not only does a business
board include the principal administrators of the company as directors, but the board and its staff have a common and single constituency in their stockholders, particularly a few large and dominant stockholders. On the other hand, regents, in representing the
people of a state, have a different constituency from that which is
most immediate for university administrators: the faculty always,
and now students too. By no means is a university administrator's
relationship to his faculty only like that of a corporation president's
relationship to his business employees. And insofar as regents assume
such a relationship for their university president, they make his task
impossible within the university. Regents appoint him along with
other administrators, but they cannot regard him only as their
agent. For better or worse, he and his staff represent faculty interests, student interests, and internal university interests generally—

often as opposed to certain external interests that regents may represent.

Another way of putting this point is to say that regents do not have any appreciable staff of their own. At the University of Wisconsin, for example, regents have a professional employee as their secretary, and he has a few clerical and secretarial assistants. Otherwise, in all financial, personnel, planning, and construction matters, regents depend for data and analysis on administrative officers serving under the president. Other universities, as far as I know, vary only slightly from this pattern, in which the board has no separate service from that of the university itself. Occasionally it is proposed that there be a large separate staff for regents. But the idea is odd because it means a duplicate administrative service. Not only would this be expensive, and hard to justify as a state expenditure, but whoever became the regents' director of their own administrative service would almost inevitably rival the power of the university president. The board itself would then lose a good deal of its supposed identification with the university, as it ceased in practice to fulfill the trusteeship conception that it be of, although not in, the institution.

Something like this may be occurring as a board assumes responsibility for a multicampus university created by extension of the original institution, or as a superboard is created for an entire state system of higher education. Although a separate administrative service for regents is not thereby created, the multicampus president and his staff become a "central administration" as distinct from the several campus administrations. It might in time come to look upon itself, and be regarded by regents, as more clearly associated with the board than with internal university interests. Regents would then have an understandable desire to enlarge the staff in numbers and in scope. The consequence is a conversion of the board, along with its staff, to a much more definitely external role, most feasibly expressed as coordination rather than government, or as a concern with "system-wide matters" (Lee and Bowen, 1971, pp. 439–440). When that happens, trusteeship, as traditionally understood, is transformed into something else.

Some transformation seems inevitable. The multicampus

university and the merged university system are not the only forces implying a change in regent status. The growing size and complexity of even a single major university campus are enough to make "governing" by regents an increasingly remote ambition. Almost always, in modern times, a gulf has developed between the broad statutory powers of regents and their capacity directly to exercise those powers. Corson (1960, p. 49) has well summarized a long-prevailing situation: board members, he notes, are dependent on others for the formulation and effective making of decisions; they are inadequately informed about basic institutional operations; and they are unable to influence the decisions, delegated to the faculty, that determine the character of the institution as an educational enterprise. Board meetings, he points out, tend to be formal affairs granting official approval for policies previously developed elsewhere. It is tempting to add that such routine action is the only workable answer to a board's problem of discharging its responsibilities. Regents simply cannot literally undertake to "fix and regulate the course of instruction and prescribe the extent and character of experiments to be made at the University," as, for example, Ohio State's board is statutorily charged with doing (Rauh, 1969, p. 3).

Over time, especially in the early 1960s, regent authority appeared in many universities to be exercised only pro forma with respect to the many academic and related matters for which statutory responsibility existed. A good illustration is to be found in personnel policy. Appointments, promotions, and salary increases of individual faculty members require board approval, ordinarily as submitted in each year's budget. Because the regents cannot possibly scrutinize the thousand or more such proposals, and because the academic community in any case claims superior judgment of academic merit, regents customarily accept the recommendations that administrators bring from the faculty—assuming that such recommendations follow general guidelines previously adopted by the board or by the administration acting under the board's authority. Yet regents, even if acting pro forma, are approving each individual appointment, promotion, and salary increase when they accept the budgetary recommendations. And no legal barrier exists to their deciding against a particular individual. In 1969 and 1970, however, when regents occasionally sought to use their power to veto a faculty appointment, promotion, or salary increase, they confronted a university community accustomed to the atrophy of that power and prepared to protest its use. The protest, in the known instances, involved faculty unwillingness to accept a regent definition of "good campus citizenship" as a criterion free from a threat to academic freedom; there is no doubt, however, that the university community also regards as wrong any criterion other than academic merit as judged by academic peers. And since regents, if exercising their power at all to determine faculty appointments, promotions, or salary increases, would necessarily be nonacademic in their judgment, they are expected to forgo the use of that power altogether.

A different status is accorded regent power over administrative personnel. Here we reach the heart of a board's evidently meaningful legitimate authority to make decisions capable of determining general policy in at least an indirect sense. Most important, regents select the university's president (or his equivalent under another title), and they can also force his resignation or dismiss him. With only slight qualifications, regent powers in these vital respects are de facto as well as de jure. They are also great in determining other important administrative appointees, although, of course, individual choices are likely to be the president's unless he has lost favor with the board. In any event, faculty objection to regent discretion in personnel actions involving administrators is not the same as it is for actions involving professors. A particular decision may be objected to, but the right of the regents to make it is seldom seriously questioned, even when faculty advice about selections is overridden (as it can be and is on occasion). Regents, therefore, can and do seek to influence university policy by changing administrators or by threatening at least implicitly to make such changes. The only plain limitation is that they cannot use the power very often without becoming ridiculous and reducing university administration to a shambles. This practical consideration means that hiring and firing administrators is less than a full-fledged substitute for the direct policy making that regents are seldom able to undertake. Even its indirect influence, it ought to be added, depends upon the effectiveness of the administrative authority, old or newly appointed, to make policy for the university. And that cannot always be assumed.

Regent relations with university administration have a

broader aspect than that of appointing individual administrators. The board also has the power to determine the structure for the exercise of their authority. The Carnegie Commission (1973, p. 33)' emphasizes and approves of this power to provide for "the governance of the institution." What is evidently meant is that the board should establish the *system* of government, acting in the manner of a constitutional convention that specifies the respective branches of government, the methods for selecting their officers, and the powers each is to exercise. No doubt it is practical and reasonable to expect regents to have the time and the competence (subject to advice) to undertake this structure-making responsibility. Its significance, however, is limited from two sides. Much of the academic structure of departments and colleges is dictated by a professional academic organization almost universal in American higher education. And much of the broad structure of a state's system of colleges and universities is determined by legislative action.

Whatever can be made of the regents' power to establish the administrative structure, it is a power that university administrators and faculty members surely prefer to having regents make administrative decisions or any policies transmitted by outside pressures. As noted earlier, the internal university view is that regents should resist rather than transmit such pressures. The farthest that university opinion goes in acknowledging a legitimate role here is to say that regents serve "as both moat and bridge between the university and the community" (Moos and Rourke, 1959, p. 311), thus transmitting as well as resisting public pressures. The sophisticated assumption implicit in this opinion is that transmitting and resisting are not alternative strategies, but that regents, in yielding to some community pressures, may put themselves and the university in a better position to resist other, greater pressures. Yet to accept any regent transmission of community pressures, even in the name of a long-run defense of the university, is difficult especially for nonadministrative members of the university community. They are likely to wonder how, with friends like these, they could need any enemies. Faculty members may not appreciate regent fears of gubernatorial and legislative actions by way of budgetary cuts, investigatory committees, onerous statutory regulations, new board appointments, or the creation of an entirely new governing board. And if professors appreciate the fears, they may still prefer the university to stand by existing policies rather than surrender even a little to outside demands. For them, yielding will almost always seem a failure of regents properly and effectively to champion the institution.

Yet from the university's standpoint, the regent performance that counts is the ability to secure the budgetary requests originating in the institution. Regents are expected not only to approve the requests but then to help obtain gubernatorial and legislative approval. As noted previously, almost half of American faculty members believe that fund raising is the only legitimate task of trustees. For a state institution, however, even regents who are most devoted to higher education and who are virtuous sentinels of academic freedom can fail to secure the funds. Perhaps the most devoted and virtuous have the most difficulty. Nor are eminence and high status, financial and otherwise, always overwhelming regent advantages. Political access is more important, and that access is severely limited by the arrangement under which most board members are politically associated not with present elected officeholders but with previous officeholders and especially previous governors. Other features of their long and overlapping terms may compensate for the handicap, but not in facilitating budgetary salesmanship. The difficulty appears inherent in the trusteeship conception. By being removed in principle from the immediate political environment, regents are rendered less capable of directly influencing that environment. At an extreme, they are so much identified with a former set of officeholders as to be positively harmful to the university case. Wisconsin experience provides examples both early in this century (Curti and Carstensen, 1949, Vol. II, pp. 71, 101, 216–217) and in the 1960s and early 1970s. The state may be exceptional in the ideological sharpness of its partisan shifts, but the greater rapidity of electoral than of regent turnover must almost everywhere limit political access.

Interestingly, however, it is not at all clear that shortening regent terms, so as more nearly to coincide with a governor's, would ensure a more effective regent presentation of a university's budgetary aspirations. A newly appointed board is most likely to share the appointing governor's view of how much state money the university should receive. If that amount is less than university administrators believe desirable or necessary, the regents themselves may make reductions before the budget formally reaches the state capitol. Or without going so far as to make their own reductions, they may be constrained, by party loyalty or personal relations with the governor, from using their political access to urge that requests be fully met. New regents are less likely than holdovers to be so identified with the university that they would want to adopt a specifically university position as against the overall fiscal policies of their fellow partisans now in state elective office. For this practical reason, as well as for other more conventional reasons, the weight of university opinion remains favorable to long and overlapping terms for regents. The probably limited political access of holdover regents seems a lesser disadvantage for the university. It can be reduced if holdover regents convert the few new members, when appointed by a new governor, to the pro-university positions of the established board. Then, optimistically, the new regents will use their political access to help obtain funds from elective officeholders. Implicitly, this is a key assumption of the trusteeship conception. Old regents, helped by the administration, are supposed to make good university representatives of their new colleagues. Together, they share a trust, and in discharging their responsibilities they are much like members of a small and exclusive club. Maintaining such a role, I have suggested, is uncertain in the political and academic world of the late twentieth century.

Durability

Uncertainty is the operative term for the views permeating the discussion of trusteeship in this chapter. I do not believe that boards of regents will or ought to be abolished. Nor do I have a sufficient basis for thinking that they will or should wither away. I am even sympathetic with the hope that they might be revitalized. Like all experienced university people, who know that there must be some public governing authority, I am more fearful of control by other state authorities than I am of regent authority. I believe that the American university has prospered in an environment in which trusteeship served partly as a buffer against more populist intervention. And I can tolerate a good deal of the ambiguity of a governing conception that vests public power in a body with only limited direct accountability to the public. But I cannot share the belief of the Carnegie Commission that "the role of the board of trustees is due for a renaissance" (1973, p. 33). Traditionally, in public affairs, the viability of trusteeship required an acceptance of the exercise of power by the good, the wise, and the rich. Into our times trusteeship survived along with an established and accepted order in which there was a broad consensus about the university and its purposes. Regents could then represent the public's interest in higher education and be accepted in doing so by the academic community—although not without increasing restiveness.

Regents are now beset from both sides. The public's interest, not just the public's tax support, has grown, and it has become more diverse. State officials respond to this interest, but they also significantly stimulate it and give it political focus. From their standpoint, regents may seem too heavily identified with the university to be readily accepted as representatives of the state. If regents are not identified with the university, however, they become absentee landlords in the eyes of the academic community. A modern faculty is especially unready to accept the credentials of lay citizens to govern their specialized professional affairs. Neither set of difficulties is entirely new. But the difficulties, in principle and practice, are now harder to solve through regent authority. Proposals for changing board membership, while sometimes useful in broadening representation, do not promise much help with the basic problem of trusteeship. Plans to load a board with educators, or with those chosen by educators, can destroy trusteeship altogether. A solution will seem even more complicated when, later in this study, the impact of collective bargaining is taken into account; regents, it can be seen, ordinarily lack the independent funding power to make binding union agreements.

In noting the difficulties that now seem inherent in the role of regents, I do not suggest that regents lack devotion to their universities and their states. My own limited observation is that they have considerable devotion. True, individual regents do not always perceive university interests as I and many other professors perceive them. And, when they do have the same perceptions, they do not always choose the same means that we would choose to serve our interests. These differences may occasionally reflect only individual differences of judgment, where right is no group's monopoly; but principally the differences flow from their attempt to represent the state's general concern with the university and to do so without the credential of most democratic representatives and also without membership in good standing within the community that regents are supposed to govern. The fundamental question is whether trusteeship provides for adequate representation of the enlarged public interest in higher education. A means for such representation, it is assumed, must be maintained in a democratic society that expects a great deal from its tax-supported universities. Yet, in the absence of a superior method, still compatible with the traditions of academic freedom and institutional autonomy, universities understandably cling to trusteeship despite its anachronistic qualities. Its endurance is likely even though it does not guarantee so effective a governmental instrument as to resist other forms of public control.

FIVE

ᘙᘙᘙᘙᘙᘙᘙᘙᘙᘙᘙᘙᘙᘙᘙᘙᘙᘙ

Managerialism

ᘙᘙᘙᘙᘙᘙᘙᘙᘙᘙᘙᘙᘙᘙᘙᘙᘙᘙ

In reflections about university government, managerialism is seldom conceived as a separate source of authority. Administrators are ordinarily understood to be agents for other more broadly based bodies. In state universities they act either for regents, representing the broader public, or for the university community, chiefly its faculty. Although they develop their own constituencies in and out of their institutions, there is no clear-cut basis in principle for their doing so. The board of regents officially intervenes between a university president and citizens of a state as it does between a president and elected public representatives. Nor are high-level university administrators responsible to their internal constituencies of faculty and students in the same legal sense as they are to the authority that appoints them.

These points of principle suggest that administration should be subsumed under each of several conceptions of authority; that university managers should be treated successively as the agents of state government, regents, professors, and students. Certainly I discuss

99

administration in each of these ways. But I also pause briefly to discuss managerialism as a separate conception of university authority. I do so for two reasons. In the first place, the public believes that administrators should have some university policy-making responsibility. In the second place, university administrators—because of their access to information and because of their dual responsibilities to external and internal constituents—often act creatively both to mediate and to formulate institutional policies. In this respect, managerialism as a topic links the discussions of the conventionally separated external and internal authorities. It reflects my desire to treat both as inextricable parts of the whole problem of university government. At the same time, the functioning of university administrators between external and internal bases of authority will display the instability of such dual responsibilities. And any such instability raises the question whether the university administrators ought to be responsible in more clear-cut ways to other authorities, some to the academic community and others to the public and its representatives.

Historically, the form and the power of American university administrations are the products of lay trusteeship. The American principle of vesting de jure sovereignty in boards of regents or trustees is "responsible for the most striking contrast between American and British university governance; namely, the existence of the administration as an estate of the university, separate from the estates of the faculty and the students. There is no administrative estate in the British universities" (Ashby, 1971, p. 67). British universities do have administrators; but they are agents of the faculty, de jure as well as de facto. Converting American administrators to de facto agents of the faculty, as professors have sought to do, is at odds not just with the de jure situation but also with the conventional belief of regents and their publics about how state universities should be managed. Generally this belief assumes a hierarchical system of authority in which each administrator is responsible to his superior and eventually to the president, who in turn is responsible to the lay board (Hartnett, 1970, p. 67). The board's will is to be done without the board's having to make many decisions. Administrators would be expected to know that will, or to anticipate it, and so make it effective in the university. Like members of corporate boards of directors, regents would look to strong executives as their agents. The management model of business enterprise looms large in American life generally, and specifically for university administration over the last century.

In major universities and probably in many others, this hierarchical view of administrative authority has long been qualified in practice. Scholars of university administration readily recognize the qualification. Corson perceives that decision-making responsibility is "more widely diffused" in universities than in other forms of enterprise and that "substantial independent authority for making various types of decisions is allocated beyond the trustees and the president to the faculty as a group, to individual teachers, to department heads, to deans, to coaches, and to administrative officers" (1960, pp. 10–11). Millett, writing both as a scholarly specialist in public administration and as an experienced university administrator, goes farther in suggesting that universities are not organized according to a "hierarchy of power" but rather as a "community of power" (1962, p. 64). As Millett understands a university, the term *management,* in the private business sense, is not properly applied to an administration whose task is to facilitate the work of the educational enterprise rather than to manage it (1962, p. 179).

This departure from the managerial pattern is appreciated by most of the principal officers who are supposed to exercise any hierarchical authority. In a very recent study of presidents, Cohen and March (1973, chap. 6–7) emphasize the realization of chief executives in universities that they cannot fulfill the traditionally heroic roles accompanying their official titles and job descriptions. University presidents work hard and long, but they know that they achieve only modest effects on policies. According to Cohen and March, a good deal of presidential work, particularly talking to people and presiding over meetings, is an assertion only of the symbols of power. The sense of presidential powerlessness seems to have grown recently. Edward Levi of Chicago reports that "the American university president in general . . . has very little power left" (1969, p. 76). And Father Hesburgh of Notre Dame says that he has only roughly one tenth as much power over the university's affairs as he had when he first became president, in 1952 (Barlow, 1970, p. 12). It is not clear whether reduced power is linked to presidential turnover or whether turnover itself has significantly in-creased in recent years. Kerr (1970, pp. 139–140) and Cohen and March (1973, chap. 8) present conflicting evidence on this point. Presidents may survive just as well with more limited powers. They can often shrewdly avoid policy making in favor of the symbolic roles that Cohen and March discuss.

The explanation for limiting hierarchical authority is im-plicit in Millett's description of the university as a *community* of power. In this community the faculty member, in his role as an indi-vidual practitioner, is not subject to orders from the president. Hierarchical command is legitimate only in procedural and house-keeping details. In whatever is academic, by faculty definition, there are no orders in the usual sense. A president can presumably direct a vice-president, a dean, and a staff of assistants to pursue his policies even in academic matters, but their effective pursuit is limited by an inability to direct faculty members to carry out aca-demic policies that are not of their own choosing. He may even find that other administrators, notably deans and department chairmen, are not really *his* administrators as much as they are the faculty's. Their response to passing along orders may be no more than nomi-nally favorable. If other administrators stop short of opposing presi-dential programs, they may still do little to carry them out against the desires of their faculty colleagues. The working of this profes-sorial power is the subject of the next chapter. Only its general char-acter needs to be stressed here. Higher education has developed much the same organizational collegiality in the United States as it has in Europe. It flows from the clustering in universities of highly specialized professionals, whose work resembles in many ways that of individual legal or medical practitioners but whose employment is collective by association with peers, in departments or institutes, and by salaried status (Wilson, 1942, pp. 72–73). The professionals themselves insist on making the policies relating to their work. Thus, they bring to an organization a basic principle that is incompatible with government from the top down and with decision making by a single head. Faculty members prefer something closer to Weber's description of a premodern structure of authority in which groups of people "are unwilling to allow any individual to hold authority over them" (1947, p. 413).

Collegial practices impose a special qualification on the effectiveness of hierarchical authority in a university. Dismissal of faculty-level administrators does not have the same consequence as do management dismissals in other enterprises. For example, a president can dismiss a dean as a dean; but ordinarily the dean, as an old faculty member himself, holds a professorship entitling him to tenure in that capacity. He may view his loss of an administrative post with considerably greater equanimity than if he had to look for a position at another institution, in administration or something else. Although this situation need not deter dismissal of an administrator, it deprives the superior officer of some usual managerial advantages implicit in the possibility of dismissal. His subordinates, especially the most important academic administrators, have less cause than subordinates in other organizations to be concerned about the consequences of losing their administrative positions. They may as a result be no less loyal, but surely they are in a stronger position to resist presidential policies, especially by the explicit or implicit threat to resign administrative posts, when they have immediate fall-back positions as faculty members. They are less dependent on a superior officer for their professional futures and for their livelihoods than are managers of most other enterprises. It is true that they would have to look elsewhere for new administrative appointments, if desired, but they retain the advantages of local professorial status while conducting any such search.

Another feature of administration in the collegial environment is amateurism. Rotating department chairmanships, often at intervals of a very few years, is an obvious manifestation of academic preferences for a nonspecialized administrator who is basically a colleague and only temporarily the first among equals. At higher levels of academic administration, from deans through presidents, where rotation or limited terms of office are not usually established as a fixed principle, the collegial thrust toward amateurism expresses itself by the insistence that appointees be academic professionals. Administrative experience and competence are not thereby excluded as requisites for office, but they must be sought among candidates who also possess sufficient academic status to qualify as faculty colleagues. In practice, this means someone who has a doctoral degree, who has taught for a substantial period in a university, and who has also established a scholarly reputation at one time or another. Consequently, he cannot have spent more than part of his adult career in administration. He would first have been trained for something entirely different, and then have spent his first ten or twenty postdoctoral years doing mainly nonadministrative academic work. Amateurism, in large measure, is thus made likely if not actually guaranteed.

To avoid any invidiousness associated with "amateurs," it is better to speak of teacher-scholars becoming administrators. They may, of course, be so gifted that they quickly overcome their late start in administration and develop all of the managerial skills of professional administrators. A few years in one administrative post thus prepares the teacher-scholar for a higher one. After several years in several posts, he is an experienced administrator, and incidentally, if now at a very high level, he will no longer seem a teacher-scholar in the eyes of faculty members. Professors, however, realistically accept this in their presidents and comparable top officials. They do not expect these officials to have much to do with educational matters anyway; faculties prefer to take care of these matters themselves, securing administrative acquiescence while avoiding administrative interference. Therefore, they are satisfied with former teacher-scholars as their presidents. Whether the teacher-scholar experience is past or recent, however, is less significant than the fact that such experience remains a minimum credential for presidents and for other administrators of direct concern to the faculty. It is a credential, along with others, that professors ordinarily insist upon when they have the major voice, as they often do, in the search-and-screen committees used by universities to nominate administrative candidates.

The search-and-screen procedure itself not only produces candidates who have been teacher-scholars; it also works (when it works as faculty members want it to work) so as to impose limits on which teacher-scholars can be named. Again the collegial thrust is at odds with the conception of hierarchical management. A university president, who may himself have been chosen from a limited list presented to a board, selects many of his principal administrators from nominees of search-and-screen committees. I do not want to exaggerate the impact of these committees. They are now widespread, but they are not universally accepted even in principle. And when they are established in principle, they may fall short of exerting effective power. My impression is that regents zealously guard their freedom to choose a president, subject more often to faculty advice than to faculty search-and-screen limitations, and that they and their chosen president exercise considerable independent judgment in choosing other administrators. In practice, they can even make search-and-screen committees their instruments by controlling or influencing committee members. It is still fair to say, however, that the search-and-screen procedure represents a strong and distinctive resistance to conventionally structured management authority.

The resistance to managerial authority, it is well to emphasize, is in *academic* administration. To be sure, the faculty will oppose presidential authority whenever the president represents the tradition of hierarchical management in educational affairs. The faculty will also oppose any such management by academic vice-presidents, chancellors, vice chancellors, and deans. Thus, the most prestigious academic administrators, coming themselves from certified faculty backgrounds, are to function with due regard for faculty prerogatives. But they constitute only a small minority of the total administrative apparatus of the university. For example, business vice-presidents (in contrast to academic vice-presidents) seldom come from the faculty, and neither do the many other specialized administrators dealing with registration, admissions, counseling, accounting, records, publicity, budgeting, construction, and miscellaneous business services. They are ordinarily professional career administrators whose appointments, although subject to promotion, demotion, and transfer to other institutions, are more durable than those of academic administrators (including the president). Hence, they secure the advantages of experience and continuity to go along with their specialized expertise. With such advantages, a considerable portion of management responsibility tends to fall into their hands, as it supposedly does in any large and complex organization with a permanent staff capable of doing the work over which a less technical leadership has been chosen to preside. In this respect, a university is hardly unique (Weber, 1947, p. 413). Like any modern organization dealing with a large clientele, it needs a specialized bureaucratic management routinely providing service regardless of turnover at academic levels of administration, notably at the very top level. Bureaucracy of this kind is to a large extent self-contained, having an internal hierarchical structure subject to overall presidential direction, but it coexists with the decidedly nonhierarchical distribution of authority in the academic realm of the university (Stroup, 1966, pp. 38–39).

The coexistence, however, is uneasy. Every sensitive observer of the large contemporary university knows that the specialized administrative or business realm impinges on academic policy making and that increasingly influential decisions are made by experienced career administrators rather than by teacher-scholar administrators. In a state institution this kind of decision making necessarily follows from the growth of externally mandated program budget procedures. They require trained, experienced, and skillful administrators more likely to be recruited from federal or state service than from university faculty ranks. In practice, their authority is harder to contain than that of the university's conventional business manager, who has also occasionally become a considerable power in his own right. It is especially difficult for the faculty to impose effective limits on administrators from outside its own ranks. Symbolically, it does so when insisting that the very top place be occupied by a teacher-scholar type and that specialized career administrators fill only positions carrying nonacademic labels, as distinguished from academic vice-presidents or academic deans. The symbolism has become blurred by the more frequent selection of senior administrators who have had specialized managerial training and who also meet the nominal Ph.D. requirement (Donoghue and Shannon, 1972). As this happens and as, in other ways, a noncollegial authority becomes more overt in academic matters, faculty members will almost certainly seek new means to resist managerialism.

The conventional collegial resistance has never precluded a considerable administrative authority. Well before the recent development of specialized program budget controls, a hierarchical control of financial resources impinged on academic affairs. Indeed, that control might have been more completely hierarchical in earlier times, when presidents and deans, while without technical administrative skills, were more formidable as the official wielders of regent authority. But allocating the university's budgetary resources remains, in our time as before, a largely administrative task. Even in an institution with the greatest faculty domination of personnel appointments and promotions as well as curriculum matters and research programs, administrators still exert considerable power in the distribution of salary increases, funds for new faculty positions, and financial support for a variety of activities of concern to faculty members. Presidents, chancellors, and deans are thus in positions to make policy. That is, through the use of the financial reward structure, they can indirectly influence individual faculty behavior (say, to do more teaching and less research, or more research and less teaching); and through the allocation of funds, they can directly support certain academic programs more generously than others. Although power employed in this way runs counter to the collegial spirit, university communities are somewhat accustomed to its presence and its impact. Officially, funds are distributed from the top down; and this distribution provides administrators with opportunities, based partly on informational advantages, to fulfill some of an employer's role.

How these opportunities have been used by administrators varies considerably with the times and circumstances. During flush years of expansion, like those of the 1960s, presidents, vice-presidents, and deans decide the portions of their increasing budgets that go to particular existing programs and to any new programs. Nothing has to be cut back or eliminated. In fact, almost everything needs more money because of generally increasing enrollments. This imposes a fairly effective limit on administrative discretion. Much of the available money supply follows enrollment. Departments that attract more and more students get more and more funds to staff faculty and related positions. Also some of the available money helps to retain prestige faculty members tempted by competitive offers in an expanding academic market. Still there are always decisions at the margins—a little more or less for this or that program or professor—that allow administrators to make a crucial impact on educational policy. What is especially hard to do in boom times, however, is to insist on any general policy that faculty members do not want to adopt themselves. Obviously, when there is a rapidly growing national demand for professors, no president or dean will succeed in increasing his faculty's undergraduate teaching load or in doing much else to increase faculty effort in meeting strictly institutional responsibilities of this nature. Indeed, in these respects university administrators do well if they just hold the line. They did not do so, in my observations, during the developments of the 1960s described in Chapter Two. Whether most of them wanted to hold the line is not clear. If they had so desired, I doubt whether they could have managed it while still maintaining high-quality faculties. There was at least a temporary erosion of the capacity of administrators to manipulate the reward structure for the benefit of undergraduate teaching.

In contrast, during a period of financial stringency like that of the early 1970s, administrators are better able to use their budgetary allocations to achieve institutional purposes—at least, to achieve those purposes that administrators perceive as institutional (Rourke and Brooks, 1966, p. 85). They have, it is true, much less money to distribute, but the little that they have is much sought after. Even with no new money, there is a power of the purse that derives from the now recognized need to cut back some departments or programs in order to maintain or expand those that have more students or otherwise commend themselves. This is not to contend that administrators welcome financial stringency. I know of none who would not prefer the prosperity of expansion. The management of scarcity—despite the one advantage cited—is unpleasant and lacks the creative policy-making possibility that accompanies growing financial resources. For this reason as well as for other apparent causes, administrators in state universities welcome and ordinarily encourage the enrollment increases that justify larger budgets to teach the additional students. By allocating so many tax dollars for each student, states encourage universities to attract more students.

With or without growing budgets, the admittedly substantial financial power and influence of administrators must be understood as subject to certain limits peculiar to the university. Often, especially in prestige institutions, professors make recommendations at the departmental level, on their own or through their chairman, about each other's salaries, within certain boundaries fixed by available funds. They demand explanations if these recommendations are overridden by less specialized administrators. Similarly, professors claim to be in the best position to judge the relative worth of academic programs in or near their own fields. Furthermore, even if faculty members defer to their judgment, administrators have only limited sums over which to exercise discretion. Most university funding is committed for each year to continuing programs that cannot be abandoned or greatly reduced. If there are too few students for given programs or courses, tenured professors still expect regular salaries and other funds to meet rising costs. Even the administrative determination of salary increases, already observed as limited to the margins by departmental recommendations, may be still further limited by legislated formulas ensuring fixed percentage raises for everyone, or fixed levels for each rank. All of this, I know, describes the incrementalism that characterizes budgetary decision making in many enterprises. It is not the equivalent of administrative powerlessness in financial matters. Marginal budget decisions are the essence of the process. They may be no more substantially restricted in universities than they are for administrators in many other enterprises. But they are restricted in a few special ways that illustrate the environment in which university management must operate.

Whatever the impact of these restrictions on managerial power, there can be no doubt about the budgetary responsibility of administrators. Their lives are dominated by it. They make financial commitments to colleges and departments on the basis of anticipated legislative appropriations, which are thus absolutely crucial for administrative well-being. Nothing seems worse than insufficient funds to meet institutional teaching responsibilities or other commitments. A level of anxiety exists here that the faculty need not and does not share, and it accounts for an administrative sensitivity about adverse university publicity, during legislative sessions, that seems unwarranted to the faculty. In this respect, administrators are a kind of separate class within the institution. Their budgetary anxiety is a common ground that they share with regents more than with faculty colleagues. And, like the regents to whom they are responsible, administrators cannot shape and present the institution's academic programs in ways of their own choosing. An administration may prepare its own budgetary requests and subsequently make most of the decisions about allocations, but it has to contend with a substantially independent faculty to carry out the programs.

The managerial implications of this faculty independence have been observed in the rejection of hierarchical authority in academic affairs. Something more than hierarchy, however, is rejected. Many professors simply question the policy-making credentials of administrators. Partly this questioning comes from an unwillingness to accord a genuine professional status to the field of university administration. The specialized staff assistant, exemplified by an accounting officer or a program budgeter, may be respected as a trained and experienced technician, but he is not viewed as a manager of the educational enterprise—only as its useful servant. Above him, it is assumed, are academic administrators, whose tasks are not technical or specialized. Their status is the crucial one. They are the transplanted professors whom the faculty wants, not only because the faculty prefers administrators to share its academic values but also because the faculty does not believe in the existence of a field of competency that can be called "general university management."

Professors live in a world of specialized scholarly disciplines, in which neither the substance nor the method of administrative work has an honored place. There is a field of public administration, often within political science or linked to business and other areas in an interdisciplinary program. Fields of educational administration and of higher education exist in education schools. Occasionally, within a university, one or another of these fields is respectable and even prestigious, but it tends to be so only when it is sufficiently academic to be removed from the training of practitioners. The status gained for the scholarly study of administration is not conferred on the practice. The academic community does not regard the one as relevant to the other, at the level of presidencies and deanships, in the manner that studying chemistry is relevant to becoming a chemistry professor. From the faculty point of view, university administrators "cannot convincingly claim, *as a group,* any distinctive expertise which might clothe their bare, formal positions with 'professional' legitimacy. In the highly professionalized organization that is a university, this alone means that their very authority is always more or less precarious" (Lunsford, 1968, p. 6). In other words, a chemistry professor or a philosophy professor does not believe that a dean or a president can possibly "know" about higher education in the way that the professor knows about chemistry or philosophy (or about his subfield of chemistry or of philosophy).

Academics in general also do not always support administrators in their belief that they decide and act in the best interests of the institution. For Lunsford (1968, p. 9) the belief is mythical and so therefore is the image of rational administration that it supports. By denying the validity of this belief, academics may be delivering the most significant of all challenges to the legitimacy of university administration. If presidents, chancellors, and deans are not entitled, by virtue of their positions, to regard themselves as institution-serving decision makers, what other basis for independent action can they have? The answer "none" is unlikely to trouble many faculty members, who believe that there should be no administrative action independent of the faculty. But such an answer would trouble virtually every administrator who wants to be more than a clerk registering the faculty's will, if and when it is collectively expressed, or more than a messenger for regent policies. An administrator who cannot secure legitimacy for his own position in institutional decision making, however, may very well become just such a messenger. He may even want to cite the authority of regents as the basis for what is really his own policy. Regents, too, it is true, have an internal campus legitimacy problem, but they may nevertheless add something to an even more sharply challenged administration. They can, more easily than a president or a dean, claim that they represent an institutional interest as perceived by the public. Therefore, they have much less reason than administrators to worry about any consequent unpopularity on a campus. Unlike regents, most campus administrators (as distinguished from the new breed of central administrators of state systems) regularly live and work in their universities. They feel dependent on the support of the university community in a way that regents do not.

Perhaps it is the immediacy of administration that produces a special faculty antipathy for its power. It seems "personal and arbitrary," in the words of a summary of professorial attitudes (Caplow and McGee, 1958, pp. 228–229). Its organizational logic, according to another faculty writer, is "insensitive to subtle matters of spirit" (Presthus, 1962, p. 240). The antipathy is old and well established. Thorstein Veblen's (1957, pp. 63–64, 68, 71) views are well known, and there are other early twentieth-century examples (Jastrow, 1913, p. 318). More recently Paul Goodman (1962, pp. 162, 169, 172) expressed the antiadministration bias in extreme form. No doubt, his desire to eliminate university administration altogether, by eliminating large and complex institutions, goes much further than most faculty members believe desirable or feasible. More often professors want only to reduce the size of university administration as a means to reduce its scope as well as its costs. Almost half of all American faculty members responding to the Carnegie Commission's national survey thought that their institutions would be better off with fewer administrators (1973, p. 97).

This response reflects considerable frustration among professors who have seen the growth of administrative positions in their increasingly large and complex institutions. Trying to limit that growth means a resistance to the evidently inevitable bureaucratization of modern society. While faculty members have therefore apparently failed in any effort to curb an administration's size, they have succeeded in limiting its power. I am thinking here of new or sharper limits developed especially in the 1950s and 1960s. The conventional inhibitions were probably rising throughout this century, as faculties progressively asserted their rights against administrations, but they were made especially strong during the years of most rapid university expansion. Professors, when in short supply, were able to win new privileges and greater independence generally —not just in budgetary affairs—from the institutional control represented by administrators. Nonuniversity sources for grants and contracts purchased a good deal of practical independence, and so did the abundance of competitive teaching and research offers from other institutions (Barzun, 1968, p. 150). The consequent weakening of vestigial hierarchical authority tended to be obscured by the growth of the administrative apparatus necessary to serve the increasingly large and complex academic establishment. New and different technical tasks had to be performed, and certain old ones had to be handled in less casual and more formal ways. But the actual enlargement of the bureaucracy—however irritating to professors notoriously sensitive to increased paperwork—should not be confused with the substantive power over academic programs and personnel. The latter power, more than ever, ceased to be feasible for administrators to exercise effectively (Riesman, 1969). Hierarchy declined even as bureaucracy grew. Or, more precisely, hierarchy declined still further in academic affairs. Now, "academic freedom is more and more interpreted in such a way as to keep the administration out of any truly academic affairs" (Lazarsfeld, 1962, p. 764). This may seem an overstatement if one conceives administrative roles in primarily faculty-representational terms; in that case, there is still room for persuasive leadership here and there. But of course such a role is hardly hierarchical. Not only does the "representative" administrator need to obtain faculty consent for his policies—probably always necessary in at least a tacit sense; he also needs a rather explicit mandate from the professorial constituency.

Most of us in an academic community regard many of the new limits on administrative authority as beneficent. Requiring explicit faculty consent, for example, seems only to bring into the open an administrator's engineering of consent, to regularize his mediating and compromising roles, and to make him publicly responsible within the university community. Also welcomed are the developing safeguards against arbitrary power, including due-process rights for students as well as for staff members. It is hard to argue that these rights are not worth the price of the corresponding diminution of administrative power. No one is prepared to defend the arbitrary exercise of authority.

More broadly, however, my description of both the conventional and the recent limits on administrative authority raises questions about the adequacy of the managerialism that remains. To the extent that campus administrators become primarily faculty representatives or virtually faculty delegates, they do not serve as agents of regent or of state authority. In practice, of course, they try to mediate between public authority and the academic community. It is as mediators that university presidents, in particular, now frequently perceive themselves. I believe that the term is well applied to the nature of the work of university administrators, as it is to administrators in many other organizations. I do not regard mediation and compromise as poor or powerless substitutes for hierarchical command. Within a campus community, skill and success in these respects are the essence of effective leadership. But the specific task

of mediating between public authority and the academic community
is not convincingly fulfilled by a campus administration identified
with the academic community. The reasons for this identification,
I have suggested, are implicit in the nature and development of the
university.

If campus officers should be acknowledged as representatives
primarily of the academic community, to bargain largely in its behalf, they would have to deal with other administrators who more
directly represent a board or a state agency of some kind. These
other administrators may be emerging as staff members of coordinating councils, multicampus university headquarters, or superboards responsible for merged university systems. The common element is the removal of administrators from a campus and from a
particular university. If not always detached geographically, the
central administrators are removed in the more significant sense of
working in a different world from the faculty's. They are a new and
different breed from the teacher-scholars in campus administrative
posts. Obviously, the detached administrators are no more able than
campus administrators to govern internal university affairs in hierarchical fashion. In fact, by background they seem less able to do
so. They lack academic experience and legitimacy. The reasonable
assumption remains that campuses cannot and should not be managed hierarchically. But this assumption leaves room for universities
to be responsive to the public interest as that interest is formulated
in broad educational policy by the public's representatives. Necessarily, I believe, this formulation involves the help of an administrative staff. The development of such a staff, removed from the university campus, is undoubtedly a threat to the traditional autonomy
of institutions; it is especially threatening to the autonomy of prestige institutions and even to their continued quality status. There
are good reasons, which I certainly share, for university faculties and
their administrators to limit the governing scope of essentially external administrators. The relationship requires an effective bargaining stance. The university has much that it ought to defend.
But in doing so, it has to face the fact that the state, or its council or
board, needs and will have its own administrative help in establishing educational priorities.

SIX

Professorialism

Choosing the right word for the conception of professorial governing power is difficult. I want a term to describe the claims of professors to make university policy in whatever spheres they believe are rightfully theirs. Since professors are working members of the institution being governed, the word *syndicalism* first seemed appropriate for the professorial sharing of power. But, derived as it is from the word for unions, in the Romance languages, syndicalism stands for worker-management through trade unions and therefore can be confused with the collective bargaining conception of the next chapter. More substantively, syndicalism implies participation not just by professors but also by the rest of a university's work force—the secretaries, assistants, maintenance crews, research associates, and many others noted earlier. Professors are no more than a substantial minority of the staff of any large university, even when their category is generously defined, as it is here, to include nontenured assistant professors along with associate professors and full professors. Often this professoriate is synonymous with *faculty,* in whose name power is asserted, but

115

the faculty may also include instructors and lecturers, plus some nonteaching personnel like librarians and administrators. In any case, the still largely professorial faculty is far short of representing the whole of a university's staff. Rather, it is an elite segment, although a large one, within that staff. Its claims to power flow from professional and academic credentials and not from a general theory of worker control.

Many professors, while classifiable as professional workers, are managers, employers, and academic entrepreneurs within units of the larger employing institution. They are supervisory participants in the academic enterprise. *Corporatism,* suggesting government by professors as a corporate or collegial body, may accordingly be a less misleading term than *syndicalism,* but it suffers the disadvantage of association with Mussolini's corporate state. Perhaps *professorial collegialism* would be suitable. Its awkwardness, however, leads me to settle on *professorialism* as an adequately descriptive term for the conception of faculty power in university government. As a word, it is only slightly cumbersome and not at all invidious. It suits the ambiguities of a conception of power that is often more implicit than explicit, more latent than regularly exercised, and more a restraining veto than a fully responsible governing force. Professorialism means faculty power whether or not it is organized for positive policy making in a university.

The point is more than a terminological nicety. In my analysis professorial power—although it emerges as a significant factor— is not ordinarily responsible collectively for university policies beyond a narrow range. It may, of course, be conceived in such a way as to be more broadly responsible, and that possibility must be explored. But I am especially interested in the implications of the current situation, in which professorial power, although fragmented and only sporadically exercised in general policy making, is nevertheless a critical element in university government. Professors, individually or in small groups, may make many important policies even while their campus senates are ineffective, and they may constrain other authorities from making broader university policies without at least tacit faculty consent. Whatever the disadvantages for other interests of this division between power and responsibility, it is likely to fulfill the aspirations of many professors, who find it neither feasible nor desirable to run the university but who do not want anyone else to run it according to nonfaculty criteria.

Professorialism is bound to seem an internally based conception whose claims to authority, like those of students, are sharply different from the claims of the state, its regents, or its administrators. I note the transition from external to internal authorities, as these are commonly understood, but I consider their relationships sufficiently intertwined to justify analysis in one volume. Thus, professorialism should be understood as elitist—not only in relation to the more numerous other staff members and students within the university but also in relation to public authority. It is an elitism, however, that rests on modern as well as ancient credentials. Professors can reasonably claim wisdom, experience, and specialized expertise, along with campus residence, as the bases for their authority. These credentials are plainly and explicitly stated in an AAUP-sponsored study: "Faculty participation in university government is not an expression of some kind of democratic principle adapted from the outside world; it is, rather, the consequence of the unique professional expertise of the professor which makes his contributions to decision making essential to the success of the university" (Mason, 1972, p. 19). A relatively democratic principle appears only when professorial decision making is compared to the process of administrative management. As befits a large elite group, professors conduct discussions and make their collegial decisions by majority vote or by consensual agreement.

Individual Autonomy

Faculty power, although also expressed at departmental and other levels of university government, has its roots in the individual professor's freedom to define his work in a fashion uncharacteristic of most employment relations. The nature of the academic enterprise justifies such freedom on the ground that it is conducive to the best research and teaching. Whether professors enjoy the freedom, as they presumably do, is not the most persuasive consideration. The relevant social consideration is that students and the community generally will benefit from the freedom accorded the professor, through his tenured status and procedural safeguards, to express unpopular or controversial ideas. Certainly such protection serves professorial interests, but at the same time it serves the public's interest in freedom of inquiry and in the educational quality accompanying such inquiry. This much seems incontrovertible in principle, at any rate for those reading this book, and accordingly worth little attention here despite the occasional difficulties in maintaining the protection in notorious cases.

Of greater present concern are the implications for university government when the professorial freedom being protected is unrelated to the controversial political and social subjects exciting the community at large. The individual professor asserts the right to decide what and how he should teach in a given course (whose content is only loosely described in a catalog statement that is probably his own), to decide what course he should teach (subject to a little collegial bargaining), and to determine his own research projects. These rights are commonplace and almost taken for granted within most large state universities. Occasionally a professor becomes aware of the significance of these rights when he realizes that teaching assistants and perhaps instructors at his own university do not have such rights, that even professors in some colleges lack the same rights, or that students are suddenly demanding new and different courses. Most of the time, however, the professor's freedom to decide what work he will do and how he will do it is unquestioned to an extent that is extraordinary for anyone who is not self-employed. Apart from a few classes each week, whose days and hours the professor usually chooses himself, his time is mainly his own to distribute between related teaching tasks, research, and various university assignments, on the one hand, and his off-campus professional, business, and recreational pursuits, on the other hand. He decides whether to work in an evening rather than an afternoon, or to work both times or neither time. He decides whether a professional conference across the country, or across the world, is more important than meeting regularly his own class schedule, or more important than simply being available on campus without classes. If this conspicuous flexibility in work time appears to have little impact on university policy outcomes except to encourage casualness in student habits, it is still a good indicator of a general professorial autonomy that does directly affect academic policy.

Note the consequences of the substantive freedom of a professor to teach what he wants to teach. The professor is a research specialist of some kind to begin with. His freedom to define his teaching subject or content means that he can and does teach his specialty. Although he may thus serve student interests, even very well, it will be as a byproduct of his own professional interests and not primarily as a result of an institutionally defined need. That need, of course, might have been defined to include the particular specialization when the professor was appointed, and stated or confirmed from time to time by departmental approval of the professor's proposal to teach a particular course. But professors, notably tenured professors, are free to change or modify their specialties. Their course proposals are usually approved routinely. And, under any course label, teaching freedom allows great latitude for changing actual course content. Consequently, a university's courses as well as its research—in other words, its academic programs—are really the aggregate of what individual professors choose to offer. In this sense, professors surely make university policy. They do so, it is true, within the overall budgetary constraints that limit the range and number of specializations, principally by limiting numbers of appointments. But such constraints do not prevent a professor from offering a course, under one name or another, that covers an area not specifically budgeted.

A professor's freedom to teach what he wants to teach is not generally interpreted, however, as meaning that a professor is free to introduce material obviously extraneous to the announced subject of the course—for example, foreign policy opinions in a mathematics course. As the American Association of University Professors has said, through its council, "It is a teacher's mastery of his subject and his own scholarship which entitle him to his classroom and to freedom in the presentation of his subject. Thus, it is improper for an instructor persistently to intrude material which has no relation to his subject, or to fail to present the subject matter of his course as announced to his students and as approved by the faculty in their collective responsibility for the curriculum" (1970). Even this statement, although perhaps regarded as unfortunate by some politically minded professors, does not materially qualify individual freedom. The use of the word *persistently* suggests that an instructor may *occasionally* intrude material that has no relation to his subject. Moreover, the AAUP, like faculty members generally, will insist that professorial colleagues are to decide what is persistent rather than occasional, as well as what is extraneous. Professors will seldom override a colleague's judgment of the boundaries of his own subject matter. In these and related matters, such as adjourning classes for a political cause, professors can be expected to err on the side of the freedom that they share. For example, the AAUP leadership itself announced in its newsletter (*Academe,* October 1969, p. 4), at the time of the Vietnam moratorium, that whether "an instructor reschedules a class for this purpose is primarily a matter of responsible individual decision." So, it can be assumed, is the professor's choice, occasionally, to discuss a political or social topic in a course largely devoted to a very different subject. Self-restraint is counted upon to keep such deviations within reasonable bounds. The likely effectiveness of self-restraint, almost all of the time, does not negate the essential freedom on which it rests.

An important aspect of professorial freedom is that it is defined and protected by professors themselves. The AAUP, for example, asserts that the faculty has primary responsibility in determining the status of a tenured professor against whom dismissal charges have been brought by administrative authorities (Joughin, 1967, pp. 43, 222). A committee of faculty peers is to hear the charges, weigh them against the professor's defense, and make the crucial recommendation subject to a hoped-for pro forma ratification by a governing board. Thus, professors will judge whether dismissal or other sanctions have the effect of abridging their colleague's academic freedom. Not surprisingly, freedom is defined rather broadly in these circumstances.

Freedom, it is tempting to believe, is defined so broadly, especially at a prestige university, as to make virtually impossible the dismissal of a tenured professor on charges of irresponsibility in an academic role. But it is not absolutely impossible. There is a well-publicized Stanford case of 1971–72, in which elected faculty members recommended dismissal of a tenured colleague, apparently in accord with AAUP procedures and standards. The case, however, was based on charges having little or nothing to do with the professor's behavior in a conventional academic role, or for that matter in a conventional nonacademic free-speech situation. More frequent exceptions to the sanctity of tenure are to be found in the unpublicized instances of forced resignations under threat of embarrassing charges. And still other actual dismissals occur in institutions that do not observe the AAUP procedure.

These are all in addition to the growing number of dismissals for financial reasons rather than on specific charges of misconduct. I mention this potentially widespread attack on tenure only tangentially in this chapter. Although an institution may try to use its lack of funds for particular programs to rid itself of troublesome professors, the attack on freedom is not direct. Insofar as it appears indirectly, the AAUP procedures are designed to deal with it. On the other hand, neither the AAUP nor faculty traditions fully guarantee tenured positions when there is a genuine shortage of funds or students to support the positions after savings have already been made in relevant nontenure positions. The most that is then insisted upon is an institutional effort to find other suitable work for the tenured professor. Granting this substantial gap in the tenure system, however, does not materially detract from the point that I am trying to emphasize. The prevailing ethos of the academic community staunchly protects the professor's freedom in his job even though it does not automatically protect the job itself from the ravages of financial attrition.

The point may be strengthened by a description of the situation of assistant professors. Typically nontenured, they share a large measure of the freedom characteristic of the more numerous tenured professors. They are protected from dismissal without a hearing procedure during their probationary contracts (which usually run for two or three renewable years up to a total of seven years at a given institution before an up-or-out decision). When contracts are not renewed, assistant professors are often able to demand explanations for the decision on grounds that do not violate academic freedom as defined for faculty members generally. To be sure, a nonretention decision is still much easier than a dismissal, and therefore actual or suspected irresponsibility is a likelier ground for action against an assistant professor than against a tenured professor. Irresponsibility may be a code word for unpopular beliefs or conduct. Everyone knows of alleged abuses. They tend to be well publicized on and off campuses. But these abuses should not obscure the fact that most assistant professors most of the time enjoy the same faculty rights as do established colleagues. They are not told what or how to teach, or just when to perform their nonteaching work. They have most of the professorial freedom and lack mainly the security for that freedom.

The difference is hardly meaningless, as everyone who has been an assistant professor well remembers. Quantitative and qualitative expectations about scholarly work must be met, and the expectations often appear to be indefinite or to shift so as to increase the assistant professor's insecurity about meeting the standards. But the scholarly expectations themselves, and certainly the judgments as to whether the expectations are met, are almost entirely those of senior faculty colleagues. Generally these colleagues may be no more fair and reasonable than any other possible judges. Yet they have the distinctive incentives, derived from their own status, to avoid encroachment on individual expression by assistant professors in much the same way as they seek to avoid encroachment on the freedom of tenured professors. The tendency may be so strong that even the appearance of encroachment is avoided, as it is when faculty members retain a marginal academic appointee of radical persuasion because they do not want to be accused of violating academic freedom (Petersen, 1965, p. 378).

This exposition of academic freedom is conventional except for my effort to stress its relevance for university government. The acknowledged and self-protected freedom of the professor is itself a kind of power. It represents a large measure of self-government, in the literal sense, and it imposes severe limits on the governing authority of anyone else (Woodring, 1968, pp. 134–135, 143). Moreover, it provides the basis for the building of collective faculty power. This development is apparent in the straightforward sense that the faculty as a whole protects the freedom of its members. But it may also appear in the claims of collegial groups, at departmental and higher levels, to make academic policy. These claims, and their different legitimacy and effectiveness at different levels of decision making, will subsequently be explored. For the moment, it is enough to note that the belief in individual professorial rights as the basis for collective authority does not go unchallenged. Ruml, for instance, has explicitly argued that faculties of colleges or departments do not rightly have the academic freedom accorded to individual faculty members (1959, pp. 86–88).

In addition to the individual professor's academic freedom, in the traditional sense, his distinctive status in other respects also has consequences for university government. Especially striking is the extent to which a professor is treated as an independent professional enjoying the autonomy associated with self-employment. This goes well beyond his freedom to teach what and how he wants; even with that freedom, there remains something of the standard employment relationship about an understanding that a professor should teach a certain amount. But teaching is only one of the tasks that a professor expects to perform during his salaried work time. It may well occupy only a minority of that time. Some other tasks are university functions of one kind or another, perhaps committee membership, part-time administration, or public service, but a great many are certainly less directly related to the institution. Professors pursue professional careers, nationally and internationally, much as would self-employed writers. They act with the assurance that this is what they are supposed to do in order to become successful scientists or scholars, thereby achieving the distinction on which salaries and other awards are based. Professional achievement is recognized by fellow specialists, mainly outside one's own institution, through invitations to deliver papers, opportunities to attend conferences, acceptance of articles for publication in learned journals, favorable reviews of published books, scholarly awards, government or foundation grants in support of research, and job offers from other universities.

External recognition is ratified locally as a professor's departmental colleagues become aware of it and convey the record to a university administration while recommending appropriate salary and promotional rewards. The decision on salary and promotion remains the university's, but the basis for making it is professional standing as determined primarily by external judgment and verified by local peers (Siegfried and White, 1972, pp. 12–13). It is hard to see how it could be otherwise, since the work being judged is fairly evaluated only by fellow specialists, mostly located elsewhere. Hence, as long as a university defines professorial tasks so as to emphasize research and scholarship, it must relate its reward structure to external recognition of professorial accomplishments. The university assumes that the accomplishments serve its institutional purposes, at least in the loose sense of having strong research programs, but it cannot impose its own institutional criteria in individual cases. By employing professors whose work is largely of an independent professional character, the university surrenders de facto a large portion of the conventional employer's role in determining the value of a staff member's contribution to the institutional enterprise.

Undoubtedly, since World War II the independent professional functions of professors have grown relative to the more specifically institutional commitments. That is, increased emphasis is placed on research compared to teaching, particularly of undergraduates. Increasingly, professors have become scholars and researchers in their specialized fields and only secondarily teachers in a particular university. A chemistry professor is really a chemist who also teaches chemistry, rather than a teacher who also works as a chemist. The professional identification is in the subject-matter field. As Jencks and Riesman remark (1968, p. 531), teaching is not a profession in the way that research is. Given this perception, the professorial specialists who hold it are likely to prefer university policies that serve research. Their own interests are closely tied to such policies. For example, the more time available for research, the greater the professor's opportunity for professional advancement. Research may be harder and more challenging work than teaching, but there is a tendency to speak only of teaching and related tasks as an institutional "work load" and to regard research hours as the professor's own work time.

Illustrating the strictly professional drive within university employment is the highly prized appointment to do or administer research without any teaching responsibilities beyond those relating to graduate students engaged in the same research. Such an appointment is less often based solely on university funds, especially state funds, than on external financing that a professor or a group of professors have attracted because of work and reputation. The result is a most obvious unusualness, even an anomaly, in the employment relationship. Now the professor receives not only his recognition from outside but also the rewards accompanying such recognition.

In effect, he is an independent entrepreneurial professional who holds rank and title in a university, adds to its general reputation, and receives certain administrative services from it. He works in the university but not "for" it except in the most diffuse sense. Although this degree of professorial autonomy is not itself widespread, it is significant because of its prestige among professors and because it represents a culmination of the general thrust toward self-employment status within the university.

Such status, however, is not automatically equated with governing power. Professors, who surely acknowledge their substantial success in achieving largely independent professional roles, may still feel that they have little authority over general university policies. There is a good deal of testimony to this effect. On the other hand, administrators attribute much more power to faculty members than the faculty members believe that they have (AAUP, 1969, p. 183). Perhaps there is a way to reconcile these apparently conflicting perceptions. It is to a large extent the practical independence of professors that administrators view as a kind of power—as indeed it is in relation to any effort to frame a policy intruding on that independence through the imposition of institutional standards. At the same time, professors, however independent in their own specialized work, may feel genuinely powerless to exert positive influence on overall policies.

Departments

A sense of powerlessness is hardly characteristic of professorial attitudes about departmental policies. In most universities no serious doubt exists that professors determine the policies of their respective departments. What may be at issue is the significance of such policies relative to those made at other levels of university government. Obviously, a department's range is limited by its specialized subject matter. Only within that range does it exercise authority over academic programs and the personnel to carry out those programs. And that authority is constrained by higher-level allocation of resources and by related general directives. But a great deal of educational decision making takes place in a department. My observation is that most educational decisions, apart from those of individual professors, are made departmentally. This is the level where professors are effectively organized to exercise collective power. Probably this level ought to be understood to include, besides the department itself, a research unit or an interdisciplinary teaching unit that also functions as a collegial group responsible for developing an academic program. The department, however, is the prototype and also the dominant agency with respect to course offerings and personnel appointments and promotions.

The starting point for understanding the department's role is to appreciate that it is a natural extension of the individual professor's interest in his professional subject matter. The department is a local version of the national peer group to which the professor belongs. It is probably not as specialized as his most highly focused national peer group (which, for example, may include only a certain kind of chemist rather than all chemists), but a large department has subgroups corresponding with the subspecializations into which a field is divided. At any rate, each department is a collection of fellow professionals having a fairly substantial common interest in a subject matter. When the common interest recedes, a department often spins off a new department.

Much more clearly than at any higher level in a university, the professor's judgments in departmental decision making are specialized ones derived from his scholarly work. They cannot be challenged on academic grounds by administrators or by any other officials outside the specialized area. Just as the individual professor has established his power to decide what he ought to teach or study, on the grounds of his professional competence, so the department asserts the similar power for its professors to make collegial decisions within an academic field. In practice, this professional competence constitutes the case for departmental autonomy within a university —that is, for specialized groups of professors to have a governing sphere of their own. As a defender of the autonomous department has said, it "is a shield for its members, a strong line of defense against the academic man doing other than what he wants to do" (Clark, 1961, p. 301).

In short, the department is the professor writ large—or perhaps writ fairly large in relation to his strictly individual domain. The department is not large in relation to the whole university. Even in the biggest institutions, its membership is seldom greater than forty or fifty, counting assistant professors along with associate and full professors. The few departments with sixty to one hundred members are more than balanced by numerous small departments of six to fifteen or twenty members. A given campus may have over one hundred departments, as many as forty of them in the liberal arts college. The average departmental membership, in such a situation, is about twenty. Until the 1960s, however, the average would have been much lower, since departments of thirty, forty, and fifty, not to mention those even larger, are mainly recent phenomena. The fact is that departmental decision making developed for the more limited membership and has had subsequently to be adapted to a larger unit. There are difficulties in this adaptation, especially when rapid growth reduces collaborative relations. But the department's total professorial membership overstates the numbers involved in the most significant decision making. At most, only the associate professors and full professors, comprising about one half to two thirds of a department, have authority to make personnel decisions; and their authority may be vested in a smaller committee.

The numbers of participating tenured staff, even if fifteen to thirty, still permit a shared concern with appointments and promotions, although it is not exactly like that of the smaller membership that established the character of departmental proceedings. That character is revealed by use of the word *colleague*. Implying a peer with whom one works, *colleague* is preeminently a professorial term. Occasionally applied by a professor to any other professor in his own institution, this usage is infrequent in a large university. Nowadays, at any rate, a colleague is another professor in one's own department or in one's own similarly situated unit (for example, a research institute or a law school without a departmental breakdown). He is a professor with whom another professor teaches and perhaps does research in an academic program oriented about a shared subject matter. Full and associate professors in a given department undoubtedly regard each other as colleagues, and the embrace may extend to assistant professors as well. But the latter are not permanent colleagues, and they are not colleagues at all with respect to personnel decisions. They are often called "junior colleagues," indicating, ironically, that they are not full-fledged colleagues. Regardless of the degree to which assistant professors are included, the colleague idea is clearly professional and, in that sense, elitist. Status as subject-matter specialists is asserted, and along with it a power to determine policies related to the subject matter. The rough equality of professors within a department implies no broader egalitarianism. On the contrary, it excludes all nonspecialists, whether they be administrators, students, or even professors in other departments.

Departmental colleagueship is the university's leading example of the more general effort of highly professional groups to manage their own affairs. Note Frederick Mosher's description of this effort: "A basic drive of every profession, established or emergent, is *self-government* in deciding policies, criteria, and standards for employment and advancement, and in deciding individual personnel matters. The underlying argument for such professional hegemony is that no one outside—no amateur—is equipped to judge or even to understand the true content of the profession or the ingredients of merit in its practice. The argument is difficult to challenge, particularly in highly developed, specialized, and scientized fields, with which an amateur—or a professional in personnel administration—can have only a passing acquaintance" (1968, pp. 124–125). The remarkable feature of this description is that it clearly fits a departmental faculty although the author's concern is not with this particular manifestation of professionalism or with any university problems. Rather, Mosher is writing about employees in standard governmental agencies—that is, about civil servants rather than professors. The civil servants that he has in mind are certainly highly educated and specialized professionals, as are faculty members, and so the similarity of aspiration is understandable. So, too, is the consequence of the self-government to which the professional aspiration leads. Within the civil service, as Mosher perceives, "professional hegemony" has the democratically troublesome effect of reducing control by nonspecialized authorities, including those chosen to represent the public. This process seems especially far advanced in university departments, where the drive for self-government has been effectively institutionalized. The departmental faculty is a model of professional hegemony, effectively excluding nonpeers from its considerable sphere of authority and consequently posing, at least in a state university, the same problem troubling Mosher: the freedom of public employees from public direction.

In stressing the department as the means for exercising professorial power, I do not suggest that the power can be exercised only through that unit. It is in fact also exercised by interdepartmental committees, whose members are slightly broader specialists reviewing the judgments of departmental specialists. And professors could develop other groupings if departments did not exist. These groups might be more highly specialized around research problems rather than traditional scholarly disciplines or fields. With *colleagues* then more narrowly defined, those deemed capable of judging another professor would belong to a subdiscipline. To some degree, this kind of subdividing now occurs in a very large and heterogeneous department, which tends to function in sections or divisions; the department itself does little more than formally ratify judgments of its several sections. The principle, however, remains essentially the same. The department is just its most common locus. Development in this respect is instructive. Originally the academic department was not a collegial structure. Rather, it was an extension of the sphere of the single professor of a given subject. He had assistants and perhaps others to help his teaching and research, but they worked for him and under him. Being the professor of a subject meant becoming head of the department for that subject. His peers were then professors of other subjects. The hierarchical pattern ceased to prevail after the department enlarged to include several professors, each with his own specialization within the subject matter of the department and so with claims to equality in decision-making powers (Dressel, Johnson, and Marcus, 1970, pp. 3–4).

Just as the growth in numbers of professors within a department makes it a peer group rather than a hierarchy, so the growth of a university tends to focus professorial power in the department. In part the sheer size of every other unit—college, campus, or anything in between—rules out collegiality above the department. But departmental collegiality is also a matter of increased specialization of professors around their subject matter. That is why departmental power is especially great in large, research-oriented universities. The point is verified in a study of academic decision making in several universities. Those with a high degree of "institutional differentia-

tion"—as determined by size, quality, and research orientation—
had greater departmental autonomy and control over policies directly related to departmental operations, including staff promotions
and chairman selection (Platt and Parsons, 1968, pp. 163–164).

In these situations, it is difficult to know just how great a
contribution to departmental autonomy is made by the quality of
a faculty and of its research. At the least, the successful professional
status of the professors in a department seems to enhance collegial
power. But that power is likely to exist at the department level in
any large university whose broader units—college or campus—
include far too many professors for effective colleagueship. With
enough specialists to constitute separate peer groups in almost every
discipline, the large university finds the department a convenient
agency for professorial power. The result, from the faculty viewpoint, may be more favorable than the situation at smaller institutions where professors are active participants at other governing levels
—for example, where professors make personnel decisions for an entire college. The claim to specialized competency of judgment is certainly harder to defend against an administrative challenge when the
professors involved are themselves nonspecialists in the area of the personnel decision. In giving up, as a professor in a large university
often does, the opportunity to influence decisions outside his discipline, a professor may well be gaining a greater influence within that
discipline.

There is a widespread belief, however, that professorial
power is somehow diminished in a large university. In one sense, the
belief is obviously true: an individual professor will tend to have
less power when he is one of two thousand than when he is one of
only two hundred faculty members—assuming that the whole faculty has some collective power. Similarly, when he is one of fifty
instead of one of ten departmental faculty members, a professor also
seems to have his individual power reduced. But this is to look at
power in too simple a way. If an effect of size is to transfer decision
making to the department, then the individual professor gains a
larger share than he had before. And if departmental decision making becomes, as I think it does, practically autonomous, then the
professor possesses more effective power than has ordinarily been
possible at a nonspecialized level. For his strongest claim to authority

derives not from his professorship in a university but rather from his professorship of a given subject—in other words, from his specialized professional status. Looked at from the standpoint of the whole faculty, approximating two thousand professors in a large university, professorial power appears fragmented along departmental lines. Yet it is also supreme with respect to virtually all academic matters. Each department manages its own affairs, and together these affairs constitute a university's academic policy.

It is true that each department has a presiding officer, usually called a chairman in prestige universities. Elsewhere hierarchical traditions, if not hierarchical practices, prescribe the title of head. But the word *chairman* fits the contemporary facts in most universities. Although technically an administrative appointee, most often by a college dean, the chairman is really the choice of his departmental colleagues, who express their preference either informally or through actual ballot. If not previously a professorial member of the department, although he usually is, he becomes a member by action of his new colleagues. He may become an effective leader, if his colleagues want him to be, but he is not expected to make any important policies without the consent of at least a majority of his colleagues. Much of the time the chairmanship is viewed as a chore carrying some but not great status, and in many large and important departments it is held for about three or four years by one professor and then passed along to someone else (Corson, 1960, p. 94). It is almost never a full-time administrative job, but rather a part-time encumbrance for a professor who is pursuing a professional career. In most instances, the chairman is not the department's most famous professor. He may even be one of the least famous. The important point is that he should represent the department in dealing with the university administration, similar departments in other universities, and various professional agencies. A good and successful chairman, while vigorous in these relations, never forgets that he is only one of several professorial colleagues and that the unit to which they belong is a collegial peer group (Demerath, Stephens, and Taylor, 1967, p. 201).

All of this discussion implies that professors accept the burdens of departmental power—that they assume responsibility commensurate with their asserted authority at this level. I believe that

the implication is correct. Professors actively participate in departmental decision making. Meetings, especially of tenured professors to
decide faculty personnel issues, are very well attended—in contrast
to many meetings of college and campus faculties. Departmental
committees as well as full staff meetings absorb a good deal of professorial time and energy. This should not be surprising in light of
the natural interest of professors in their own specialized field and
of the intimate relation of departmental policy to that interest. How
the department develops, particularly through its choice of other
permanent members, will certainly affect a professor's own academic
prospects, both materially and intellectually. Although a department is thus an aggregation of individual interests, there may also
emerge at this level a common educational enterprise whose quality
and reputation are of concern to the participants who share in it.
Certainly the department provides a regularized opportunity for
professors to use their power for mutual purposes. For example,
each professor, while interested in teaching his own specialized
courses, has a stake in a balanced program that provides other related courses and thus attracts good students to the department.

Ordinarily, enough of mutual concern remains to sustain
professorial participation in departments despite the conflicting
loyalty that comes with large-scale external research funding
(Schneider, 1971, p. 269). But even if substantial fragmentation
occurs as a consequence of such funding, the new research groups or
institutes serve as collegial decision-making units in much the same
manner as departments. The financial status of the research units
may make them more independently important in their spheres,
and so contribute to "the great growth of faculty power" since
World War II (McConnell, 1971a, p. 99). In any case, that power
in its present highly developed form is most plainly expressed in the
relatively small and specialized collegial units at no higher level than
that of the department or the interdepartmental committee if not in
the department itself.

Other Levels

Beyond what is loosely regarded as the department level,
professorial power faces policy questions that, as I have already sug-

gested, are not resolvable as specialized professorial issues. They are unlike questions for chemists about chemistry or questions for historians about history. At a level as broad as a college or a campus, there are only a few marginal cases in which a specialist contributes as a specialist. For example, a chemist may draw on his knowledge of chemistry to help a college faculty decide which chemistry course should be required for a general degree program. Here he seems on as firm professional ground as he is when planning his own department's major. Most of the time, however, a professor's participation in college, campus, or university-wide decision making rests on a different basis altogether.

Not as a specialist but simply as a professor, the faculty member claims a share in general governing power in a university. Of course, this basis is also in a sense professional even if it is not highly specialized. Being a university teacher, on a permanent basis, may well be thought a profession in itself, although that is not the ordinary usage among professors in a large university. Regardless of the term, teaching status is the common characteristic of professors. "Teaching status" need not mean actual teaching. A research professor may not teach at all; but, because he is eligible to teach by virtue of his rank and title, he shares in the status. Nevertheless, almost all professors teach some of the time, and it is fair to regard this function as characteristic. It is easy to see how this function establishes professorial credentials, even at a campus level, for decision making with respect to certain academic matters. In maintaining general policies about examinations, grading, and graduation requirements, for example, those who regularly teach appear to have the relevant experience and wisdom. The qualifications are less obvious in relation to other matters.

Whatever the professorial qualifications for making general university policies, there is, as previously observed, much less persistant faculty involvement here than at the departmental level. Only rare decisions of college or campus faculties attract the attention of large numbers. The professor's interest is not regularly engaged as it is in his department's affairs. The very good reason is that the general policy making seldom affects what he regards as his vital interests. The department protects these interests. The effect may be readily observed on a campus that holds general faculty meetings.

They are poorly attended. Except in the most dramatic crises, no more than 5 to 20 percent of the faculty members appear. Most professors are ordinarily content to leave the general university policy making to the handful of regulars—faculty statesmen, administrators, and a few gadflies—in a mood that is truly one of benign neglect. The attitude should not be confused with an indifference to the condition of the university. Professors care about that, but they usually assume that it is being properly watched by enough of their colleagues. After all, professors are not primarily governors of their university. As a distinguished faculty member (Dahl, 1970, p. 51) has aptly said, professors do not want to spend much time deciding what a university ought to be. They want it just to *be,* so that they can get on with their own work.

Yet professors collectively claim a right to share in governing a university. At a time when universities were smaller and professors much less numerous, the entire faculty established policy in a meeting of all its members (Mooney, 1968, pp. 183–184). Although it must long have been cumbersome, the town-meeting idea remained attractive for professors wanting the opportunity to represent themselves, even if only occasionally. Its feasibility, however, is drastically reduced for a campus with two thousand professors, or even for one with half of that number. In the rare crisis, when any large proportion of such numbers actually attend a faculty meeting, it is hardly a manageable deliberative body. It may not even fit in an available meeting room. And in the more usual case, when only about one hundred professors appear, the decisions reached by the meeting lack credibility as faculty policy. A third difficulty for faculty meetings in large universities is not peculiar to the general-assembly format. It is the absence of a sense of common purpose and common problems—which, presumably, the much smaller faculties of another era had. Although this feature of present-day universities undoubtedly reduces the feasibility of policy making by general faculty meeting, it also raises doubts that even an elected representative assembly of one hundred or two hundred professors can effectively make policy for their campus. They, too, are less likely to have the broad institutional knowledge and interest of professors of another day. In fact, if they should have such knowledge and interest, they would be so untypical of most specialized professors as to be unrepresentative of the colleagues who elected them.

Regardless of this problem, general faculty power is now usually asserted in large universities through some kind of elected senate. Although a senate does not have the most obvious difficulties of the town meeting, it has a few of its own. The first is the unit of representation. Any at-large election of faculty senators for an entire campus means that many candidates will be unknown to those asked to cast ballots. The same tends to hold for any large unit, like a liberal arts college or a broad spectrum of disciplinary fields. Only at the departmental level do professors usually know each other. It is tempting, therefore, to have senators elected by their departments. That is what the Madison faculty did in 1970, when it finally established a representative senate to replace, except on rare occasions, its old monthly town meeting. With this election method, professors know their candidates and remain in subsequent departmental contact with those whom they elect. The departmental constituency seems, then, the most realistic way to try to fulfill professorial desires for intimate representation. On the other hand, the department, as a grouping of academic subject-matter specialists, is not itself an interest that is supposed to be represented in broader policy making. For example, why should chemists as chemists hold particular positions on most questions decided by a campus senate? Although elected exclusively by chemists, the senators from a chemistry department supposedly represent their departmental colleagues as professors rather than as chemists. The department is merely convenient as a constituency because it is the place in a large university where professors regularly know each other well enough for representational purposes.

Another question concerning the composition of a senate is how to settle a proper apportionment. Assuming that the senate is exclusively a faculty body, without students or other members, it still can be argued that senate seats should be apportioned not in relation to the number of professors in a department, college, or other campus unit, but rather in relation to the number of students in the teaching unit to which professors belong (Kammerer, 1969, pp. 295–296). The result would be to give relatively more senate seats to units with high student-faculty ratios. The principle justifying such a distribution is that professors, in making campus policy, represent students and not just themselves. Even if students should be excluded from helping to choose senators, their interests might be represented by professors. And, if so, the interests could be represented on an equitable basis instead of the one-professor-one-vote system assumed for the usual faculty senate. The idea has been seriously proposed, but its unlikely adoption tells us a great deal about the nature of professorial power. It is as professors, rather than as representatives of anyone else, that faculty members assert their claim in assemblies or senates. For this purpose, all professors are equal.

The point can be taken for granted as long as the object of professorial power is the kind of professional self-government described in the departmental situation. Then naturally what is expected is "one professor, one vote." So it is also with respect to certain decisions above the departmental level. Some of these, like interdepartmental clearance of faculty appointments or promotions, are evidently extensions of the professional self-government more regularly asserted in departments. The same holds, in another respect, for any faculty body hearing individual professorial grievances against administrative or other official university actions. A committee of professors, elected by professors representing only themselves, is the proper authority to protect the freedom of faculty colleagues and the decision making by individuals and departments that flows from that freedom. It is worth noting that such protection is a signal mark of successful faculty government at prestige universities. But there are kinds of policy issues at the campus level that do not represent straightforward extensions of professorial freedom and independence. For example, what justifies faculty policy making with respect to nonacademic disciplinary codes for students? Even if it be granted (as is by no means universal) that some authority other than students should develop such codes, why should it be the faculty? "Self-government" is obviously not involved. And neither as scholar specialists nor as teachers do professors have convincing qualifications in this area. Only by uniquely identifying themselves with university authority, and with the university itself, can professors emerge as the rightful makers of a policy so far removed from their own expertise and professional interests. That is exactly what professors do when they speak of the faculty as though it were the university. In many ways, the faculty's character—generally famous or mediocre, good in certain areas and not in others—does significantly distinguish a university. Whether it does or should justify professorial power to make broad university policy is less certain.

So also is it doubtful whether professors have succeeded in developing a means for effectively exercising such policy-making power. A representative senate does not guarantee results any more clearly than a town meeting. Numerous new faculty constitutions in recent years testify to the effort to improve upon older mechanisms (Mason, 1972, chap. 2). During the crisis years of the late 1960s, those mechanisms almost always seemed inadequate: they vested authority in too large a body, especially the town meeting; or they provided for a body that represented too small, too senior, and too unrepresentative a portion of the faculty; or they did not provide for an all-campus faculty assembly or senate at all. Even when such a body existed, and even when it was relatively unflawed in representing the whole of a faculty, it seldom seemed to perform effectively in establishing policies to deal with campus crises or with the issues underlying the crises. Mostly, of course, any body representing professors simply reflected their divergent positions. Whether backing or opposing an administration, or trying to mediate between an administration and student militants, a faculty tended to be so sharply divided that it could not impose an authoritative decision on its own members and certainly not on the university as a whole or on its students. No likely constitutional mechanism will overcome this kind of difficulty. It appears inherent in faculty attempts to establish policies outside the usual limited academic sphere in which, as I have noted, professorial credentials are widely accepted and professorial decisions are customarily made.

Within that academic sphere, new faculty government constitutions may be useful and perhaps necessary. Certainly a campus or college senate, when determining such matters as degree requirements and the academic validity of proposed new programs, can improve its performance. A senate limited in numbers and yet fairly representative is one essential. So is a structure of carefully chosen specialized subject-matter committees, with ample time and staff

help, plus a willingness of faculty senators to respect and accept
committee work and recommendations (Huitt, 1971, p. 180). A
strong case can also be made for a small general executive committee
or council to serve as the faculty's leadership during and between
senate sessions.

Both this committee and the senate itself will, in a way, go
beyond the academic sphere in which its authoritative legislative
power lies. The faculty through its senate will almost certainly express opinions by passing resolutions on many broader university
affairs, and it will want its leadership to present such opinions to
the administration, the regents, and state officials. Fulfilling this
function, however, is much more modest than any professorial ambition to exercise final legislative authority on a policy question like,
let us say, the total undergraduate enrollment. A faculty can be
organized to express a considered opinion and to exert influence in
behalf of that opinion, but without claiming for itself the power to
make the policy. At most, and it is a good deal, professors may hope
for decisive influence. This is essentially the AAUP position expressed in the phrase "shared authority." Apart from strictly academic matters, where full professorial power is asserted, the faculty
is to have only something to say about university policies. The same
principle would seem to apply when faculty power is partially integrated with student power in a university senate, in contrast to a
purely faculty body.

Perhaps on certain broad policy questions, if not on strictly
academic ones, professors and students together may exert more influence on regents and state officials. But a combined faculty-student
senate, now established in some institutions, is no likelier than an
exclusively faculty senate to have the greater legitimacy necessary to
challenge effectively the power of public authority in broad university policy making. This is not to speak of a senate dominated by
superior student numbers; such a body raises other questions, to be
discussed in Chapter Nine. Domination by students is not what most
professors have in mind when they join a faculty-student senate.
While often willing to allow preponderant or even sole student
power in purely student affairs of a nonacademic nature, professors
conceive a university senate as representing faculty primarily. They
would add just enough student votes and voices to increase faculty

influence without overwhelming it or seriously diluting it. Indeed, there is a well-grounded fear that bringing students into a faculty senate, in order to increase senate influence in general policy making, will dilute professorial power even in conventional academic affairs. Because of a similar fear, faculty members desire often to exclude most nonprofessorial staff members from any representative academic body (McConnell and Mortimer, 1971, p. 81). Only limited numbers of administrators, especially those also holding professorial titles, are ordinarily given membership privileges. Anomalously, however, in many universities the president or chancellor is the senate's presiding officer. Perhaps this symbolizes "shared authority."

However exclusive or nonexclusive their memberships, faculty senates exercise in practice a more limited authority than professors are able to exert in their departments. Their "share" in general university policy making at the campus or university level is only to exert influence; even in the academic areas, where professors do make campus policy, they cannot also administer it as they do their departmental policy. At most, they critically review campus administration, occasionally second-guessing the administrators whom they have helped to select through the search-and-screen process. Professors may thus, as I have noted, successfully convert administrators to de facto faculty representatives. But, much more than department chairmen, higher-level campus administrators remain answerable directly or indirectly to regents as the appointing authorities. Given this standard arrangement, the faculty cannot and does not assume responsibility for governing the university as a whole. To do so would be very different from the prevailing situation, in which professors have the power to make it difficult for anyone else to govern effectively. Now professors do not regard administrative or regent decisions as expressions of their own collective will. They assume that many of those decisions are made in behalf of or in response to nonfaculty constituencies. And they know that a university president seriously at odds with his board of regents will not long remain in office, even with considerable faculty support. Professors may have a strong hand in selecting a president, and they may also play a part in destroying his effectiveness. But he is not their man in the sense of simply executing the faculty will.

Moreover, the faculty's legislative policy making can be, and occasionally is, overridden by regent action. There is still room for
considerable faculty influence; at the same time, it is possible to
understand why many professors think of a campus or university
senate as "sandbox government."

Dissatisfaction with this situation sometimes leads to the
drastic proposal to make faculties fully responsible as corporate
bodies for governing universities. A proposal of this kind represents
the full reach of professorialism. It would give professors the same
power at campus and university levels as they now have in their departments. Presidents, chancellors, and deans would become professorial agents just as clearly as are department chairmen. As in
some European universities, professors would elect these administrators for fixed terms. The more radical version envisions the possibility of nonfaculty staff and students also participating in the
election process (Wallerstein, 1969, p. 86). Faculty election of
administrators, however, is not exclusively the proposal of radicals
or of isolated other-worldly scholars. One recent advocate, John
Searle of Berkeley, writes from a perspective that is both ideologically moderate and keenly knowledgeable about university affairs.
His own experience makes him critical of faculty behavior in under-
cutting his university's administration (of which he has been a
part). His remedy is to make the faculty responsible for administration by eliminating regents or trustees as power holders and by
having professors elect their own administrators (1971, pp. 109–
110, 134, 226–227). No longer, then, would the faculty have an
adversary relationship with the administration. And no longer
would the faculty be able to overlook the political consequences of
its own policy-making efforts. It would, presumably, itself confront
any adverse public reaction that a board of regents now attempts to
meet. The governing model, as Searle explicitly suggests, is the department, where professors in the fullness of their power act re-
sponsibly and even conservatively.

With only slight qualification, I grant this favorable perception of professorial decision making at the departmental level; but
I cannot accept it as an appropriate model for faculty government
at the campus or institutional level. Justification for professorial
power in the department rests on the specialized subject matter of

the decision making. A similar justification, derived from professional expertise, cannot often or generally provide the basis for faculty supremacy at other levels of government. But are there no other justifications? One is the absence of any other actual or prospective governors who seem more experienced or better informed about universities than are professors. Bolstering this view is the old tradition of corporate collegiality associated with the great medieval universities. Curiously, in the United States corporate collegiality emerges as though it constituted a democratic claim against administrators or regents seeking to represent the public interest. Such a claim characterized one of the earliest professorial proposals for full faculty power (Cattell, 1913, pp. 17–21, 61–62). And there are similar implications in any proposal for the policy-making supremacy of academic people. The attractions are stated in Galbraith's opinion: "The college and university community must retain paramount authority for the education it provides and for the research it undertakes. The needs of the industrial system must always be secondary to the cultivation of general understanding and perception" (1967, p. 379). Here, by implication, is the heart of the case for full faculty power: professors know best what a university should do with the taxpayers' money. If they have different values from those of the rest of the community, perhaps even from the students as well as their parents, all the more reason to maintain faculty supremacy. Friedenberg (1970, p. 68) almost explicitly makes the point.

In an American state university, almost any proponent of faculty supremacy must appreciate that there will have to be an institutional accountability to public authority. Professors collectively, or through their elected administrative leadership, have to secure state funds and for this and other purposes make a case for their managerial policies. Without a board of regents, the university would make its case directly to general state authorities or perhaps to a special state board of higher education. In some respects, as I suggested at the end of the last chapter, we may be moving in this direction; that is, campus administrators may become de facto faculty representatives as distinct from both central university system and state officials. This is not precisely the result that proponents of faculty power have in mind. Although it eliminates the power of the traditional single-university or single-campus governing board and its administrators, it substitutes not just the preferred professorial administrators at the campus level but also a set of off-campus administrators plainly responsible to a superboard or other state authority.

Inevitably, it seems to me, professorialism will thus fall short in reaching for full power. If campus administrators were to become professorial delegates, as they surely would if elected by professors, they would not exercise authority as agents of the state or of its trustees. They might find it even more difficult than they do now to exercise any active managerial authority. But no matter how effective or ineffective their leadership turned out to be, it would lack credentials to represent the public interest. Professors would simply have to ask the public to trust faculty government on the ground that it functioned according to professional academic norms, as defined by those who share the norms. Except in specialized academic areas, this asks too much of a democratic society supporting and benefitting from an important service. The society's representatives would, as they should, find other means to express the public interest in university policy making.

SEVEN

Collective Bargaining

Starkly stated, collective bargaining is a conception of government in which staff members organize as employees to exercise power through bilateral negotiations. In the process, professors do not act as quasi-independent practitioners who share managerial authority. Defining collective bargaining in these terms should not obscure the practical likelihood that university staff members will seek to play both roles. The starkness of the statement remains analytically useful in distinguishing this governing conception from professorialism and especially from the full reach of professorialism. Collective bargaining requires that there be an identifiable management apart from employees and their representatives. Organized staff members must negotiate in an adversary relationship with somebody. Negotiation may be limited to bread-and-butter issues, with other matters left to older governing mech-

143

anisms, or it may extend to broad policy-making questions. Either way, collective bargaining introduces a measure of bilateral government distinguishable both from unfettered hierarchical authority and from pure professional self-government (Oberer, 1969).

Nevertheless, the degrees and the kinds of bilateral government accompanying collective bargaining are of the greatest importance in understanding the impact on universities. Collective bargaining can change the roles of professors and other staff members, and it can affect the powers of state officials, trustees, administrators, and students. I shall try to show that the development of collective bargaining tends to diminish the authority of any strictly campus or university management—specifically, of boards of regents and their administrative agents in state universities—and to be compatible with an increasingly direct exercise of fiscal authority by other state officials. My analysis is mainly of faculty unionism, because professorial collective bargaining is likeliest to change established governing arrangements. But all staff members, not just the visible minority of professors, are organizable employees. In particular, nonfaculty professionals may have reason to turn to collective bargaining for more than bread-and-butter gains. They may want some of the independence that professors have already secured by traditional means (Kruytbosch and Messinger, 1968). In this as in other respects, collective bargaining is a university game whose employee-players are not only professors.

It should be evident that I am adopting the now customary American usage in which collective bargaining means the legally recognized process for conducting relations and settling issues between employer and employees. It includes binding contracts as well as negotiations, and it operates on the principle that all workers in a given unit of employment shall be represented by a single organization chosen by a majority of those workers voting in an election. The federal government provides for the process in large private enterprises, now embracing private colleges and universities; the relevant authorities are federal statutes, the National Labor Relations Board, and the federal courts. State laws regulate employment relations in state governments; and there is an increasing tendency for states to provide explicitly for collective bargaining by their employees, sometimes including faculty members. The legal and historical principles of collective bargaining are more fully stated by Carr and VanEyck (1973, pp. 1–37) in their generally useful study of the application of these principles to universities.

Well established though collective bargaining is in the United States generally, it is very new among professional employees in higher education. In the late 1960s, faculty bargaining agreements began to be made, first in two-year community colleges and then in a scattering of four-year institutions. By June 1972 faculties at forty four-year institutions, including the multicampus CUNY and SUNY systems, had selected bargaining agents, but only "about fifteen" had signed agreements (Carr and VanEyck, 1973, pp. 18, 54). Ten months later a news story listed 59 four-year institutions, plus 226 two-year colleges, with faculty bargaining agents, but gave no indication of the number of contracts (*Chronicle of Higher Education,* April 30, 1973, p. 4). Interest in collective bargaining has grown rapidly and suddenly, but at this writing it still does not extend to the great majority of American colleges and universities or to many major institutions. Besides the large and important New York systems, only Rutgers and Wayne State among major universities are in the list of 59 institutions whose faculties had selected bargaining agents by mid-1973. None of the leading prestige state or private universities so far appear on the list. Nor are there bargaining agents at many large institutions of any kind outside an extended New York metropolitan area and the state of Michigan. Even in Michigan, where professors at both Wayne and Central Michigan chose bargaining agents, the faculty at Michigan State voted two to one against collective bargaining in October 1972. Hence, it remains possible that faculty collective bargaining thrives only in distinctively hospitable circumstances, institutionally and geographically, and that it will not dominate American higher education. No one, however, holds this belief with great confidence. At the moment, a wait-and-see attitude is widespread among professors. What they are waiting to see, among other things, is how collective bargaining works where it has been adopted.

To adopt collective bargaining is a more evidently difficult decision for a faculty at a prestige institution, public or private, than it is for a faculty at a two-year community college or at a four-year state institution without major university traditions. The more

limited adoption of collective bargaining in prestige universities
accords with the differences in polled preferences of faculty members at the various kinds of institutions. Doctoral-granting universities have the smallest majorities agreeing that collective bargaining has a place in higher education, and two-year colleges the largest
such majorities (Carnegie Commission, 1973, p. 42). In the two-
year colleges professors are likely to have both lower salaries and
lesser status as self-governing professionals. They may well perceive
themselves as employees because they have long been treated primarily as employees. In addition, many professors at community
colleges are linked by their own backgrounds, as well as by the financial base of their institutions, with secondary and elementary
school systems, and it is natural for their unionization to follow the
pattern of teachers in these local systems. Like the American Federa-
tion of Teachers (AFT) in New York City (Cole, 1969) and in its
other strongholds, the National Education Association (NEA)
facilitates the process by extending its organizing effort into higher
education from its large established membership of elementary and
secondary teachers. The NEA also provides a ready organizing path
at state four-year colleges or universities that developed from state
teachers' colleges. But the consequent nonprestige faculty unionism,
more likely than prestige faculty organization for the several reasons
indicated, may in some states force the pace and provide models for
major universities. However reluctant a prestige faculty is to turn to
collective bargaining, it may decide that it must do so in order to
protect its economic interests against the claims of unionized professors at other state institutions of higher education.

Similarly, professors at a high-status university will have to
consider their own unionization as a protective mechanism when
and if other professional staff members at the same institution organize to bargain collectively. So far, however, these other professional staff members do not seem to be effectively organized in
separate nonfaculty unions. If they should be so organized on a
major research campus where their numbers are large, they could
conceivably threaten faculty power by competing for scarce budgetary resources or by trying to influence academic policies. The effect,
of course, may be for professors to respond as managers and employers rather than as rival employees about to defend their interests

in their own union. In this, as in other aspects of collective bargaining in universities, there is almost no substantial recorded experience with the problem. I know of only one even approximating case. It concerns the unionization and bargaining of teaching assistants at the University of Wisconsin–Madison. It is only an "approximating" case because the organized professionals are graduate students holding part-time appointments and, almost necessarily, for a limited number of years. In these transient circumstances they are an unlikely group to organize for collective bargaining. Evidently they have organized effectively only at Madison, despite sporadic efforts elsewhere during the late 1960s and early 1970s. In what must, therefore, have been unusually favorable circumstances, the Madison Teaching Assistants Association (TAA)˙ achieved recognition as the bargaining agent in 1969, conducted a strike for more than two weeks in early 1970, secured a contract meeting some of its strike demands, and subsequently continued a contractual arrangement with the university.

The very novelty of the experience makes for an interesting academic story that ought to be told somewhere, but only one feature is significant in the present context. It is the conflict that emerged between the TAA and the professorial faculty. Although the university administration was the target for the TAA's economic demands as well as for much of its original rhetoric, the sticking point in the negotiations to settle the strike was the TAA claim that assistants and other students should have a share in "educational planning." Professors resisted on this issue—in sharp contrast to their acquiescence in the administration's concessions on work loads and length of appointments. Specifically, they reacted against a proposal that tripartite committees of professors, graduate teaching assistants, and undergraduate students be established to make decisions about courses in which professors had always been the final authority. By a two-thirds majority vote, the Madison faculty insisted that departmental planning mechanisms for teaching-assistant participation "shall not infringe upon the ultimate responsibility of the faculty for curriculum and course content" (April 6, 1970). It was on these terms that the TAA and its student-power following had to settle. No wonder that the TAA leadership concluded that professors were the real enemy. Their firm stand in behalf of faculty power confirmed the conflict of interest that had been evident as professors regularly crossed TAA picket lines to teach their own classes.

This kind of conflict is at least as likely to emerge between professors and organized full-time nonteaching professionals as between professors and teaching assistants. In the one instance as in the other, professors have a conventional policy-making power (as principal research investigators, for example) ordinarily denied to other professional staff members in a university; furthermore, professors are the immediately supervising managerial employers, with practical authority to appoint and reappoint. Demands for grievance procedures, therefore, will seek to eliminate alleged abuses primarily by professorial supervisors rather than by any other administrators. And any demands for broader participation in determining the nature of research work will also threaten established professorial power.

These managerial roles of professors may conflict with the interests of other professional staff members and so help explain faculty reluctance to accept employee status and union organization. That reluctance cannot be explained solely by high professional status since a similar status has not always deterred nonuniversity professionals from organizing unions. Nor can it be explained solely by high salaries since the higher pay of airline pilots has not precluded their effective unionization. Perhaps, however, the late start of faculty unionism can be accounted for, in a special way, by the unattractiveness for professors of the distinctive weapon of unionism: the strike or the meaningful threat of a strike. Because professorial strike experience is limited so far to a few nonmajor institutions, its usefulness is still uncertain. But there is reason to doubt the effectiveness of a classroom teaching strike in a university. Professors must know that their institution, when backed by state authority, is in a strong position to take such a strike. Public opinion is not going to force or induce concessions. Professors have salaries and other advantages hardly conducive to widespread public support for increased benefits. Unlike many schoolteachers, professors do not serve as all-day babysitters in place of working parents. Nor do professors perform an essential day-by-day service in the manner of policemen, firemen, nurses, bus drivers, and sanitation workers.

Hence, for at least three or four weeks a university and its students will lose little that cannot be made up after a strike. Not until later will tuition fees probably have to be refunded and the educational enterprise possibly suffer irreparable damage. This is another way of saying, I realize, that professors have to be ready for a long strike in order to be effective in pressing demands.

In any event, professors until recently seemed to have less sacrificial means to get what they wanted. The American Association of University Professors (AAUP) long championed these other means and eschewed collective bargaining. It is, therefore, a measure of the new strength of countervailing forces that, after only a few years of experience at the fringes, the AAUP announced in December 1972 that it was committed to collective bargaining as a major organizational method. This change in position indicates that the AAUP, which traditionally drew many members from prestige faculties concerned generally to protect academic freedom and to extend "shared authority," was responding to new or prospective members in less highly developed institutions and also to any collective bargaining aspirations of its older chapters (for instance, at Rutgers and Wayne, where the AAUP won bargaining-agent elections). The AAUP, or perhaps an independent association, is likeliest to succeed at such established universities as Rutgers and Wayne or at high-status liberal arts colleges, where faculties have enjoyed considerable professional status and are unattracted by the schoolteacher base of the NEA or the AFT or by the AFL-CIO ties of the AFT or of other competing unions. In these circumstances, the AAUP's very chariness about collective bargaining as the sole means for faculty representation is an asset. Its continued commitment to shared managerial authority is compatible with the ambivalence of faculty members at many institutions. Thus, in a limited sector of higher education the AAUP may be a more formidable rival to the larger and wealthier NEA and AFT than its less than wholehearted and considerably less than unanimous adoption of collective bargaining would suggest. At any rate, the availability of the AAUP as a collective bargaining agent is a significant landmark in the development of American higher education.

The AAUP's conversion, whether or not it means success for the AAUP itself, seems to corroborate the view that certain underlying factors impel even the most reluctant faculties to consider collective bargaining. Some of these factors operate distinctively at state institutions. Everywhere, however, there is a considerably greater receptivity of younger than of older faculty members to collective bargaining and to the use of the strike weapon (Carnegie Commission, 1973, pp. 94–95). Just as pervasive as the generational factor in encouraging faculty unions is the financial stringency that afflicts colleges and universities in the 1970s. Following the palmiest years in both the private and public sectors of higher education, this stringency imposes salient relative deprivations on faculty members who, when there was a seller's market for their services, became accustomed to easily won improvements in their status and salaries. With the new surplus of prospective professors, individual bargaining ceases to be effective for most faculty members. If salaries are to increase and teaching loads be reduced, or just maintained at the levels achieved in the 1960s, collective action appears much more useful than a decade earlier. It will impress many professors as especially relevant when they find that even their tenure status no longer guarantees jobs against budgetary cutbacks. Nothing is likelier to produce a unionized response among older as well as younger professors than an institution's intention to lay off or terminate tenured appointees. The alarm bells ring loud and clear from only a few such cases, based on narrow financial grounds, and still more ominously from proposals for a periodic review of the continued competency of and need for tenured professors generally. Although unionization in higher education, as elsewhere in the economy, cannot guarantee jobs, it constitutes a defensive reaction capable at least of imposing regularized seniority principles and perhaps of limiting the adverse effects of financial cutbacks.

At state institutions the first special factor conducive to faculty collective bargaining is the widespread unionization and bargaining by nonfaculty state employees, in and out of universities. The economic benefits secured by these other employees may prod professors to organize, especially if the benefits come at the expense of unorganized faculties. Also the various existing unions of state employees set precedents in public employment, both for legal recognition of collective bargaining and for at least de facto toleration of the strike weapon.

A second state-related factor is the increasingly detached and specialized university management described in previous chapters. Notably but not only on major state university campuses now included in multicampus systems, a formerly intimate teacher-scholar administration has been partly superseded by detached authorities administering fiscal policies in behalf of the state's interest in higher education generally. Although I regard this development as inevitable and probably necessary if the public interest is to be adequately represented, nevertheless I decidedly share the professorial perception that faculty members thus lose managerial influence as *their* campus administrators lose autonomous decision-making power. In this respect, despite the maintenance of professorial power in broad and important academic areas, faculty members have a new sense of powerlessness. Senior professors accustomed to influencing budgetary management at the highest campus levels are most likely to feel the loss of power.

A third factor conducive to collective bargaining by state university professors is their large numbers. These large numbers will be especially helpful when professors, like civil service workers, bargain at the state level. Several thousand professors on several university campuses constitute a politically substantial bloc capable of hiring lobbyists and otherwise mounting campaigns in behalf of their economic interests. The advantages of strategic geographical dispersion as well of numbers are so apparent that professors employed by several separate state institutions will be tempted to pool their organizational efforts even if the state itself does not merge the institutions under a single board or council.

The previous observation, concluding the list of likely causes for a continued spread of faculty collective bargaining, also raises one of the new problems that unionization brings to campus government and notably to professors at a major university. For faculty members at a prestige campus, the cost of joining a single state's higher education bargaining unit may seem so high as decisively to outweigh the in-union-there-is-strength argument. If such professors are going to bargain at all, they have good reason to prefer their own union—a union dedicated to preserving their status as relatively well-paid research scholars and also to preserving the special distinction of their university. They do not want to be a minority within a union of all professors in a state system of higher education. From what I have heard from my own Madison colleagues, both informally and through official representatives, I am convinced that they and similarly situated professors will fight to have a separate bargaining unit, at least for a cluster of doctoral-granting campuses if not for their own campus, and that they will resist unionization altogether unless that alternative exists. This attitude does not exclude system-wide collaboration with professors at more exclusively teaching campuses, where common ground between unions can be found, but it insists on an independent decision-making organization for a campus or campuses committed to research. Whether such an organization will be possible at Wisconsin or elsewhere is doubtful. SUNY and CUNY, where two-year and four-year colleges are lumped together, are cases to the contrary, since each large multicampus system is a single bargaining unit. On the other hand, each of Michigan's unionized universities, consistent with its considerable autonomy in other respects, has a separate bargaining unit. The key to resolving the problem one way or the other does not lie with campuses or their faculties. At most, they may exert pressure for separation or togetherness. The authoritative decision will be made by state statute or by administrative ruling of an employment-relations commission, and the decision will be subject to the crucial influence of state managerial authorities who occupy employer bargaining roles. Their desires, understandably, are to negotiate with only one statewide faculty union.

The same influence from the same source has much to do with determining the membership of the bargaining unit on a given campus. Professors will not always be free to decide for themselves how narrowly or broadly to define "faculty" membership in a collective bargaining election. I have already discussed the competitive consequence of leaving large numbers of nonteaching professionals to form their own union. But this is a risk that I suspect professors at a prestige institution will prefer to run rather than to dilute their interests in one big professional union, where they would be outnumbered or nearly outnumbered by staff members with less status, salary, and independent power. This likely professorial preference is consistent with the staunch tradition of a teaching faculty that occupies a separate and special position within a university, but it is at odds with collective bargaining principles as ordinarily administered in state employment. Of course, these principles are not immutable. They could be modified to allow or even encourage professorial exclusiveness. Yet so far the tendency is in the other direction. At SUNY and CUNY, operating under state employment-relations statutes and rulings, the bargaining unit in each system is a single association that represents all teaching and nonteaching professional staff members. Each association's embrace is wide enough to include librarians and postdoctoral research specialists as well as part-time teachers below professorial rank. Similarly, the Michigan state employment-relations commission has placed nonteaching professionals in a faculty unit (Carr and VanEyck, 1973, pp. 93–94). The dynamics of competition between the AFT, the NEA, and the AAUP also work in this direction. Each seeks to maximize its membership and its vote in a bargaining-agent election. Accordingly, the AAUP—historically a professors' organization, as its label indicates—amended its constitution in 1972 so as to embrace "any professional appointee included in a collective representation unit with the faculty of an approved institution" (Carr and VanEyck, 1973, p. 128).

In spite of decisions of this kind—by the AAUP or other unions or employment-relations boards—bargaining units that are exclusively or overwhelmingly professorial in their membership still can exist. Such units now exist, and they are bound to exist at colleges where nonteaching professionals are small minorities relative to professors. Nor do significant inclusionary decisions always cause professors to turn away from collective bargaining. They have not done so at SUNY and CUNY. In any such situation, however, professors probably will seek to limit the scope of the professional association's collective bargaining so that it leaves to older established faculty mechanisms the policy-making power that professors are accustomed to exercise in academic affairs. They probably prefer to retain such mechanisms in any case.

Less significant for university government in the usual sense is the adaptation of collective bargaining for employees who have enjoyed highly effective individual bargaining opportunities in highly inegalitarian circumstances. Especially privileged faculty members—grouped, for example, in law or medical schools—show signs of wanting their own bargaining units if they organize at all. At prestige universities many professors besides those in law and medicine will insist on continuing to bargain in what remains, for them as individuals, a favorable competitive situation. By their ability and willingness to move to another institution, star senior professors and their younger ambitious colleagues secure for themselves higher salaries, special research support, lower teaching loads, additional secretarial help, and other fringe benefits. These practices are not insurmountable difficulties in the way of collective bargaining. Like musicians, professional athletes, actors, and communications-media workers, professors can negotiate collective contracts for minimum salaries and other general benefits, and simultaneously negotiate as individuals for higher and special rewards commensurate with personal talents and contributions. Professional unionism can be meritocratic. This is not to say that it is always so in practice or in principle. Indeed, it is specifically antimeritocratic for schoolteachers when it insists on regular salary steps in accord with years of service. Union customs here also reflect preunion traditions of an employment much less securely professional than that of older university faculties.

Certainly AFT egalitarianism, applied in public school systems and in state colleges and two-year colleges closely aligned with such school systems, strikes a jarring note for many university professors. The note is clear in this statement by an AFT leader arguing for college unionism: "We are appalled at the practice of making secret individual deals for the favored few. . . . We encourage faculty members to remain at an institution and engage in its reform rather than to become academic entrepreneurs who hop to other institutions that are ready to pirate them away with the lure of individual betterment" (Kugler, 1968, p. 417). The most that is conceded to merit is somewhat more rapid advancement for the meritorious individual who is recognized as such by his colleagues. One would expect a greater concession than this to the individually competitive environment of professors at a prestige university if the AFT expects to organize successfully in competition with other associations or unions more closely attuned to the particular professional customs. Whether these customs would survive long-term unionization is another question. It is arguable that the democratic context of union membership generates a leveling process in which a representative leadership serves primarily a majority of less well-paid and less privileged members by seeking across-the-board benefits. This possibility is more resistable by professors at a prestige university who succeed in having their own union undiluted either by nonteaching professionals or by professors from less highly developed institutions. Then, although some professors are less well paid and less privileged than others, most of them are accustomed to a meritocratic system and expect to be able to benefit from it in the future if they have not done so in the past.

The problems of faculty collective bargaining may not always be solved in ways compatible with many customary professorial prerogatives. But it is surely not beyond the ingenuity of faculties to plan for this outcome. Nor is it beyond the realm of political probability that faculties might succeed in persuading reluctant state authorities to allow the desired outcome. Similarly it is reasonable to expect professors, even while accepting unionization, to be able to defend their governing roles at the department level, where, as I stressed in the last chapter, the collegial power of professors is indeed dominant. I see nothing in department policy making that has to be, or is likely to be, significantly changed as a result of faculty collective bargaining. At this level the one controversial possibility so far to emerge is the role of the department chairman. In those universities where he has been effectively elected by his colleagues or otherwise serves primarily as their representative, it is a radical departure to make him a managerial agent in bargaining collectively with professors. It converts a shop steward with incidental foreman duties into a foreman. Or, in university terminology, it turns a professor serving also as a part-time administrator into a full-fledged administrator. Top university management has sometimes proposed such a transformation with the advent of collective bargaining, but it has not often succeeded in thus excluding chairmen from faculty bargaining units (Carr and Van-Eyck, 1973, pp. 100–111). The National Labor Relations Board has ruled that generally chairmen are not supervisors, in the meaning of federal labor law applied to private colleges, and this ruling is in accord with the tendency of most state board rulings.

Where any choice is left to faculties, they can be counted on to insist on the continued collegial status for chairmen, just as they will insist that their departmental power remain intact in other respects. Professors will want this power protected rather than diluted by a collective bargaining contract. There is no compelling reason to surrender any of their present governing authority at this level. Its continuation is compatible with higher-level collective bargaining relationships. Insofar as a bargaining contract negotiated elsewhere has to be administered departmentally, it can be done by nondepartmental managers dealing with chairmen as shop stewards. For example, salary recommendations now made by departments through their chairmen, in accord with administration guidelines as to total amounts and distribution formulas, can be made in the same way under a union contract that sets these total amounts and distribution formulas.

Even at the next level above the department, I am not certain that any established professorial power has to be abandoned in return for collective bargaining. Unionism need not disturb the customary policy making of college, campus, or university faculties in strictly academic spheres like curriculum planning and course requirements. Nor should there be much argument about the personnel-reviewing authority of faculty committees with respect to departmental recommendations on promotions, appointments, or salaries. "Reviewing" here, like the departmental recommendations themselves, often carries great weight, but it does not constitute a state university's final legal determination. Rather, it provides another set of recommendations forwarded to managerial administrators and regents. Continuing such a practice seems as feasible under a negotiated collective bargaining contract, setting the general terms within which recommendations will be made, as it is when the guidelines are established unilaterally by nonfaculty authorities. I realize that I am thus suggesting, as I have for the departmental level, the maintenance of an important de facto managerial power for professors at the same time that they participate in collective bargaining with another tier of managers. No doubt, this will appear unusual in comparison with the roles of most other unionized employees. But it does not appear unreasonable.

What would appear unreasonable is an inclusion in a professorial union of any full-time academic administrators who are supposed to represent managerial authority in evaluating faculty recommendations. In this perspective, college deans and campus chancellors or presidents, along with their principal associates, are properly outside the ranks of organizable professors. They are to be part of the management with whom a faculty union establishes an adversary relationship. At many institutions faculty and administration separateness is in any case a preunionized fact of life. But at campuses where professorial power is traditionally highly developed, and where the principal administrators are themselves teacher-scholars, the sharp faculty-administrator dichotomy accompanying collective bargaining is an innovation in certain respects. In particular, it is at odds with the view that the teacher-scholar administrators at college and campus levels are representatives of their professorial colleagues in a manner analogous to the roles of department chairmen. The representational character, it will be recalled, is institutionalized through the search-and-screen procedure that gives professors a strong voice in selecting administrators. Maintenance of this faculty power, it seems to me, will be hard to justify in the case of any administrator with whom a faculty union intends to bargain. There is something wrong with the notion that employees should be able to select not only their own bargainers but also management's. The incompatibility with the thrust of collective bargaining is recognized by one of the most active proponents of faculty unionism (Lieberman, 1969). His reasons are different from mine, since he minimizes the significance of professorial management generally; but the impropriety of unionized professors' choosing the representatives for their managerial adversaries is clear, especially in a public institution. Therefore, under collective bargaining, college deans as well as their superiors are ordinarily relegated to managerial roles plainly distinguished from faculty roles. In fact, with department chairmen treated as professorial members of a union, the college and campus managers would probably assume a few of the strictly managerial tasks now left to departments.

I want to qualify this developing picture by suggesting another possible outcome for a campus whose administrators are now de facto faculty representatives. They may remain so and even become de jure representatives of professors, in the manner of department chairmen, and leave the managerial side of negotiations to other administrators. College deans in particular perform essentially as faculty leaders. If campus presidents or chancellors were also to do so, managerial power would be transferred to off-campus agents in the ways discussed in the two previous chapters. I do not regard this as inconceivable. Indeed, it is the only way that a faculty could have both collective bargaining and an effective voice in choosing its campus administrators. The AAUP may well be headed unde-liberately in this direction. Coupled with the AAUP's recent com-mitment to collective bargaining is its continued insistence, through Committee T on College and University Government, that faculties have a greater role in decisions relating to the appointment, reten-tion, and dismissal of administrators (*Academe,* October 1972, p. 1). The price to be paid is unacknowledged by the AAUP, but I believe that it is inevitably a greater off-campus power in the con-duct of collective bargaining negotiations. Management in behalf of the public must and will emerge somewhere.

I emphasize the point although I largely accept the com-patibility of professorial governing power with professorial union-ism. I go at least as far in this respect as the Carnegie Commission appears to in its critical assessment of the impact of collective bar-gaining on university government (1973, pp. 39–51). Perhaps I go farther by suggesting that professors have little to lose if their col-lective bargaining thrust encourages the shift of certain nonaca-demic and nondepartmental managerial roles to off-campus admin-istrators or to campus administrators who are also removed from faculty representational roles. In state universities these roles are shifting anyway, and collective bargaining is as much a response to the shift as it is an encouragement of it.

In concluding, more attention should be given to the ways in which collective bargaining encourages the change in governing re-lationships. Professors may be left their main bastions of academic power in the departments; but the same cannot be said for other state university authorities. Campus budgetary officials lose decision-making power whenever institutional autonomy is reduced, and that autonomy is bound to be reduced as it becomes plain that union de-mands can be met only by those who control the state's financial resources. Neither university administrators nor university regents can commit state funds without their appropriation and authorization through the legislative process. Hence, faculty unions, like other public employees' unions, will negotiate with legislators, governors, and their staffs. Regents and their administrative agents will have only limited leeway in distributing appropriated funds so as to meet salary-increase demands, for example, instead of allocating money for other purposes. Few state universities enjoy that much autonomy now, and recent governmental developments, as we have seen, are decidedly against increasing it. Consequently, boards no less than presidents will have to expect state officials to be heavily involved in negotiations. I do not see how it can be otherwise. The belief that collective bargaining will strengthen trustees relative to university administrators (Carr and VanEyck, 1973, p. 250) seems to me applicable mainly to private rather than public universities. Supporting my interpretation is the evidence from SUNY, where the governor's agent rather than the university board was the managerial negotiator. Probably regents of a state university will try to handle the negotiations. They may even succeed in reaching settlements in some places. But sooner or later union demands for economic benefits will reach the state's elected officials. Only authorities with the power to tax can meet such demands.

Reaching these authorities is essentially a lobbying process for faculties as it is for other state employees. Professors have been known to try to help their own cause by informal lobbying without being organized into a union for the purpose. Doing so now in a more concerted way through a professional association may be an alternative to full-fledged unionization. That kind of effort resembles unionized pressure except that it is unaccompanied by a strike threat or by any eventual formal contract. Professors may sometimes find it more comfortable and convenient to exert their organized pressure in this nonunionized way. It too is compatible with a recognition that state authorities, not university boards or administrators, are the ultimate source of fiscal decisions. No doubt, however, collective bargaining in its usual statutory form tends more sharply to bypass the intervening authorities and to deal squarely with off-campus public representatives in advancing financial claims of employees.

EIGHT

Individual Consumer Sovereignty

Student roles in university government are the subject of this chapter and the next. The participatory demands of the late 1960s, familiarly conceived as student power, are discussed in the next chapter. Here the subject is the unorganized aggregate power of *individual* student decisions with respect to enrollment in particular institutions, programs, and courses. For reasons that I hope will become apparent, the limited subject matter is important enough to deserve separate consideration. Conceiving students as individual consumers places them in a special kind of relationship to university governing authority.

Treating students as consumers in any sense probably requires a brief defense. The marketplace imagery can be offensive to all of us who believe that education involves much more than pas-

160

sive student consumption of a product. Viewing students as consumers, however, does not deny that they are also much more than consumers in the ordinary sense of that word. I use the term because their economic position as consumers provides students with one kind of basis for asserting influence. This consumer basis is more widely acknowledged as legitimate than are the various ideological bases recently discovered. Its effectiveness, however, is not often acknowledged or readily demonstrated.

Having borrowed the term *consumer sovereignty* from the language of economics, I should acknowledge an economist's qualification. University students, or their parents, are investors in, as well as consumers of, an education (Schultz, 1961, pp. 52–53)`. They do not literally consume—that is, use up—the product that they buy with their contribution of actual dollar payments or postponed earnings. Rather, they acquire a kind of capital investment that will pay off later in increased earnings or personal gratification. But since personal gratification can also coincide with the educational process itself, at least some consumption occurs along with the investment. The word *customer* may better indicate the combination of investing and consuming roles. I refrain from shifting to that term because *consumer sovereignty,* despite the technical qualification, remains widely understood as embracing buyers of investments no less than of consumable products.

Much more substantive by way of qualifying the conception is that the student or parental buyers of education are not paying its full cost. Whether or not there is scholarship money or subsidized loans, most students pay considerably less than cost because of endowment funds or government funding, or both. Undoubtedly, these nonconsumer sources of support, notably state sources, challenge the influence of student consumers as against a generalized public interest in the products of higher education. Nevertheless, the students, and/or their parents, pay enough of their education bills to be able to claim at least portions of the sovereignty ordinarily attributed to purchasing consumers. Certainly they feel that they pay a great deal more than tuition fees even though the institution may collect nothing else. Room and board, plus forgone earnings, are also real costs for students and their parents.

Despite the monetary basis for student sovereignty, earlier

studies of university government tended to ignore its impact on the decision-making process. And, in fact, before the late 1960s students did not participate in the university's formal governing structure except in a few marginal areas. Although they might have exerted a significant influence simply as individual consumers, such influence was not considered an aspect of governing. Instead, studies of campus power structure focused on administrative relations and on the university as a managed organization. In one of these studies, published as late as 1967 but evidently written a little earlier, the authors bluntly declared that they "regard students not as members of universities but as one of several clienteles we choose to put to one side as far as our studies are concerned" (Demerath, Stephens, and Taylor, 1967, p. 4). Given the authors' limited purpose, they ought not be criticized for the exclusion even though it would have been unthinkable a few years later, when everyone writing about university government realized that students had indeed become active participants. My view is that as a consuming clientele they have always actively participated.

The Historical Buyer's Market

Higher education in the United States historically provided the opportunity for consumer influence. During most of this century, prior to the 1960s, the numerous American students financially able to attend college—that is, with effective demand for higher education—were in a position to choose to attend one among several available colleges; they were also free to choose, within a given institution, which program and which courses to pursue. Choice, in that sense, was widely institutionalized by the elective system, serving as American higher education's equivalent of free trade. Altogether the system was extraordinarily free and open for those who could afford it. College and university admissions were made available to a degree unknown elsewhere in the world. Apart from an exceptional circumstance like that of the enrollment bulge at the end of World War II, American colleges and universities collectively had more places than students. Not every applicant could always be admitted to Harvard, even if able to pay the tuition, but he could be admitted somewhere. All but the most prestigious of the private institutions almost always sought to add students. Many state institutions, responding to actual and projected increases in demand, usually sought more applicants than actually enrolled.

For American students, then, higher education was historically a buyer's market. In that situation, with colleges wanting more students, the buyers would seem to have had an opportunity to influence the product by enrolling in certain schools or courses rather than in others. They might at least have tried this consumer-power route in the absence of any established means for direct influence. The idea is hardly novel. Within universities it was well understood that student choices of courses and subjects played a large part in determining which would grow and which would decline. Not all professors liked the outcome. Writing over half a century ago, Thorstein Veblen complained about just such university responsiveness to student interests: "A decisive voice in the ordering of the affairs of the higher learning has so been given to the novices, or rather to the untutored probationers of the undergraduate schools, whose entrance on a career of scholarship is yet a matter of speculative probability at best" (1957, p. 143). The result, Veblen thought, was to expand practical vocational courses at the expense of more scholarly fields. Other professors worried more, then as now, about the popularity achieved by dramatic and simplifying rivals.

Yet at the best of times for the usually prevalent buyer's market, universities cushion themselves in ways peculiar to the market for educational services. Certain institutions are so attractive that they can restrict their services to a clientele of their own selection; and many others manage to impose academic standards for admission and continuation despite their need and desire to attract students. True enough, institutions vary sufficiently in the rigor of their standards that almost any financially advantaged undergraduate aspirant finds a place somewhere. But the aspirant has to meet certain academic requirements, including prior course work, at least a few nonelective college courses, and a modest qualitative level of performance. Moreover, the general nature of the standards, in contrast to their varying degree of rigor, tends to be remarkably similar at any period of time among American colleges and universities. Nor does the content of higher education in the United States vary greatly from institution to institution. In fact, certain colleges and

universities set the standards for the others—both by force of prestigious example and by direct influence of their graduates who become professors elsewhere. Intercollegiate accrediting agencies rein-
force these tendencies. Altogether, few institutions have broadly
experimental curricula, and even fewer persist with such experiments.

If these observations appear to do an injustice to the range of
subject matter offered by American colleges and universities, let me
be clear that I am talking about something else. No one would deny
that every conceivable academic subject, along with a large number of dubiously academic subjects, is available to the prospective
student. The sameness, or at least the basic similarity, is in the content and method of instruction of the given subject, no matter where
presented. Although students can select virtually anything from
poultry raising to classical archeology as a major curriculum, or as
a field for an occasional course without a major, each of the many
institutions that offer a particular subject present that subject in
about the same way. Some institutions, of course, have larger, more
advanced, and more specialized offerings than others; but such differences, as long as a full-fledged major curriculum exists, are not
ordinarily material for undergraduates.

Strictly qualitative differences are another matter. Suppose
that these exist in a substantial way between one institution and
another. How would prospective students know about such differences, particularly about the quality of teachers and their courses,
when choosing among institutions? Do college students, particularly
prospective college students, have the requisite knowledge to make
reasonable choices? The questions are plainly consequential. The
leading economist writing about student sovereignty recognizes that
if it "has an Achilles' heel, it is in the domain of information, a long-
standing controversial issue as unsettled today as it was when classical economists divided on this issue" (Schultz, 1968, p. 342). Prospective students, in this economist's view, are even more obviously
disadvantaged in calculating the relative value of various educational services than are most consumers in choosing among competing products. It is hard to disagree with this opinion. Comparative
shopping is bound to be restricted to a few brief campus visits, parental experience of an earlier time, conversations with a casual as-
sortment of experienced students, advice from high school counselors

whose own first-hand knowledge is slight, review of the largely un-
revealing college catalogs or their recapitulation in commercial
guides, and overheard gossip about reputational prestige rankings.
From one or another of these sources, a prospective student may
happen to secure excellent and relevant educational information for
his decision making. The student may even choose to act on such
information. But the process hardly makes such a well-informed
decision a likely outcome, although it may lead to considerable
switching in midstream from one institution to another or to drop-
ping out altogether. Such comparative shopping, in which one
literally tries out how well a particular college education suits one's
interests and talents, is inadvertent and often wasteful.

Nevertheless, the switching between institutions, like the
original enrollment decision (however slight its educational informational basis), does confirm the existence of formal choice by the
consumer. Whether or not one uses any relevant knowledge about
significant differences in educational programs, he does make a
choice. And that choice may be important to him regardless of specifically educational values. In fact, on certain noneducational matters the prospective student has a great deal of knowledge decidedly
relevant to his tastes. He knows whether schools are large or small,
in large or small towns, socially permissive or restrictive, athletically
successful or failing, and near or far from home. He also knows how
much each institution costs in tuition as well as in room and board,
although he may not know the educational value, or the possibly
related long-run economic value, of what he is buying. The worst
that can then be said about consumer sovereignty in this situation is
that the student does not act as a fully rational economic man when on
the basis of noneducational concerns he decides that it is worth paying more or less for a particular university enrollment. But undoubtedly he is exercising some kind of choice that he believes rational
for his immediate purposes.

This much, as suggested earlier, has been possible for the increasingly large number of Americans with effective demand—that
is, with sufficient purchasing power to buy admission to colleges and
universities. The United States is unusual in this respect. Most other
nations have not had, even recently, enough university and college
places for all their secondary school graduates who want degree-

granting higher education. In Britain, for example, only an academically well-qualified minority (though lately an enlarged minority) of secondary school graduates are able to enroll in standard degree-granting institutions. A fixed number of students are admitted each year to British universities, although an additional number attend other kinds of postsecondary institutions (Caine, 1969, p. 231). Within the university category each institution itself takes only a fixed number. Furthermore, quotas are often fixed by general fields of study. In sharp contrast to this controlled and rationed educational economy is America's conventional competitive market, in which almost all students of even modest academic qualifications, with even modest financial resources, can enter some degree-granting institution to study in the field of their undergraduate preference.

However, the American pattern, in which students must usually provide *some* financial resources, is less generous than the fuller subsidies by European nations of many if not all of their enrolled students—a select group, to be sure. The American characteristic has to be taken into account in qualifying the significance of consumer sovereignty with respect to choice of institution. The poorer the student, or the poorer his family, the less wide his effective choice almost always. And one need not be very poor in order to have to rule out (unless earning an unusually rich scholarship) most private colleges of high or middle prestige, as well as public institutions outside one's own state. Only a fairly small minority of prospective students come from families well enough off to provide the resources for a genuine choice among all collegiate institutions.

This substantial inequity, however, hardly renders meaningless the opportunity for choice associated with the usual availability of more college places than student applicants. A high school graduate with only modest resources need not have a chance for admission to all institutions, or to all kinds of institutions, in order to have some choice and especially to *feel* that he has some choice. Large numbers of aspiring college students now as in the past have such a choice, if only among public institutions in their own state and perhaps also among certain private colleges that cost relatively little because of their convenient location or church support. A smaller although substantial number are forced or strongly persuaded by limited finances to enroll in a strictly local institution so that they can live at home as a means of saving money. But even among the large number who are able to choose among at least a few institutions, a question about the significance of the choice can still be raised. This is not so much a matter of the quality of the less prestigious institutions from which most students have to choose. These students suffer no necessarily large and clear quality disadvantage in having their choices somewhat limited by their financial means. But, with respect to their remaining choices, they probably lack useful information about the value for them of particular educational programs.

Less uncertainty arises about the informational basis of consumer choice within an institution. In selecting courses, majors, and teachers, a continuing student has much greater access to information than he could have had before actually enrolling. He talks with other students about their experiences, tries out various courses and teachers, and also uses the occasional systematic course evaluations published by student organizations. Despite obvious communication problems in a large university, the student should find that the diversity of programs provides a greater choice than does a small college. More fields of study, more courses, and more professors are available for the shopping student. A straightforward example comes from the presence in a large university of a large enough departmental faculty in a given field to have two or more professors, rather than just one, teaching similarly specialized courses from which a student can make his choice.

The great breadth of intrainstitutional academic choice is a reality that no one familiar with large American universities will challenge. But the meaning of this choice for university government may remain dubious. How, it will be asked, can the students' selection of courses, majors, and teachers influence the educational program offered by the university? The simplest answer is that a faculty is influenced to offer what the students are willing to take, and that it is constrained from offering much of what students are unwilling to take. Or at least a faculty will be so influenced if its institutional reward structure provides sufficient incentives to respond to consumer demand. I believe that these incentives can be made reasonably sufficient despite acknowledged limitations against cheapening the educational product in order to attract students. Specifically, in my state university teaching experience of the early 1950s, the incentives were sufficient for me and my departmental colleagues to try to develop a set of courses as well as our own individual courses in ways that would meet student interest and, at the same time, observe intellectually respectable standards. We knew that our success in this respect would have favorable budgetary consequences for us individually and for the department's potential growth. We realized particularly that we needed to enroll large numbers of undergraduates because they provided the basis for administrative allocation of salary money for new positions. In this situation students indeed exercised power by voting with their feet.

Admittedly, the departmental faculty response depended heavily upon the recognition of a collective professorial interest. Not every individual faculty member could be counted upon to subordinate his specialized professional interest in order to teach large numbers of students who wanted or needed a nonspecialized course. His self-interest might have led him to focus almost exclusively on work to enhance his national scholarly reputation. Even in the early 1950s this conflicting incentive system existed. But it was not dominant in many instances. Mainly it yielded to the counterpressure of colleagues responding to administrative control of fiscal resources. Only a rare and universally respected scholar of the very top rank could afford to evade departmental teaching responsibilities when their effective discharge helped determine the esteem and so the salary-increase recommendations of his colleagues and his dean.

Reversal

On the other hand, this situation, with its significant student-consumer power, requires the historic buyer's market. Only when the supply of professors, potential professors, and educational facilities generally is sufficient, or more than sufficient, can students expect their course preferences to have appreciable impact on what is offered and by whom. But the buyer's market ceased to exist in the late 1950s and 1960s. For at least a decade, not just for a year or two as after World War II, the historic situation was reversed. Coinciding with the massive increase in demand for higher education was a shortage of Ph.D.s to serve as professors. This shortage would have existed simply because not enough professors were being turned out to teach the increasing number of undergraduate students, but it was aggravated by the simultaneously expanded opportunities for Ph.D.s to do research in and out of universities instead of teaching. The new and largely unprecedented situation was clearly described by John Millett early in the decade: "The demand for admission greatly exceeds the supply of college and university facilities for residence and instruction, especially in many of the best-known and most popular colleges and universities. The result is that many colleges and universities are little concerned about economic competition at the moment. The demand for their services is far greater than they are willing to meet. In a seller's market the consumer—in this instance, the student—finds his economic power considerably lessened" (1962, p. 120).

Although Millett was addressing more directly the student's reduced choice among institutions, the seller's market of the 1960s had just as serious consequences for student influence within an institution. The consequences were especially serious in a large state university, where individual consumer choice had played a part because student numbers were used to justify increased legislative funding. Now, when numbers had become overwhelming at almost all state institutions, students were without any established means to exert influence. New restrictions on total enrollment at some of these institutions symbolized the situation: more than enough applicants were at hand. With or without fixed enrollment limits, however, each state university's major campus was crowded. Its problem was having too many students for the available and recruitable staff. Neither administrators nor professors had to be concerned with low-enrollment courses. If students did not like a course or a professor, other students were at hand to take their places. The competition was for faculty, not for students. Therefore, the subjects taught, the methods of teaching, and the times of teaching tended to be arranged to suit professors rather than students. This was part of the heightened professorial power described in Chapter Two. As a critic of this power remarked, "At no time in American higher education have students been as powerless vis-à-vis their institutions as

they were from 1955 to 1965" (Hefferlin, 1969, p. 147). He might
have added that at no time were administrators as powerless to do
anything about it if they had wished to do so.

In addition to its direct reduction of responsiveness to consumers, the seller's market of the 1960s also lessened the availability
of information that students could use in helping to determine their
choices. Professors had become so much more mobile, not only between institutions seeking their services but also between teaching
and research leaves, that they were much less likely to offer the
same courses, or any courses, term after term and year after year.
Staffs changed rapidly for this reason as well as because the enrollment growth brought many new professors, themselves highly
mobile. Hence, a student had to choose from among teachers who
were often unknown to him and to his fellow students, and even to
each other. This recital does not exhaust the story of the deteriora-
tion of consumer sovereignty in the 1960s. The seller's market provided the opportunity for universities, especially their professors, to
pursue specialized disciplinary interests which, while always present,
flourished spectacularly in the quarter century after World War II.
These interests led professors to research, consulting, conferences,
and graduate training—all closer than undergraduate teaching to
their professional commitments as historians, chemists, and other
subject-matter specialists. The inherent professorial pressure in this
direction simply encountered much less resistance in the 1960s. Administrators joined their faculties in emphasizing prestige-laden goals
associated with advanced specialized knowledge. Convincing evidence of the agreement of administrators and professors on the importance of professional academic quality is reported from a massive
questionnaire-survey by Edward Gross (1968, pp. 530–531).

When this drive of the academic community resulted, as we
know, in fewer professorial undergraduate teaching hours, the
seller's market made it virtually impossible for students as individual
consumers to exert an effective countervailing influence. Since they
lacked relevant alternatives, they could hardly reject larger lecture
classes and teaching by more numerous graduate assistants. Administrators worried much more about keeping their faculties happy
even when they knew that students now had some reason to com-
plain about their new powerlessness as consumers. Clark Kerr, when

he was president of the University of California, is a good case in point. In the early 1960s, before the outbreak of student protests, Kerr observed that undergraduate students were "restless," that "recent changes in the American university have done them little good," and that "there is an incipient revolt" against the faculty (1966, p. 103). At the time, however, there seemed nothing for the multiversity and its leadership to do than to march on toward greater successes as defined by the specialized academic community.

New Student Demands

Admittedly, universities in the 1960s began to face an apparently new kind of consuming student—one whose demands are difficult to meet within conventional educational standards in any kind of market situation. The kind of student that I have in mind is not the political protestor, whose concerns are reserved for the next chapter, but rather the type identified with a youthful counter culture that may or may not involve political activism. The phrase *counter culture* is not precise but is used to describe interests that first appeared on a fairly large scale on campuses in the 1960s. Other youth cultures preceded the new one and often continued to coexist. The best known if not actually the most typical of the older youth cultures at American universities is the "collegiate," symbolized by fraternities, athletics, proms, and nonintellectual pursuits generally (Rudolph, 1962, chap. 5). It remains alive if not well. Clark and Trow (1966), in their familiar study of campus life, list it as one of four student types; the other three are the academic, the vocational, and the nonconformist (or the counter culture). Neither the academic type, consisting of a small number of undergraduates already devoted to specialized scholarship, nor the much larger vocational group, for whom college comes closest to being exclusively an economic investment, constitutes a youth culture in the usual sense of the term. Nor do the interests of either group make it inherently difficult to serve according to American higher education's accustomed standards. The vocational type has long been welcomed for its diligent upward mobility via career-oriented courses and simple degree-earning status achievement. The academic type is obviously what a university, especially much of its faculty, prefers.

Perhaps it posed some problems in the 1960s because more students, often more highly prepared and more demanding, were of this type at the very time that universities, generally overburdened as they were in the 1960s, found it hard to maintain quality undergraduate programs suited to unusual scholarly aspirations. But surely a more numerous and more intense academic type should in the long run produce an ungrudgingly favorable response from the university.

The collegiate type, however, has had to be served in less straightforward academic ways, and these are worth noting for their success relative to the later experience of universities with the newer youth culture. Universities were, and still are, willing enough to help provide the fun and games that the collegians want, and sometimes to provide them so bountifully that football and social events become more prominent than any other campus programs. But, apart from an unfortunately nonacademic image, universities suffer thereby little harm to their educational enterprise. Collegians, by definition, are not interested in it, and they exert no pressure to change it. They play by the academic rules—to study enough for a respectable gentleman's C. The worst characteristic, even when the collegiate culture dominated, was an annoyingly great sense of consumer power identified with wealth. So it was that Yale students of the 1920s seemed, to one young professor, to treat him "like a servant." The young professor, Ernest Lawrence, later to become Berkeley's famous physicist and the epitome of the new entrepreneurial academic, noted that a student's father had tried to bribe him to help the boy pass an examination and that a campus swimming pool had an "undergraduates only" sign (Davis, 1968, pp. 9–10). But such student attitudes reflect no hostility. Neither the university nor its professors are resented. Collegians have no cause for disappointment in what the university offers them. They receive what they come for even if they have to pass some courses along the way.

The new counter-culture type, called nonconformist until too numerous for that term, is not so readily satisfied. Its many pursuits are harder for a university to provide than the more widely accepted and even popular diversions afforded the collegian, and no extracurricular opportunities can entirely suffice. Something new and different is demanded from the academic program itself. Like most professors, I confess that I am not sympathetic to most of the demands. But I believe that it is a mistake to brush all of them aside as transient or minor phenomena. Their importance might have been exaggerated in the late 1960s, when the new youth culture on campus was augmented by draft-induced college enrollments and by politically inspired revolts against all established institutions. Nevertheless, the numbers that remain in the counter culture are a substantial consumer sector demanding some attention from the university.

Insofar as the counter culture is anti-intellectual, the difficulty it poses is plain. Much if not all that a university teaches will seem wrong or irrelevant. I believe that this is the message of the public champion of the counter culture, Theodore Roszak: "What the counter culture offers us, then, is a remarkable defection from the long-standing tradition of skeptical, secular intellectuality which has served as the prime vehicle for three hundred years of scientific and technical work in the West. Almost overnight (and, astonishingly, with no great debate on the point) a significant portion of the younger generation has opted out of that tradition, rather as if to provide an emergency balance to the gross distortions of our technological society" (1969, pp. 141–142). Elsewhere Roszak, himself an academic historian, tells us about the "healthy instincts" of the young, and about the need to subvert the "scientific world view" in favor of "a new culture in which the nonintellective capacities of the personality—those capacities that take fire from visionary splendor and the experience of human communion—become the arbiters of the good, the true, and the beautiful" (1969, pp. 41, 50–51). A more recent student, Mark Gerzon, places more emphasis on the psychological orientation of the new student and on his desire for learning to come to terms with himself rather than for learning in an educational or training process; specifically, technology and hard science are of less concern, as are any subjects demanding critical detachment or objectivity as opposed to involvement (1970, pp. 65–66, 190). A strong romantic antiorganizational bias is apparent, as in Paul Goodman's (1960) early and attractive testament to the rising counter culture.

No doubt the spirit of the counter culture is traditionally humanistic in its Wordsworthian complaints about material society.

Universities may respond with more courses in the humanities and fine arts, but these do not meet the new demand if taught conventionally as academic subjects. Scholarly learning, involving objectivity with respect to any subject matter, is not entirely appropriate. Neither are the mechanics of teaching—lectures, examinations, and grades—although they are inevitable if there is to be any organized learning at least in a large university. More and even differently taught courses in the humanities can meet only part of the new demand. The social sciences and probably the natural sciences, assuming that they are tolerated at all, are expected to address themselves to the immediately relevant and often to abandon the study of phenomena apart from ideological values. Perhaps this demand is met by the adaptation of established subject matter to topical concerns. It is at least possible to do this successfully so long as the counter culturist does not reject, in the name of individuality, all organized and disciplined learning. But such a rejection is often approximated by the common-culture student who becomes solely and literally a consumer of education. He wants immediate personal satisfaction, even enjoyment, from his courses. His purchase of education is not as an investment to be paid off in future earnings or in future career satisfactions of a nonfinancial kind (Schultz, 1963, pp. 38–39). Thus, the counter-culture student differs from the scholarly academic type and from the vocational type. And his desire for particular kinds of courses distinguishes him from the collegian, who has been content to seek his satisfactions from other university facilities.

Stating matters this way helps to explain the difficulty a university faces in contemplating the demands of the counter culture. Not only is a university's educational program, by tradition and I believe by its nature, committed to a mode of learning rejected by some of these new students, but no likely basis exists for a university to justify using public funds to develop courses meant only to provide present consumption satisfactions. Even most endowment funds seem inappropriate sources for this purpose. Admittedly, all universities have long offered some courses promising personal gratification. Art and music appreciation come to mind. But they are not justified or ordinarily presented primarily, and certainly not solely, as immediate pleasures. Rather, they are supposed to provide the learning and background to enhance subsequent aesthetic satisfactions. Otherwise it would be reasonable to expect students themselves, or their parents, to pay the full cost of courses defined strictly as current-consumption items.

The counter-culture problem is sometimes enveloped in the larger problem of enrolling increasing numbers who lack aptitude for or interest in university learning. Many who attend a university may not care for the counter culture any more than for conventional scholarship. Such students (almost nonstudents) are not new on American campuses, but their huge numbers date from the 1960s. Newly recruited ethnic minorities—really some members of these minorities—may provide a small portion of the total. Their special difficulties, when they occur, should not be confused with a more widespread resistance to learning. The new large numbers of students reflect the general movement from mass toward universal higher education, in Trow's sense of the term (1970), or from a still self-selective attendance toward a nearly involuntary enrollment. Unwilling students are assumed to become resentful if not actually hostile toward the university and its conventional academic offering. As consumers, if they do not adopt the counter culture's demands, they may want simply less academic course work—less reading, less intellectual analysis, less writing, and (contrary to the counter culture) less humanistic appreciation of the arts. Some prefer more directly practical or applied learning, especially of a kind to be absorbed through experience in a work situation rather than through classes and books. In that case, a university may be asked to provide course credit for off-campus projects that it cannot properly evaluate by its traditional academic standards.

It is common to argue that universities should be more flexible in dealing with this kind of demand (U.S. Department of Health, Education, and Welfare, 1971, pp. 21–22), but the desired flexibility seems so great that its achievement by many established universities is doubtful. More likely is the fuller development of other kinds of institutions to meet most of the demand for nonintellectual learning. In fact, this is the educational growth industry of the 1970s. Colleges and universities are no longer so clearly on their way to universalizing higher education as they were in the 1960s. Consequently, unwilling students may recede in significance. Still they are numerous enough to complicate a state university's effort to satisfy its consumers. When they are not attracted to vocational or technical schools, or to special kinds of colleges, older universities will have to consider adding nonacademic tracks to their conventional programs.

Prospects

By discussing in the last few pages certain new student demands of doubtful academic standing, I seem to detour from my main concern with the efficacy of consumer interests in universities. Underlying that concern is an assumption that many student interests ought to obtain institutional responses and that our universities in this respect better served their clientele in the early 1950s than they did a decade or so later. I detoured to note the counter culture and other nonacademic student demands in order to make it clear that my argument stops short of advocating that universities should respond to any and all consumer interests. This qualification should not detract from my operative premise that most student demands are educationally reasonable and legitimate.

Returning to the question of the efficacy of individual student consumer power, it is now realistic to discuss it in the context of the restoration, in the 1970s, of the buyer's market traditionally prevalent in American higher education. Universities again have cause to respond to their students and prospective students—not to mention the taxpaying public, whose desires in matters of educational programs tend to coincide with those of large numbers of students belonging to that public. Moreover, all reasonable projections of university enrollments and of qualified university teachers (Ph.D.s) indicate that the restored buyer's market will prevail over the next few decades and, in one degree or another, almost indefinitely. Although they have economic cause to respond, universities still may not respond to their individual consumers. Even if they did so in earlier times, and not all critics would agree with me that they ever responded in significant degree, they may now be so settled in the nonresponsive habits of the 1960s that they cannot as readily accommodate to student interests as in times past. The habits, it must be realized, are those of specialized academic professionals,

many of them new faculty members in the 1960s and hence unaccustomed to any pattern other than that of largely uninhibited professorial power. A return to the traditional attitudes of the early
1950s, therefore, cannot be an immediate reaction to harder times
in higher education. But I recognize an increasing pressure, which
produces an increasing response. It takes time for an institution's
budgetary pinch to have first departmental and then individual impact. Inexorably, however, it begins to influence professors, individually and collegially, to pay more attention to students and
notably to undergraduate students. Or, to state the point govern-
mentally, the budgetary pinch enables administrators, in ways discussed earlier, to encourage faculties to be responsive.

In addition to the growing effect of the restored buyer's
market for higher education, other economic changes in the students' situation may be developing so as to strengthen consumer
power. The most evident of these is the greatly increased tuition
charge now essential at public as well as private universities (Cheit,
1971, p. 13). Year by year, the charge becomes higher—not only
absolutely but also relative to the share of the costs contributed from
institutional funds. To be sure, nonresident tuition at state universities remains smaller than the taxpayers' share. Nevertheless, even
further modest increases, which are most probable, will make
public tuition seem high enough to fortify a student's argument for
greater influence in determining the product that he purchases. The
fact that the student can borrow the money through a federally
guaranteed loan program does not mean that he is any less the
purchaser.

Nor is the student clearly deprived of his purchaser status by
receiving general federal or state scholarship grants. True, these
grants, if large enough, can mean that the student need not use his
own or his family's money to buy his higher education. But the
grants may still be designed to increase student influence in the
marketplace. Congressional provision in 1972 of scholarships for
low-income students, although on a modest scale, displays such
a design by allotting sums to colleges in proportion to the sums
awarded to scholarship holders attending the particular colleges.
The scheme resembles the more ambitious proposals of the Carnegie Commission (1970). In effect, the student is given double pur-

chasing power. He has government money with which to pay tuition; at the same time, he carries with his enrollment an additional payment to the college that attracts him. Stated the other way around, a college has a double financial reason to attract and to please the federal scholarship-holding student: his enrollment brings in twice as much money as the college can collect from anyone else. A variant of this method of strengthening student influence has been attempted on a small scale by state governments that have chosen, often with federal aids, to develop scholarship programs that provide at least a portion of the tuition money needed for enrollment at private institutions within a given state.

A more far-reaching proposal is for states to change their basic method of financing higher education, particularly for undergraduates, so as to support students and not institutions. The proposal, while still unlikely to be adopted, has in one form or another been seriously advanced in a few states. Its leading professional advocates are two economists, Hansen and Weisbrod, who drew on their critical study of California's university financing (1969) to recommend that Wisconsin require its public universities to fix their undergraduate student tuition charges at full cost (1970). If the state stopped appropriating money to cover most of that cost, public institutions would compete among themselves and with private institutions in offering academic programs to prospective students. Understandably, the Hansen-Weisbrod proposal receives a warm and happy welcome from private institutions and from ideologically conservative champions of private enterprise in general. Many conservatives, however, may be less enthusiastic about the other side of the proposal: that state funds no longer appropriated to state universities be distributed to students. In this distribution, low-income and lower-middle-income students would be favored—indeed so favored, in the Hansen-Weisbrod formula, as to make the proposal a decidedly redistributional measure, ordinarily unpopular among conservatives.

The formula, however, is of less import for consumer sovereignty than the general principle of giving state money to students rather than to institutions. We should not expect the proposal, if ever adopted, to be as rigorously redistributional as Hansen and Weisbrod advocate. In other respects, too, their policy suggestions and their economic analyses are open to persuasive criticism (Sharkansky, 1970; Pechman, 1970; Hansen and Weisbrod, 1971b). But whatever the general merits of the proposals, it includes an attempt to increase the consumer power of individual students, or, more specifically, to increase the number of students with such power. Relatively affluent students already have the power to choose between expensive and less expensive institutions. One may disagree with Hansen and Weisbrod in principle and in many particulars and still appreciate the attractiveness of state subsidy directly to students of modest income. Strong political pressures operate in this direction; and legislatures, while unlikely to stop direct institutional funding altogether, may well be willing to appropriate any additional money to students rather than to universities.

I am far from regarding either this or other economic means for strengthening the students' positions as sufficient to create an entirely satisfying or effective consumer sovereignty in university government. Insofar as the means only broaden the range of choice among institutions, the effect is limited by a student's lack of useful and understandable educational information at the time he first selects an institution. Subsequently, when deciding that he is dissatisfied with his choice and wants to contemplate transfer to another university, he is better off informationally, but the option may be expensive in time and money. In any event, I cannot argue that the choice among institutions, initially or on reconsideration, is of great educational significance so long as American curricula remain basically similar. Instead, I believe that the important pressure point for students as consumers is within a given institution. Here, bolstered admittedly by any strengthened economic power allowing them to threaten transfer of their business elsewhere, students have a chance to influence the quality of programs and courses. The longer that the restored buyer's market is with us, the better the chance. As universities respond in this circumstance, students seem to exercise at least a modest and indirect policy-making power. They may still want to try other avenues promising more direct and perhaps more successful governing roles than those of consumers.

ordinarily share the institution's legal power in proportion to their numbers. Their organized pressures are not associated with electoral power except perhaps outside the university. Other and largely nonstudent constituencies choose university governing authorities. In this respect, students as members of a university resemble a disfranchised population in a less than fully democratic society. Protest, peaceful or violent, seems the right word for pressure exerted in this situation. It is a form of organized power especially appropriate for university students even if they also have power-sharing representational channels.

Certainly student protest has a long-standing tradition on American campuses as it has in other nations. Student senates or other student government bodies have often passed resolutions protesting university policy, although their main function, at least until the 1960s, was to manage certain social and other extracurricular programs and thus to belong, as minor pieces in university governing machinery, to the representational form subsumed under the heading of the next section of this chapter. More typical of the customary campus protest mechanism, now as in the past, is the ad hoc organization dedicated to a particular cause or reform. The old familiar example is mobilization to abolish compulsory military training, but students have gathered around other causes as well. Meetings and rallies to further protest have not been unknown; but the campus newspaper, often student dominated if not actually student owned and operated, has almost always been the most important outlet. Although most of this past campus protest was peaceful, it involved, as far back as the nineteenth century, a spirit of revolt against established authority (Rudolph, 1962, pp. 97–99, 118). The pre–Civil War colleges faced agitation against their rules and suffered the hazards of student disobedience, ill temper, and disorder (Metzger, 1964, pp. 32–42). Later in the nineteenth century and during the first few decades of the twentieth century, the situation bore some resemblance to this earlier picture if we can judge by the history of one state institution. According to its records, in 1877 a student revolt disrupted military drill; in 1889 students demonstrated against university discipline of students involved in a hazing incident and, later, against the use of police; in 1899 students participated in a mob action to stop the performance of a play; and in 1913–14 a student feud with local police resulted in student-police fights and a protesting parade of over one thousand students (Curti and Carstensen, Vols. I and II, 1949). Most such incidents, as well as the social revolts of the 1920s, raised no issues of university policy except the vexed ones related to discipline. Nor did the actions of the 1930s, when more overtly political causes originating off-campus led students to protest without significant violence and without attacking campus institutions, apart from ROTC.

In the few decades just before the middle 1960s, student protest was especially, even abnormally, peaceful: "Despite the glaring contradictions in its character, the university thrived and, between 1930 and 1960, experienced less difficulty in managing its students than in any period of the same duration, either before or since then" (Handlin and Handlin, 1970, p. 80). This was a period without overt difficulties between students and their universities. Not only were disciplinary problems minor or unknown, but rebellion seemed confined to annual exhibitions of youthful high spirits associated with the rites of spring. Organized political protests remained in pacific channels. Ignoring the past record, many of us who were students and faculty members through those three decades thought of this era of good feeling as the permanent state of student-university relations. Even after the violence of the late 1960s, we may be correct in believing that peaceful protest is the usual state of affairs. The relative calm after 1971 lends support to this optimistic view. But in historical perspective one may regard the 1930–1960 period as an exceptional time. First, an unprecedentedly severe economic depression deflected protest to noncampus causes, and then our greatest war and its very extended cold-war aftermath tended to suppress any spirit of revolt. Coincidentally, the college-age population was not greatly increasing. Also the previously described buyer's market, pervasive in higher education for most of those years, encouraged institutional responsiveness (or the appearance of responsiveness) to individual consumer demands, and so gave less cause for collective protest.

But in the 1960s, while facing an educational seller's market, students were presented with appealing external political causes most readily fostered by organized protest movements. The civil rights campaigns legitimized at least passive disobedience, and, as time went on, so did the peace campaign against the Indo-China war. The war, unpopular in principle, was also of intimate concern to college students as long as the draft threatened to deprive them of the good life promised by a higher education and even threatened in the late 1960s to interrupt their actual education. More general factors might have changed student moods, capacities, and inclinations so that the nation itself if not the world looked sick in the eyes of many college youth. Perhaps a generation was coming of age during an almost uniquely different historical period—different by virtue of affluence, technological advance, nuclear capacity for annihilation, psychological insightfulness, television, international jet travel, or some combination of these and other characteristics of postindustrial society.

The truth is that we cannot be confident about what caused our campus turmoil. We had not predicted its occurrence, and we did not predict its apparent disappearance. We know that it happened, and we know also that it happened at about the same time in almost all other western and westernizing nations. In fact, student rebellions in West German and especially Japanese universities preceded ours by a few years (Altbach, 1963). The Indo-China war, while opposed by other student groups as well as by Americans, could not have been primarily responsible for European campus uprisings. Nor could the civil rights movement have served as a stimulus in most other nations. In a comparative perspective, therefore, it is fair to look for a common cause of campus revolts in the whole western and westernizing world. The most obvious characteristic directly associated with universities is the rapid expansion of enrollments during the 1960s, when higher education institutions almost everywhere sought to meet the demands of an enlarged age cohort (born during the post–World War II baby boom), of more affluent societies, and of rapid technological changes. Yet perhaps the United States, because of its resources and its previous experience with fairly large university enrollments, would have met the new demands well enough to preclude at least the most forceful student revolts if it had not simultaneously been afflicted with special off-campus causes for a generation's political rebellion. So we are back to the point of contemplating the possibility that the war in Indo-China, plus civil rights and later black-power movements, was necessary to produce the new scale and intensity of American student protest.

Observation of American student protest in the 1960s does not establish many direct links to student discontent with higher education, however great that discontent actually was. The most spectacular mass revolts, while conducted against universities and their administrations, used their campus bases primarily to participate in national politics. Plainly this was true for peace movements even when they sought to drive ROTC and defense research from campuses; while these were campus objectives, involving university government decisions, their impetus was not dissatisfaction with education as such. Campaigns to enroll ethnic minorities and especially to develop ethnic studies programs came closer to direct engagement with academic affairs, although the dissatisfaction reflected in the campaigns was not with higher education generally. For the protest years persuasive evidence exists that the majority of college students regarded their education as basically sound, and that it was from this majority—specifically, from the most intellectual—that political activists disproportionately came (Keniston and Lerner, 1971). Their dissatisfaction was demonstrably less with their universities than with national and international affairs (Gusfield, 1971). But this demonstrated absence of a simple linkage in the 1960s between antiuniversity attitudes and propensity to protest hardly makes it tenable to assume that significant student dissatisfaction with higher education did not (and does not) exist. Perhaps the dissatisfied minority, however small, was larger and more intense than in times past, for which we lack historically comparative findings, and perhaps the satisfied majority was less fully satisfied than students used to be. Many more students might have become dissatisfied with noneducational aspects of university life. Size, now often greater than ever, and its accompanying anonymity, impersonality, uniformity, and institutionalization readily come to mind as symptoms of the "dehumanization" cry raised by protesting students.

Because the campus revolts of the late 1960s were unprecedented in scale and forcefulness of protest, their occurrence may have to be explained by special circumstances of the sort that I have noted. But student protest generally is a natural feature of university life. This view does not require acceptance of the controversial and sweeping theory that middle-aged professors and administrators, serving as surrogate parents, are targets for the misplaced hostility of psychologically emancipated children. Nor is it necessary to believe that parents and their whole generation have lost their moral authority in a historical process leading to youthful resentment and uprising (Feuer, 1969, pp. 12, 528). I am content with the simpler, nonpsychological interpretation that at certain times and places political causes will stimulate youthful protest, and the modern university is a likely setting for mobilization and expression of this protest. Large communities of young people with ideas, energy, and relative leisure are themselves propitious. But in other ways too the university's situation makes protest activity a most relevant form of organized student power. The argument has two facets: (1) that protest is suited to youths who happen to be at universities and (2) that protest is suited to certain social or cultural features of university environments.

The first facet is easy to describe. It rests on standard assumptions about bright young people: impatient, romantic, innovative, idealistic, uncompromising, and optimistic about human and social improvement. These attractive qualities are readily associated with action, not just with thought or ideology; and so, accompanied by youthful energy, they make for participation in marches, mass confrontations, sit-ins, and other physical manifestations, including those that are intentionally or unintentionally violent. Spontaneity as well as action itself is a youthful quality, and not just an ingredient of the student radicalism of the 1960s despite a tendency of observers so to regard it at the time (Spender, 1968, p. 55; Novak, 1969, p. 46). Moral outrage is another characteristic leading to direct action in a way that an unyouthful sense of political complexity tends to inhibit (Kennan, 1968, pp. 190–191). At its revolutionary extreme, the youthful protesting outlook is well and sympathetically described by Erik Erikson: "The 'self-evident' truth of simplistically overdefined alternatives and the omnipotence promised in a radical course of action permit the young to invest their loyalty and to offer their very lives" (1970, pp. 162–163). Reduced to the campus context, where revolution in the usual sense rarely arises, the best-known equivalent radical action is physical confrontation posing masses of students against the authority of the university and, preferably, of external police and military forces. As a Berkeley observer, John Searle, remarks, "Confrontation is dramatic, exciting, and meaningful." He says unkind things about it as "enormous fun" for the young middle-class student, but one can still appreciate that physical confrontation is a natural expression of strong, perhaps quasi-religious, youthful political commitments (1971, pp.30, 69, 73). Appreciation should also extend to the relative utility of the tactic. For radical student purposes—that is, for programs seeking such far-reaching objects as the end of war and racism, objects plainly unachievable within university channels— the drama of confrontation serves to call attention to the issues in a way that an otherwise equally inefficacious representation would not. Confrontation thus carries out a radical student newspaper editorial by other and more compelling means. Like the editorial, it too is a form of protest activity. And, even more than the editorial, the confrontation's frequent repetition can nullify its impact.

The second facet of the suitability of protest activity in university situations is more complex. Only in some crucial ways is the campus environment hospitable to protest. Certainly it tends to be hospitable to purely verbal criticism in meetings and in newspaper editorials, where student expression is encouraged at least by the faculty as an extension of its own academic freedom against any administrative repression. But as communities devoted to learning and reason, rather than to action, universities are unlikely places for encouragement or even toleration of physical protest. Scholarly traditions and habits of universities do not themselves foster political action. They may, on their own, tend to inhibit it. But countervailing campus forces are present. Besides the sheer dynamic of energetic young people whose scholarly commitments are often only partial, the faculty plays an important though ambiguous part. Its members do not ordinarily initiate student protest, although a minority may provide ideas and subsequently participate (Lipset, 1972, p. 198). The sympathy of professors is the significant factor requiring elucidation. Many, to be sure, are not sympathetic even to verbal protest, and some become openly hostile to physical actions in behalf of the protest. Nevertheless, during the late 1960s as much as one third to one half of a large university's faculty seemed at least to tolerate student protest activities involving incidental if not deliberate disruption. The political objectives of the activities, it ought to be said, were ones that these professors happened to share, as they shared too in the students' sense of powerlessness in national and international policy making; and this may help explain their toleration of tactics that very few professors would ever have been willing to employ themselves. One professor, for example, writing in evident agreement with student protestors, treats the seizure of buildings and the blocking of recruiters not as "the instrumental use of force" but as having "a symbolic and expressive character" (Skolnick, 1969, pp. 71–72; see also Becker, 1970, p. 9; Zinn, 1968, pp. 105, 119).

Granting that special political circumstances might have produced an unusual professorial toleration of physical protest in the 1960s, I still believe that the position of a faculty, or a large portion of it, leads to considerable toleration of protest activity almost any time that it mobilizes many students. Teachers are reluctant to become adversaries of their students. They leave such roles to administrators when protest issues have nothing directly to do with teaching or with educational programs for which professors feel responsible and self-interested. For younger professors an additional incentive to tolerate protest comes from a generational solidarity, especially with graduate students close to their own age. But older as well as younger teachers of certain humanities and social science courses, where politically charged issues are discussed, often consider it important to avoid destroying their student rapport through anything less than toleration of protest activity. Altogether, then, a university faculty is a source of indulgence for politically motivated campus protest even when it uses forceful tactics. The indulgence means that many professors are unlikely to penalize active students for absences or uncompleted work, or to indicate disapproval in more subtle ways. But faculty indulgence has another important impact when it discourages a university administration from taking effective disciplinary action against students or from resisting confrontation demands. There need be only a fairly large minority of liberal and perhaps radical professors seeking to mediate between an administration and militant students, as the ad hoc faculty group did when Columbia students were occupying campus buildings, to risk prolongation of conflict by raising student hopes for the achievement of extreme demands (Cox Commission, 1968, pp. 149–152; Avorn, 1969). At the very least, a gathering of sympathetic professors can partially legitimize student protest activity. Imagine a comparable situation in a business corporation confronted with a strike of blue-collar workers—that is, a situation in which the junior executives and professional employees, attempting to form a committee to mediate the strike, initially concede the righteousness of the strike cause. The unlikelihood, indeed the absurdity, of this business parallel should help to make clear the special advantage for student protest activity that the faculty provides in a campus situation.

Nor is the faculty the only internal campus factor providing relevant advantages. Another is the campus newspaper. News and commentary about campus affairs, especially about student activities, are circulated principally through this newspaper, which students edit and often fully control with respect to news coverage and editorial policy. In large universities the paper appears either daily or several days a week, and consequently reports events more quickly than any official university memorandum or bulletin. Furthermore, most interested students read the campus newspaper, not official mimeographed statements or the local newspapers, for stories of campus affairs. To a lesser extent, faculty members too are dependent on the campus newspaper if they wish to follow student affairs. Although not every campus newspaper is consistently radical or otherwise committed to the objectives of activist student protest, that source of bias need not be present in order to produce sympathetic accounts of the protest activities. Generational peer-group solidarity is sufficient for at least a friendly neutrality. Much more than neutrality, however, turned up in some campus newspapers of the late 1960s—probably because similar political viewpoints were held by student activist leaders and student journalists.

The dominance of students in intracampus communication about student affairs is related to the separateness of the university community, especially a residential as opposed to a commuting university community. The extent of the separateness is perhaps surprising in modern educational institutions that are large, diverse, and highly adaptive to external purposes. But their very size and internal diversity allow self-containment for students. If their professors now function in circumstances different from those of medieval cloisters, many students may still constitute an insulated community of the young (Spender, 1968, p. 169). This community, whose ethos the faculty supports, is fertile ground for organized protest of the confrontation variety. Furthermore, students are in college so short a time that immediate action is more relevant than any other means of attempting to exert influence (Goodman, 1962, p. 285).

Another characteristic favoring organized protest activities on campus is the special difficulty that a university has in responding to physical expressions of protest. *Special* is the operative word, since almost all other institutions in a democratic society also find it difficult to respond to such expressions. It is never easy to decide how much if any legal counterforce to use against a forceful organizational presence that defies law and/or custom by occupying buildings, blocking entrances, or simply marching in massive numbers against the flow of traffic. Prompt and vigorous police reaction in any circumstance may offend a crucial portion of public opinion. But in a university it is virtually certain to offend, probably grievously, a major share of the campus community—nonparticipating as well as participating students and many faculty members. (The external public is less offended; indeed, much of it is not offended at all. This too complicates the university's decision making.) Universities may also have troubles of their own in dealing with other kinds of physical acts—destruction or theft of property, for example—because they have not customarily been well equipped for security or policing. These troubles, however, do not seem peculiarly unmanageable as a result of strictly campus attitudes. Students and professors, like most citizens, will sanction legal violence against illegal violence that is plainly criminal in character. But something less is involved, or perceived to be involved, in what I call physical expressions of organized protest, by students or by others. It is a type of passive civil disobedience, sanctified intellectually and politically by previous heroes of respected causes. As "nonviolent violence" it is well suited to the university as an institution (Aron, 1969, p. 293). Physical obstruction without overt violence is readily mounted from the large reservoir of student power, and it gives campus protestors their one chance to make a purported strike, really a boycott, at all effective against the university. Only by preventing students who still want to attend class from attending and by preventing professors, administrators, researchers, and other staff members from carrying on their work can "striking" students inflict noncriminal damage on a university in any degree comparable to the damage suffered by an establishment whose producing employees are on strike (Fisk, 1969, p. 423). When students, whose tuition has already been paid, voluntarily stay away from classes, a university is hardly damaged at all. Even if impressive numbers are peacefully persuaded to be absent for several days, the effect is slight as long as university facilities are not blocked for those who want to attend. Most of the voluntarily absent students, it is correctly calculated, will soon return.

But mass student obstruction of a university's daily activities poses a crisis for campus authority. Options are limited and unhappy. Calling the police, as observed, has disadvantages, among them an increased number of sympathizing students and so an escalation of legal counterforces that may have to include state patrolmen and national guard troops, who—even more than city and county police—are unwelcome intruders in the university community. Military and police uniforms, not to mention rifles and tear gas, violate more evidently than violent student demonstrators the campus's sanctity as perceived by its denizens. To those who are in and of it, the modern university is a secularized church whose precincts are off-limits to certain agents of the state. Of course, the position is legally and politically untenable in a public institution and of dubious persuasiveness in a private college. Only in very favorable circumstances, evidently present at the University of Chicago even in the late 1960s, can a university administration expect to have an external constituency that tolerates a flat refusal to call for police to end a prolonged mass obstruction. Certainly administrations of state universities learned during the crisis years that they can only briefly negotiate with obstructive demonstration leadership before calling for, or at any rate receiving, outside help.

The remaining options are more apparent than real. Securing a court injunction against specific obstructions, apart from objections on constitutional grounds, can be only as effective as a university is willing to make it through enforcement by marshalls, police, and other agents of the law. Strictly university disciplinary action—specifically, the old weapon of expulsion—has become a paper tiger. Once used in a summary and often dangerously arbitrary fashion by deans, it was tamed by federal court decisions that applied the Fourteenth Amendment's due-process clause, along with the First Amendment's freedom guarantees, to students in state institutions (Wright, 1969). These decisions, first taking shape in the early 1960s to protect the rights of black students in southern colleges, turned out to be broadly applicable later in the decade, much to the consternation of northern state university authorities. The courts, however, insist only on procedural due process and on protection of peaceful dissent, and these requirements impose no insuperable barriers to modernized disciplinary codes. More material is the task of gaining internal campus legitimacy for serious penalties; namely, expulsion or suspension of students engaged in politically inspired protest activities. Faculty-student committees may attain such legitimacy, but they can hardly be counted upon for severity in crisis situations. Moreover, neither such committees nor any external courts can be presented with cases against protesting students unless they are identified, much as they would be in an arrest, for committing overt acts against laws and regulations.

A last possible university response, apart from surrender of one kind or another, is a tactic seldom considered in the United States but employed in the winter term of 1969 at the London School of Economics and Political Science. The LSE administration closed the school—not under pressure of a successful student "strike" but as a measure against student disruption of the educational program. In the language of industrial relations, it was a lock-out by management. It lasted three and a half weeks, after which time the school was reopened on conditions promising, correctly as it turned out, no further disruptions (Minogue, 1969). In the prevailing British situation the closing was punitive or potentially so, since students were not only prevented from using the school's facilities for their education but they were also threatened with the loss of government scholarship grants, which most of them regularly received as long as they pursued their studies in an institution of higher learning. Places in other universities being prohibitively limited, students of the LSE had good cause to want their institution to reopen. Only the most politically involved could calculate otherwise during the three and a half weeks' intermission, and they were subject to overwhelming pressure to desist from continued confrontations by students less involved in politics and more involved as students. The American situation is not similarly propitious with respect to economic incentives for students. Moreover, an American state university may be politically unable to take the initiative to close down for an indefinite period.

Altogether, then, it is reasonable to conclude the analysis of the protest mode of organized student power by saying that universities do not have satisfactory means of coping with its physical manifestations. Given this fact and also the case for the suitability in other respects of physical protest to the campus situation, one may well wonder why the confrontation tactic has become relatively obscure after its highly developed expression in the late 1960s. Perhaps its popularity waned because of repeated use and because of a sensed anticlimax following the massive demonstrations during the Cambodian affair in the spring of 1970. Or perhaps external political factors reduced the potential. Such matters are reversible, and hence it is of more than quaint historical significance to contemplate the seriousness of student confrontations. Surely the broad suitability of campus circumstances is not altered. Like protest generally, always characteristic in one form or another of student expression, mass mobilization remains appropriate. The revival of physical confrontation, possibly in ingenious new styles, cannot be excluded.

Representation

Although protest itself represents student opinions, *representation* is defined more narrowly here to mean the formal and regularized mechanisms through which a university attempts, within its own structure, to take student opinions into account. The opinions may still be protesting ones, but they are expressed in recognized governing positions held by student representatives. The positions, elective or appointive, include membership on departmental, interdepartmental, college, and campus committees; seats in a university senate or assembly; assignments on a governing board; and even membership in a strictly student senate that is formally integrated in the broader university governing structure. On the other hand, representation of students, as I use the term, does not mean control of university government by students as the most numerous members of an academic community. Such control, which I call *communalism*, rests on principles of equality of all residents of a university and of the ultimate authority of these residents. Neither principle is essential to a conception of student representation.

Indeed, representation may give so little authority to students as to seem no better than tokenism or cooptation of students into a governing process run by others. But it may be carried far enough to give students fairly substantial powers in certain areas. The crucial defining element is that governing authority is not generally distributed to students in accord with their numbers. Some may not be distributed to students at all, and some authority may be so rationed that students have only a minority of it. Aside from areas like "student affairs," deemed to be of relatively little concern to anyone else, representation is supposed to provide student participation and influence but not control over university policy making. The rationale for such roles varies from time to time and situation to situation. The most straightforward is that students have something useful to contribute to the decisions, even to those dealing with strictly academic issues, over which professors retain the dominant authority by virtue of their specializations. The usefulness of the student contribution is derivable either from substantive knowledge and experience or from the mere fact that student opinions, however well or badly informed, must be taken into account if not fully accepted. Another kind of rationale is that students will find it easier to accept decisions whose making their representatives have had a chance to observe as intimate though noncontrolling participants. They are more likely to understand the motives for an otherwise objectionable policy and to appreciate that the motives were not malicious even if mistaken.

The latter rationale suggests a connection between the increased volume of protest activity in the late 1960s and the greater representation of students that universities began to extend in those years. The relationship is clear in an action taken by Columbia university. After a report specifically favoring student involvement in decision making as an alternative to the then growing belief in the usefulness of disruption (Cox Commission, 1968, p. 197), Columbia actually inaugurated a more generous representative system in the wake of a violent crisis. Undoubtedly other universities acted to give students a greater role in the hope that such actions would forestall campus crises. The idea of student representation, however, was hardly a new one in the late 1960s. Not only had it waxed and waned in various colleges over many prior years, but a waxing was discernible in the early 1960s even prior to the first major student uprising at Berkeley. On the Madison campus, even before there were any dramatic confrontations, students began asking for greater representation on faculty committees; and some of these requests were met. It would go too far to say that this development had nothing to do with the subsequently increased protest activity. Still the student desire for greater representation originated mainly with campus issues, including educational ones, and not from external causes.

Whatever the reasons, student representation became an accepted principle of university government by the late 1960s. It is included in the "Joint Statement on Rights and Freedoms of Students" developed out of an earlier document of the American Association of University Professors but drafted and adopted in 1967 by college administrative councils and the National Student Association as well as the AAUP. "The student body," the statement declared, "should have clearly defined means to participate in the formulation and application of institutional policy affecting academic and student affairs" (AAUP, 1967, p. 367). The words are not precise about either the means or the degree of student participation, and their inclusion in a statement mainly devoted to student political freedom and procedural safeguards indicates a greater concern with the right of participation than with the mechanics of it. Any concern with mechanics concentrated on the roles of student government and student publications. Nevertheless, the principle is clearly enunciated so as to reflect the current consensual view within universities that students should have representative roles. The way in which the principle is enunciated implies that these representative roles were undergoing considerable redefinition in the direction of greater student participation.

The simplest redefinition promised an increase in the powers of an already existing body ordinarily elected in one way or another by students. The joint statement assumed that student government is the starting point for greater student participation in the affairs of the university. Usually if not always, however, student government is not government in any conventional sense of that term. The elected senate, assembly, or council made up wholly, or almost wholly, of students does little governing itself or through officials responsible to it. Even in plainly student affairs of a nonacademic nature, like disciplinary codes, it is unlikely to have final authority. In some universities, it is true, student-government agencies manage various extracurricular activities. Except, however, for campus newspapers, whose student control is often fortified by principles of freedom of the press and by administrative desires to avoid responsibility for embarrassing published material, any extracurricular activities assuming a large scale tend to move into the hands of a university staff able to provide administrative and fiscal continuity. Intercollegiate athletics are leading cases in point. More recently developed service functions such as health insurance, charter air flights, and bookstores may remain in student hands; but they reflect activities of voluntary associations rather than of governing authorities. Nor do elected student bodies "govern" through their resolutions protesting or recommending particular policies of the university and the external community. These resolutions constitute pressure-group activity, not representative governing authority; and insofar as they relate to off-campus causes, they politicize the elected student representatives in positions different from those ordinarily relevant to most university business. The politicized student representatives may perceive themselves and their ideological positions as decidedly relevant even to educational programs. But they seldom seem so to most established university authorities, including the faculty, whose positions on educational programs reflect academic subject-matter outlooks and constituencies (Trow, 1970, p. 37).

    Despite this current problem as well as others inherent in student government, many universities attempt to build on this existing representative base when they increase student participation in campus government. The attempt takes two often complementary forms. One is to consign certain areas, or more of certain areas, to the elected student agency. Since this devolution is ordinarily

limited to well-defined student affairs, it is less significant than the
second means of legitimizing student government's role in the exercise of general university authority: the use of already student-
elected representatives as the source for recruiting student members
of various campus committees. The elected representatives may
themselves join the committees, or they may appoint other students.
Either way, student government gets a slice of the established authority. It is a more logical arrangement for some committees than
for others. Those whose jurisdiction is campus-wide obviously coincide with the total student constituency supposed to be represented
by a campus-wide student senate, while school, departmental, and
other specialized area committees do not. Also the committees
whose subject matter includes broad student concerns, like those for
residential living arrangements, are better suited to representation
from student government than are committees devoted to the curriculum of a particular college or school.

No matter what the jurisdiction or subject matter of a
committee, it is always possible that the student government will
consider its committee representatives as delegates rather than as
independently individual participants in the style of faculty committee members. In that event, student representatives may regard
themselves as effectively mandated by the elected body from which
they come. University administrators and professors hope that student representatives will not thus be mandated delegates, and they
have had a great deal of experience with students whose committee
behavior is as individually determined as any professor's. Yet no one
can deny that turning to student government for representatives
opens the possibility of the mandated delegation and at the same
time legitimizes it. On what basis can university authorities object
to students' behaving as delegates when they are chosen by an
elected body whose constituency is potentially political rather than
academic? Of course, a student government's constituency can be
structured on departmental or college lines, within the total campus,
and the method is not unknown in American universities. But more
usually, because it suits the other and original purposes of student
government, its senate or assembly is chosen at large, by residential
areas, by various component student interest groups, or by some
combination or variation that is politically more meaningful than

are academic disciplinary clusters for the numerically preponderant undergraduate students.

Consequently, university committees can in certain circumstances become confrontation sessions between administrators and/or professors, on the one hand, and student-government delegates, on the other. When that occurs—no doubt a very small portion of the time but critically when it does happen—representation is not serving its usual function but is instead a peculiar variety of collective bargaining. Its peculiarity lies in the absence of effective legal power on the student-government side. Like students generally, their senate leadership has no labor to withhold, or even tuition payments (given the virtual impossibility of organizing students before a given term begins and tuition payments are due). About all that the student-government delegates can threaten, short of violence, is to withdraw from participation from university committees. That is hardly an intimidating bargaining counter, but it dramatizes the breakdown of student representation as a governing mechanism and the reconversion, at least temporarily, of student government to protest activity.

On or off university committees, student government can negotiate what it regards as student claims. In the university systems of other nations, student representation more openly takes this form, both locally and nationally (Ashby and Anderson, 1970; Duster, 1968). The student association, instead of bearing the name *government,* is actually called a union of students; and, since it employs a professional staff, it at least resembles a trade union. The development of a similar apparently workable arrangement is difficult in the United States, where students are much more numerous and are located in diverse political and fiscal constituencies rather than in a single national system of higher education. More clearly than in Europe, student unionism, if operative at all, would be an alternative *outside* the university structure itself and therefore sharply different from the customary American efforts to integrate student representation in the governing structure. The alternative, or something like it, may be sought if I am correct about the limited efficacy of student representation now developed in the United States.

Helping to explain the limitations of institutional representation is the understandable unwillingness of present university power holders to surrender their dominant roles in educational and related policy matters. For them representation of students is as I have defined it at the start: minority participation in the vital academic areas. Anything more, it ought to be emphasized, would change the nature of the university and of its assumption of authority based on knowledge and experience. The view can also be understood through a realization that any power given to students must come from some other group. Authority is finite; or, in the already hackneyed terminology of the new political science, competition for university power is a zero-sum game. Whose present power, and over what, is to go to students? The only easy part of the game is to reallocate or abandon the regulation of strictly student affairs. Disciplinary powers of deans of students suffer from atrophy; in any case, these powers had been assumed by universities, especially their faculties, only because of once more widely prevalent societal expectations. At the other extreme, universities, especially state universities, do not seriously propose giving students any large part of the power of governing boards or of administrators responsible to those boards.

This leaves, in the middle, the abundant academic power of the faculty. That power is fragmented and decentralized, but it is therefore harder rather than easier to dislodge. It has never been as good a political target as the more readily observed power of top administrators. Therefore, when students first demanded power during the revolts of the 1960s, they sought to make the policies that they thought administrators were making. Most of the faculty could then be indulgent of the demands. But later student claims for representation—in curriculum planning, personnel policy, grading, course requirements, and research emphases—are all mainly at the expense of faculty power. Probably these will continue to be the areas of contention because of their direct and immediate concern to students and to professors. The political realism of the context is apparent to anyone who knows how much of a major university's decision-making power is now exercised by organized clusters of faculty members as well as by individual professors. It may be less apparent in universities and colleges where professorial roles are limited by hierarchical authority in determining educational programs. But it does not necessarily follow that professorial resistance to potentially dominating student power will be less at institutions where professors have less power to lose. Everywhere they have something to lose.

Professors may not enjoy making departmental and committee decisions; but by being able to make these decisions, they determine the nature of their own teaching and research. Professors would fear, in certain probably transient political circumstances, the use of student power to impose an ideological doctrine on what should be taught and studied; but they much more regularly fear the largely nonideological pressure of undergraduates to reduce research commitments generally in favor of classroom and related teaching. This threat can be realized either by student dominance of committees regulating programs and reward structures or by student constituencies choosing and so influencing middle-range academic administrators. However it arises, any such diminution of faculty power would, it is assumed, change the nature of the university in ways that many professors regard as crucial to the quality of the academic enterprise. They doubt whether students would share the same perceptions, particularly in the short run.

Not every faculty member, however, is consistently resistant to the growth of student power in academic affairs. Even in prestige universities younger faculty often support considerable increases in student participation. Perhaps it is easier for them to do so because it is not yet their own power but that of their senior colleagues which they are willing to share with students. Also, being closer to the age and concerns of students, younger faculty members may genuinely identify with their discontent and believe that student power would change the system for the better. But differences with older faculty members are not so sharp as to portend any future willingness to transfer power in a vital decision-making area like that of personnel appointment and promotion. The Carnegie Commission's data from its national survey confirm this limited impact of age on professorial attitudes toward student power (1973, pp. 120–121). The differences between age cohorts are not insignificant, but they are less impressive than the overall resistance to student power in academic areas customarily occupied by faculty authority (p. 67). Except for disciplinary matters, students want more power than the overwhelming majority of professors are willing to concede. This holds for power in the sense of substantial voting strength.

Almost as pervasive as faculty resistance on this score is faculty willingness to consult students about courses and degree requirements and to have students evaluate teaching performances. These consultative roles, when formalized, provide a kind of representation, but they only slightly dilute professorial power through the requirement that student views be heard before decisions are made. Even when students are given minority representation in the decision-making unit, the dilution may still be so limited as to be accepted by many professors. But student advocates of such representation may want so large a proportion as to tip the balance against the majority of professors when only a few professors defect from their colleagues. This becomes a distinct possibility when students have as many as two fifths of a committee's membership and when they vote together (by no means a certainty). Having, however, so large a student proportion of an academic policy-making committee is unlikely. Even Earl McGrath, a devoted educator-champion of student representation who regards about two-fifths student membership as reasonable for some committees, does not suggest this large a fraction for the most professional academic bodies (1970, p. 82).

A popular device for student representation in broader university affairs developed in the wake of the disturbances of the late 1960s. It is a campus or university senate, as distinguished from an exclusively faculty (or academic) senate, and also of course from a student senate. The idea is for all major campus constituencies to be represented in one body. These constituencies may include nonfaculty staff as well as faculty and students. Having a campus senate of this broad nature need not preclude separate faculty and student senates at the same time. These may even select representatives for the campus senate. But the tendency is to conceive the broader representative body as taking over some of the functions of the other bodies if it does not supersede them altogether. For students in particular, representation in a campus senate is often a specific alternative to the continued existence or the creation of a student senate. It is an evidently attractive alternative in some instances, even though students are assigned only a minority of a campus senate's seats rather than the dominance that their numbers would justify on a one-person-one-vote principle. The Columbia University senate, established in 1969, is a good case in point. Students regarded strictly student government as involving so little real government that they settled for about one fifth of the membership in the university senate and for varying minority shares on most of the senate's committees except those having to do with largely nonacademic affairs of students (Columbia University, 1969, p. 12). Interestingly, student members of the Columbia senate, like faculty members, are elected from school and college constituencies rather than at large or from residential living units. An example of a campus senate with different arrangements for student representation is found at the University of Kansas. Here the whole of the old established student senate, numbering just less than one hundred, is included along with the existing faculty senate in the total membership of the new body. The faculty senate, consisting of all staff members at each of the three professorial ranks, is much larger than the elected student senate, and so the faculty is numerically dominant in much the same proportion as is Columbia's. Moreover, the Kansas faculty senate itself retains functions of its own (University of Kansas, 1969). Many other arrangements exist elsewhere. The broadly based senate is now widespread, although little is known of its effectiveness (Hodgkinson, 1973).

The usefulness of a campus senate for the exercise of student power may be more closely related to the jurisdiction of the senate than to the numbers of student members in the senate. The more basic question is whether the campus senate will have the kind of jurisdiction that allows many significant policy decisions. One is certainly entitled to doubt on this score. Even where a faculty senate has been relatively strong and where its strength is transferred to a campus-wide senate, the students are not thereby accorded a share of the most important professorial power. That remains at other levels of faculty representation. As I have emphasized in discussing faculty power, professors themselves acknowledge the greater importance of departmental policies in particular by being much more regularly attentive to them than to campus business. Students may be more interested than professors in certain of the general issues taken up by a faculty senate or a campus senate, but they will be no slower to perceive their limited effectiveness. They may well be especially impatient with the fact that senate action remains subject, in the most important areas, to regent or trustee approval, as is the case now and as is likely to remain so almost everywhere.

Other levels of university government do not pose exactly this kind of problem. These levels provide less dramatically newsworthy opportunities for student representation, but they may possess more independent power. This brings us back to the stronghold of faculty authority in the department and in similarly situated agencies of academic program administration. Apart from the likely reluctance of professors substantially to dilute their real power in areas of academic program administration, other difficulties emerge for student representation at the departmental level. Chief among these is the definition of the constituency to be represented. This is resolved for graduate students, who usually are present in sufficiently limited numbers and for a long enough period in a department so that they become an identifiable, interacting group capable of meeting to choose representatives. Undergraduates, at least in a large university, are not so conveniently clustered. Freshmen and sophomores seldom have any departmental identities, and juniors and seniors have only those loosely associated with their major subjects. Some of these majoring juniors and seniors, it is true, do interact a good deal with each other and with the departmental faculty, and they, particularly those intending to pursue graduate work, are the likeliest representatives. Certainly they can be discovered by the departmental faculty. Whether they will be discovered by their fellow students majoring in the same department is another matter. My observations suggest that the constituency is not a live operative one. Few undergraduate students attend meetings called to elect departmental representatives (for an undergraduate curriculum committee, for example)', and few vote even when solicited by mail. Yet no plainly better method of securing student representatives exists at this level. Neither a campus-wide senate nor a student senate is an appropriate source for nominees representing a department's own students. Therefore, undergraduate members of department committees tend to be self-selected. Their lack of democratic credentials does not prevent useful contributions. As the most interested students, they probably have the most to suggest. And the suggestions are often highly congenial to professorial interests. But whether these suggestions are what many students want is not clear. Professors, especially in a large university, ought to be skeptical.

An altogether different level for student representation in university government is the board of regents or trustees. The board may include one or more students as voting or nonvoting members, in accord now with congressional intentions expressed through an amendment to the Higher Education Act; or the board may just provide student leadership with a regularized opportunity to present its viewpoints. The latter falls short of representation by allowing students only the roles of protesting pressure groups. Even non-voting membership is marginal, although it includes participation in discussions leading to policy decisions. Voting rights, while hardly out of the question, are no more readily justified for students than for faculty in a state university. As I argued in Chapter Four, regent voting membership for any representatives of the university community is at odds with the conception of a board acting for the state in governing the institution. In any event, when seriously proposed as when actually instituted, student voting memberships on governing boards are so limited in numbers (usually one or two students on a board of at least a dozen members)' that the inclusion is bound to be regarded as tokenism, albeit high-level tokenism.

Although student representation, as conventionally understood, has definite limitations, I do not regard it as useless. Universities and their components benefit from regularized student input, and I prefer more of it if it can be obtained without student dominance in crucial academic matters. The latter proviso, of course, is one of the limitations, or one of the factors contributing to the limitations on student representation and so to its observable and definable power. But would greater power through representation suit many students? Taking part in all the ponderous deliberations of faculty committees, Bettelheim contends, "is not the active life youth hankers for" (1969, p. 41). It is not surprising that increased student representation in the 1960s failed to diminish protests. Certain protest activities, as I noted earlier, are more relevant to the student situation—partly because protests are more occasional or sporadic. It asks a good deal of students to spend their time regularly helping to govern the university. It is seldom proposed that they be paid for their service, either in dollars or in course credits (McGrath, 1970, pp. 96–99). Doing so might help recruit student representatives, but probably from a rather special group that is professionally concerned, like professors, with educational matters. They might be nearly as self-selected and untypical as are unpaid interested students whose academic programs and affluent status allow them a great deal of leisure time.

Communalism

Before the late 1960s virtually no one seriously proposed the communal conception for American university government. Not many will take it seriously now. But from the heady days of campus revolt a left-wing communal doctrine emerged to be considered in comparison with the likelier and less radical expressions of organized student power. *Communalism* is not a usual term for the conception, and it may have certain unfavorable connotations of soviet communism or bohemian living arrangements. I intend neither set of connotations. Nor do I use the term to include various neighborhood residents, otherwise unassociated with a university, in the government of the institution. I realize that this inclusionary idea was confusingly labeled *community government* when discussed at Columbia in 1968. But the community that I have in mind as the basis for communalism in university government consists only of members of the university; that is, of students, faculty, and other staff. It is a residential definition, but not one that embraces citizens who happen to live in the campus neighborhood but have no other connection to the institution. Participants in communalism, as understood here, qualify through employment or enrollment in addition to campus or near-campus living. "Being in residence," in the campus's sense of that term, is still crucial. Definitionally excluded are all former students or other citizens who support a state university through taxes or private gifts. Technically the exclusion applies even to those of student age who drop out for a term or two but remain in the campus neighborhood, perhaps as street people. In practice, however, proponents of communalism may not be this strict about the definition.

It seems fair to regard communalism as the most extreme conception of organized student power worthy of discussion, although it is less extreme, in principle, than giving students alone all of the power. Communalism falls short of this by including faculty and other staff members in the governing arrangements. But it does not fall very short. Under the one-person-one-vote formula, students would always have the majority of votes at a mass meeting, a referendum, in an elected assembly, or a committee. Thus, communalism is distinguished from representation as an expression of organized student power. No policy-making bodies would, in principle, either exclude students or limit their membership to minority status. Most notably students would be able to dominate educational policy making with respect to faculty personnel as well as courses and curricula. By no means is it evident that many American university students want this much power, or that they consider it good for themselves or their education. Note that only a small percentage of the Madison students whose opinions are reported in Table 4 (Chapter Four) opted for student authority as the principal locus for governing decisions. More persuasively, the Carnegie Commission's national survey of student opinion, while reflecting a desire for greater student governing roles than faculty opinion allows, shows that only about one quarter of the sampled undergraduates go as far as favoring their own voting power or control over faculty appointments and promotions (1973, p. 124). Only among self-described left-wing students does this proportion sharply rise (in fact, to 70 percent). In their still limited ranks, the communalism doctrine originates and is propagated on campuses. If accepted on left-wing terms, the ideological purpose of student power becomes plain—as it has, for example, at the Free University of Berlin, where dominant Marxist students impose their educational programs (Schoenbaum, 1973, p. 8). But if American students were persuaded to assert power, they might not have the same ideological purpose, or any ideological purpose at all. We cannot be sure that they would exert control over the political content or import of their courses. In the United States, with little known experimentation with anything approaching university communalism, the doctrine must be discussed apart from much illustrative material. That means a discussion of its general principles, apart from specific Marxist overtones.

Of leading concern among these principles is communalism's implicit and often explicit rejection of the assumptions of other established conceptions of university government. By asserting their claim to a dominant voice in university policy making, students overwhelm by their numbers the established claims of professorial expertise; they also challenge the state agencies, regents, and administrators who are supposed to represent the public's interest. Although student power ordinarily appears to oppose mainly the internal campus authority of professors and associated administrators, its full-blown demands deny the legitimacy of all noncampus authority over a university. This denial follows from the cardinal principle that those actually participating in the educational process should control it. The participants are both students and staff. Their credentials, however different they may be in other respects, are based on the standard of immediacy. Students may still claim superiority over staff, including professorial staff, on the grounds of their status as paying consumers or perhaps because of inherent advantages of youthfulness; but such superiority need not be claimed in order for students to be dominant, given their numbers, once authority is granted to all the immediate participants. The democratic principle here is for "local" power and for majoritarianism within the local community.

On these grounds the case for communalism differs from the case for professorialism. Faculty power, while also leading toward autonomy for campus-based authority, is asserted in the name of an academic expertise uniquely capable of assuming responsibility for a state service. Professors do not claim power for themselves simply as participants, but rather as the specially qualified participants. Occasionally, it is true, a professor changes the terms of the traditional faculty claim by joining or supporting organized student power. Wolff seems to do so when he makes the case for the involvement of students primarily because they are members of the university community, and then declares: "The fundamental principle of governance in American colleges and universities today must be

All Power to the Faculty and Students" (1969, pp. 126, 133). How much power Wolff would give to each of these campus categories is not clear, and he does not argue for communalism as such. Wolff, like most professors, probably prefers to preserve faculty power in academic matters and to settle for substantial but not overwhelming representation of students.

The point, therefore, in citing Wolff is only to display an important ideological contribution to communalism that is not exclusively associated with student power. Wolff is concerned with the autonomy of the university—specifically, with its capacity to reject certain government programs associated with military purposes. Professors and students, he contends, should make their own judgments of the value of such programs, resisting those they regard as wrong even though the government wants them undertaken (1969, p. 40). The impression is that Wolff would have such decisions made by the whole community of professors and students, presumably with authority, by majority vote, to outlaw objectionable programs for any individual professors or students who might want them. Whatever is to be said one way or the other for this particular kind of social control (admittedly, universities have always drawn the line somewhere against programs they regarded as unsuitable), Wolff undoubtedly believes that students as well as professors possess, by their presence in the university, a rightful power that is not possessed by any external authorities.

Like many other advocates of complete university autonomy, communally or noncommunally achieved, Wolff writes chiefly in the context of the private university. Insofar as a university remains private, the case for strictly internal policy making is probably easier to argue, although by no means self-evident to trustees believing themselves responsible for the continuity of an institution endowed by earlier generations. In a state university, or a university heavily supported by federal or state funds, any argument for "all power to students and faculty" is certain to clash with the established democratic doctrine, which, even in education, provides for a measure of control by public representatives over a public facility. Yet the student advocacy of communalism seems to make no distinction between public and private institutions. The elitist implications of this advocacy are fairly plain. It is not "the people" generally who are to make university policy, but only those people who are in the university, here and now. They are inevitably a privileged group from the standpoint of everyone else, and they can hardly claim that they represent the population at large. Students are not trustees but beneficiaries. And they are not specialists, managerial or academic, managing an enterprise in behalf of the public. Yet the policy-making power that communalism assigns to student power—what should be taught and what research should be undertaken—is the kind that the public expects to have exercised by its chosen representatives or by the academic specialists whom those representatives depend upon.

Although American experience with communalism is decidedly limited to a few small-scale private ventures of little relevance for large state universities, some note should be taken of the approximation to communalism at Antioch College. This famous and well-established private college has a community government, whose council, with a student majority, exercises broad decision-making authority in many noneducational matters and a more modest role in developing courses. In addition, students participate on an unusually generous basis in the academic policy-making bodies, separated from the community government. Three students are members of an eight-person administrative council, evidently a significant academic body. These three students participate in interviewing and deciding whether to hire candidates for the faculty as well as in contract-renewal discussions (Antioch College, 1969). "Representation" here is so substantial as to make it seem different in kind from the devices discussed in the previous section. Yet it appears to fall well short of the communalism found, for example, in Latin American *co-gobierno,* where the effective power of students is associated, rightly or wrongly, with corruption, lowering of standards of performance, and danger to professorial academic freedom (Albornoz, 1966, pp. 252–254).

Without substantial American experience with communalism, and certainly without any in our large universities, it is dangerous to assume that its coming would bring the worst consequences attributed to it in Latin America or elsewhere. Such consequences are possible, but I am content to concentrate here on the less uncertain difficulties of principle that are inherent in communalism.

These difficulties emerge from the challenge that majoritarian student power poses both to public authority itself and to the professorial expertise that exercises some of that authority. Other difficulties flow from the nature of the student constituency. Especially at a large university the problem of obtaining adequate regularized student participation, observed with respect to the election of even a few representatives, would be more serious if elected students were to have majority power rather than only minority representation in educational affairs. Most students are as improbable participants in the one situation as in the other, either to serve themselves or to elect others to serve in their behalf. They do not form a stable electoral community. Each student belongs to a given university for only a few years. High and rapid turnover means that both potential voters and potential elected leaders, if they are at all typical of their fellow students, will be but short-term residents. Availability for reelection then becomes unusual, since those elected, ordinarily upperclassmen, cease to be students within a year or two of election. Responsibility in the accepted democratic electoral sense is thus impossible. Accordingly, the legitimacy of organized student power will be doubted, probably by many students as well as by others in the university. The doubt constitutes a much more commanding obstacle to student hegemony through communalism than it does to the more limited power of organized students through sporadic protests or through minority and consultative representation mechanisms.

Another Route

Organized student power does not emerge from this chapter as both effective and acceptable in any one of its modes. Protest, natural though it is to the campus situation, seems to accomplish little in its usual nonforceful manifestations, and to be at odds with regularized governing arrangements when it involves physical confrontation. A peaceful student "strike," it should be stressed, has no real effect. Representation, widely accepted by universities in its minority and consultative forms, does not satisfy or even interest many students. Communalism, or anything like it, cannot be reconciled with other values on which university government is based. Must students then look principally to their roles as individual consumers in order to influence university policies? Even in a restored buyer's market, such roles must appear of limited efficacy within the university itself.

More promising, however, is another student-power route, which I have not described until now because it lies outside the campus's institutional structure. The route is nevertheless clearly political in its relation to government of any state university. It is for students, as citizens themselves, to seek to influence state policies toward higher education. They may do so from campus organizational bases or from home communities along with their parents. Either way, students act as consumers. Now that voting eligibility is fixed at eighteen and students are able to cast ballots either in campus or home residency, they are a formidable power in certain legislative constituencies and indeed in whole states. They may try to influence regent election or appointment, fostering candidates sympathetic to student viewpoints if not actually promoting student candidates. Students may similarly participate in the election of legislators and governors committed to their interests. And plainly they can function through their own lobbying organization, as they have already done especially in California, to influence budgetary and other legislative outcomes. Often this kind of student influence might simply support university administration proposals, but occasionally a separate student influence might be exerted in behalf of a distinctive student interest. In thus seeking to help determine university policies, students in many states are not only a sizable bloc on their own, but they have natural allies in their parents and in the parents of prospective students.

In principle and in practice, students are less disadvantaged in the state's broader political arena than they are in the university's internal governing structure. They have the same right to participate as any other citizens; and, although they constitute only a large minority of the whole community, their numbers are greater than those of other educational interest groups. They may be capable of getting the attention of politicians ordinarily pressured by smaller, more intense groups. In the larger political world students cannot be dismissed because they lack the professional qualifications of faculty and administrative staffs. The decisions of governors and legislatures, or even of regents, presumably do not require such qualifications. Academic matters are not contemplated as the subject of the off-campus state policy making in which students as citizens should play a part. Nevertheless, many of the matters that are and can legitimately be decided by state authorities have an important impact on the educational enterprise. They are becoming more rather than less important as state governments seek to manage their systems of higher education.

TEN

Pluralism
Restated

S tressing in each of the last seven chapters a distinctive conception of university government, I have occasionally treated versions of particular conceptions as incompatible with other conceptions. Generally, however, I assume only conflict rather than a mutual exclusiveness among the different theories of distributing university governing power. The conflict, although seldom dramatically overt, is of long standing. The legitimacy crisis of the late 1960s brought to the surface not only an old and smoldering conflict between public authority and institutional autonomy but also an internal campus conflict. From both faculty and student groups new conceptions of power emerged, often as doctrines designed to challenge an established order. These new conceptions involve some claims that can and should be accommodated, along with older claims, in university government.

No one conception, standing alone, provides either the theoretical or the practical basis for governing a large and complex state university or, for that matter, a modern private university in which the public has a substantial interest. The reason should be plain: each conception is one constituency's claim to power in a situation where other constituencies also have claims. The consent of more than one set of participants is essential for successful government of the enterprise. Legitimacy, in other words, is in the eyes of the beholders, and the beholders of state university government do not have a single perspective. Far from it. This is why we have such varied and often conflicting conceptions of university government. Even to categorize claimants, as I have done by identifying conceptions with their proponents, is to reduce the actual variety. Well-known differences emerge within faculties, student bodies, regent boards, and elected officialdom, as well as between them. But— except in a few general instances, such as the difference between faculty governing roles and faculty collective bargaining roles or the difference between the students' individual consumer power and organized activity—I have not chosen to stress the varied conceptions that evidently exist within each category of concerned participants. This seems a pardonable analytical simplification in an effort to identify the principal thrusts of each major set of claimants to authority. No conception rests on a pure abstraction. Rather, each is a product of empirically observed interests, opportunities, and capacities of possible power holders. The participants are understood to interact as contending and bargaining members of a political system.

Perhaps I can more clearly make the point by summarizing the different perspectives that I associate with the sets of claimants and with the purposes that each group perceives as the university's basis for existence. Taxpaying citizens, through elected officeholders and to some extent through regents, are likely to want tangible benefits, such as effective (often vocationally oriented) undergraduate education and state-oriented services, and so to want a governmental arrangement that ensures priority for these concerns along with fiscal economy in meeting these concerns. Most undergraduate students can be expected to share a good deal of this perspective, but without the same desire to limit the taxpaying costs; in addition, at least some students have more purely academic goals and others the contrasting counter-culture concerns, both of which are at odds with pragmatic vocational purposes. The purely academic goals are also those of many if not most professors, whose subject-matter devotion leads to research and specialized teaching and to a conception of university government that enables professors themselves to arrange the priorities to suit their academic purposes. They may try to fulfill their purposes through faculty government or collective bargaining, or some combination of the two. But, in one way or another, professors, like students and representatives of the taxpaying citizenry, will want a governmental arrangement suited to their views of what a university ought principally to be and to do.

Not surprisingly, professorial perceptions in this respect differ from those of many students, citizens at large, legislators, other state officials, regents, and even university administrators. The last two categories, regents and university administrators, exhibit intermediate, compromising, or even mediating perceptions of university purposes, and yet have distinctive qualities too. Most regents are likely to perceive a university as their public trust to be governed with minimal control by other state officials but yet for the benefit of the citizens of the state. In this perspective, regents regard administrators as their agents—not agents of the governor or the faculty. Administrators, while sharing the regents' desire for institutional autonomy, may be more directly responsive to their faculties and perhaps to students; but increasingly they have their own managerial values of institutional prestige and performance. More directly than anyone else with a governing stake in the university, administrators are devoted to achieving harmony, gaining publicity (and avoiding bad publicity), building a favorable reputation for institutional programs of all kinds (academic and nonacademic), and increasing financial resources.

The very different perspectives of the several sets of power claimants, and also the different perspectives within each set, provide a basis for the occasional argument that the American state university—particularly the multiversity—is ungovernable and generally unworkable. Its purposes, it is said, are too varied, and it tries to serve too large and too diverse a public. Much the same case can be made against large private universities that combine major research and graduate training responsibilities with undergraduate teaching, especially now that those universities resemble state institutions in carrying out specifically governmental programs—national if not state. Even before the late 1960s, critics believed that the multiversity neglected its undergraduates. But the subsequent challenge to politically controversial research, and the simultaneous demand for new programs for new kinds of students, revealed much more clearly the different perceptions of a university's proper mission. The differences were so sharp as to threaten the governability of an academic community continuing to maintain the established diversity of functions—particularly mass undergraduate education along with an open-ended governmental service. The consequent crisis caused many to reappraise the previously assumed compatibility of the university's effort to combine the highest-level graduate training and research with a large liberal arts college for undifferentiated, unspecialized, and often academically unmotivated students. The new turbulence of undergraduate students actually interfered with graduate training and research, and it raised long-suppressed doubts, in the minds of primarily undergraduate teachers as well as of research scholars, about the strictly academic desirability of one institution's trying to serve such different purposes.

This reconsideration of the nature of the university leads in the direction of settling problems arising from different governing conceptions by liquidating, or decartelizing, the institution to be governed. Although I reject this final solution to the problems that I have posed, it is worth critical examination. Alternatives to the maintenance of the large multipurpose American university do exist.

The simplest proposition is that the American university is too large and that its educational missions at all levels would be better served in smaller units than those with 30,000 to 40,000 students. Certainly a persuasive case can be made against unlimited growth and in favor of an academically optimum size well short of the largest American universities (Gallant and Prothero, 1972). But it does not follow that a university of 20,000 would be appreciably easier to govern than a university of 40,000 if, as is usually believed, the present governmental difficulties flow from diversity of purpose and not from size as such. Ordinarily those who think of an optimal size of 20,000, or even 10,000 or 15,000, still assume most of the established diversity. Only one mission would be drastically diminished, if not eliminated, by a reduction in size of the enterprise. It is the servicing of nonserious undergraduate students. Such students would tend to be excluded by more highly selective admission procedures, British style (Halsey, 1962), as a university reduced its total enrollment. Fewer would thus mean better students, at least at the prestige universities. The less serious, or the less able or the less well motivated, would in these circumstances be shunted to other colleges or universities. Much can be said for and against this kind of separation; but even if it were achieved, along with fixed limits on enrollments in particular places, it probably would not ease governing problems in a major way. The evidence from California, which has had ceilings at its largest university campuses and considerable differences in admission standards between those campuses and certain other state institutions, suggests no advantages for internal government.

Stemming also from objections to great size is the proposal to decentralize university authority. Large size and diverse functions in a given geographical location would remain, but their problems would be met by establishing component units to govern themselves as though they were geographically separated (Scranton Commission, 1970, p. 14). Certainly a measure of this kind of decentralization is workable, either through innovative means like cluster colleges or through departments and programs. In fact, the American university has already achieved substantial decentralization of its authority. It will no doubt attempt to achieve something similar for its campuses within any merged state system of higher education. Admittedly essential to academic well-being and probably inherent in the nature of the enterprise, this decentralization is really part of the problem of university government rather than a new solution for it. The task of governing a large and diverse enterprise cannot be escaped by decentralization; it is just made more or less difficult. Escape is clearly conceivable only through secession—for instance, small learning groups of about 150 teachers and students surviving in anarchical simplicity without any of the usual governing necessities (Goodman, 1962, p. 323).

Short of so drastic and utopian a reorganization, there is another alternative to the multiversity. To protect, preserve, and invigorate humanistic undergraduate education, many believe that it must be separated from most of the other missions of the modern university—from graduate and professional training and from related research—and that this separation requires a liberal arts college whose departments or other units are divorced from the specialized, discipline-oriented departments offering more advanced work. Champions of this viewpoint include the philosopher Robert Paul Wolff (1969, pp. xiii, 17) and reform-minded writers associated with educational research (Dressel, Johnson, and Marcus, 1970, pp. 229–230). Not far from the same position are traditional academics like Jacques Barzun (1968) and Robert Nisbet (1971). They do not specifically advocate an exclusively undergraduate teaching institution, as does Wolff, but they prefer a restoration of the pre-1940 situation, in which university departments concentrated on liberal arts education and treated graduate training and research as ancillary rather than as dominating activities. Much of the university's current research load and associated training would be peeled off for location in noneducational institutions of one kind or another. The university's diversity, not merely its size, would be curtailed.

The champions of undergraduate liberal arts are not the only proponents of this division. Occasionally the very academics least interested in teaching undifferentiated and unspecialized undergraduates come to the same conclusion. What they are trying to save is research and graduate training from the encroachment of mass teaching concerns. They would keep the university, physically and symbolically, as their preserve, peeling off the undergraduate work for lesser organizations to manage. But the result would be much the same: two kinds of institutions instead of the present multipurpose university. The idea is not a new one. As early as World War I, when the large multipurpose university was just developing, Veblen regarded the burden of mass undergraduate teaching as incompatible with higher learning and inquiry (1957, pp. 12, 17). Over fifty years later, Carl Kaysen writes to the same effect: "The present universities should, to the greatest possible extent, abandon the function of undergraduate socialization and certification to institutions primarily engaged in them, and reserve their own efforts for higher levels of training, the tasks of adapting scientific and technical knowledge to the solution of difficult social problems, and those of the creation of new knowledge and incorporation of it into the existing body of learning" (1969, p. 79). Unquestionably these words, in the late 1960s, struck a sympathetic note in the minds of many beleaguered scientists and other academics, who found their research challenged both ideologically (because the research was oriented the "wrong" way) and educationally (because it distracted from undergraduate teaching). Whatever his own intentions, Kaysen offers a way out: send most of the troublesome undergraduate students to places where there would be no research.

Besides the proponents of disaggregation, who would save either undergraduate education or high-level research and training, other academics state a similar case less clearly derived from a commitment primarily to one purpose or the other. For example, Amitai Etzioni's quite specific proposals reflect an apparent concern with both kinds of purposes and perhaps with others too. He would have three types of institutions: one, consisting of the great majority of present colleges and universities, to have an exclusively teaching mission (including instructional service to the community); a second, consisting of less than 10 percent of present colleges and universities, to provide all the basic research and graduate research training; and the third, consisting of new and established research corporations, to perform the applied research and development work that is now, in many fields, done within universities. This "process of differentiation," as Etzioni describes it, is meant to clarify what he views as "complementary but still quite distinct missions of three knowledge-processing institutions," and to enable each more effectively to fulfill its purpose by concentration on that purpose (1970, IV, p. 26). Such concentration quite evidently includes separate government according to standards and rules relevant to the separate mission. Yet the complementary relationship of the three missions is readily conceded by Etzioni; it causes him to suggest that the three institutional types would continue to benefit if they were associated in academic "cities" rather than being geographically separated.

Of course, such association would perpetuate the current uses of buildings and other facilities now on a single multipurpose campus. In addition, governmental and physical relations within the academic cities would probably be maintained in order to have the full benefits of the association. After all, it is reasonable to suppose that the multipurpose university itself developed to provide such mutual benefits. The case for its division is weakened once one recognizes the need for other means to achieve the collaboration now established. Foreign and especially Russian experience without the multipurpose university is instructive, since difficulties arise from the separation of academies of science, research institutes, and universities (Vicinich, 1956; De Witt, 1955, 1961). It may have been a historical accident that the United States developed its science establishment within teaching universities (Wolfle, 1972, p. 15), but this location now appears advantageous relative to the other possibilities.

At any rate, disaggregation proposals are unrealistic if only because of the enormous investment in the large American multipurpose university. The investment, besides its obvious financial and physical dimensions, is also heavily cultural and psychological. We are accustomed to functioning within a given institutional framework. I share this view, but I also believe that the multipurpose university is so desirable academically that I should prefer to establish it if we were starting from scratch. Undergraduate teaching can and does benefit from its association with graduate training and research, and the latter need not suffer because of the association. Similarly, an institutional mixture of basic and applied research strikes me as fruitful for both kinds of work. At the same time, I do not ignore the strains. An evident constant strain was exacerbated in rapid growth years, when professorial resources became insufficient to meet the simultaneously expanded demands for both teaching and research. But that strain, while most salient within the multipurpose university, can exist between institutions just as well; an essentially national shortage of faculty resources adversely affects students in exclusively teaching colleges no less than students in prestige universities. The consequences are just less apparent, and perhaps they linger less significantly than in large universities after expansion has ended.

A second evident strain, dating from the late 1960s, may turn out to be more transient. It arises from the ideological, political, and moral objections to certain programs of applied research under federal and occasionally private contract or grant. Although only a relatively small number of programs, mainly military in character, thus became controversial, they constituted the focal points of major campus crises of a sort peculiarly difficult to resolve. Except when security classification of research findings was involved, so as to clash with traditional academic values, a university found it virtually impossible to pick and choose on policy grounds among scientifically respectable projects that some of its professors wanted to undertake. Yet the accustomed posture of institutional neutrality, allowing faculty members to pursue under university auspices whatever legal research they thought worth doing, ceased to be accepted once the nation (and the campus)' no longer had a broad consensus about the legitimacy of government policy and so of the research conducted on its behalf. Substantial restoration of that consensus, either by a change in government policy or by another change in public and campus attitudes, would almost surely eliminate the problem. In the meantime, the university community, unable to constitute itself a court to judge the political and moral virtues of each research project, may at the worst of times be tempted to avoid its difficulties by abandoning applied research generally, or at least a large category of such research (Skolnick, 1969, p. 121)'. The temptation, however, is not nearly great enough, or durable enough, to overcome the significant external research commitments of the American university.

Finally, beyond thinking of the large multipurpose university as both practical and desirable, I believe that such a university is governable. Most of the different governing conceptions, derived from the different purposes of the university, are potentially reconcilable although uneasily so in some cases. That point, reiterated here, is meant to emerge from the analysis of the preceding chapters. It should also have become clear that the conceptions are not now reconciled in practice and that changes in their accommodation may well be in order. Something needs to be said about the nature of these changes. I have no radical proposals for the exclusion of any present claimants to power, nor for the distribution of power according to any single all-embracing governing conception. On the contrary, I have a conventionally pluralist view of university government, distinctive mainly by taking into account certain new external and internal forces that shape the contemporary university.

The first of these forces is new only, but most significantly, in its form and strength. It is the public's concern, reflected through elected and appointed officials, with a now large and expensive higher education serving a substantial proportion of the college-age population. Gone are the days when the public university, standing virtually alone as a given state's institution of higher education, spent but modest sums needed to serve the relatively small numbers of students able and willing to enroll in what was the alternative to the numerous private colleges. With many more students at the original state university campus and even more at new or revamped state institutions accorded a similar status, and with each institution providing more expensive per-student education than before, it should be easy to understand the growth in citizen concern for the enterprise. Although it is simplest to appreciate this rising concern as taxpayer response to larger appropriations, the budgetary factor is really an index of a broad public stake in a service that now reaches many citizens directly and indirectly. Quality as well as cost of that service is a legitimate state concern. Even if many rank-and-file voters often seem uninterested, legislators, governors, and other officials responsible for state government can hardly afford to overlook the substantial share of their budgeted resources going to higher education. Of course, they did not ignore this share even when it was smaller. Cuts in university proposals were always common. So were various state interventions in university management. But recently these interventions have become more systematic, reflecting both a new expertise and a determination to develop a kind of accountability of higher education to state authority resembling that of other state services. In this development the emergence of collective bargaining by university staff members plays a reciprocating role. Faculty unionism itself is partly a response to any transfer of decision-making authority from a campus to a higher level of state government; it also provides an additional reason for that transfer, since only those able to speak for the state's taxing and spending powers can make the contractual commitments sought in collective bargaining.

The developing state intervention that I am discussing should not be confused with politically motivated campaigns against the academic freedom of professors or students or with transient

overreactions to student disorders. Public concern for higher education need not be of this kind. There is a legitimate interest in the
ways in which tax money is spent. At times this interest may seem
inordinately directed to the organizational structure, as in the creation of coordinating councils or superboards over previously separate university units of one kind or another; but the purpose, almost always, is to achieve economy and efficiency in administration
and particularly to allocate funds without unnecessary duplication
of programs. Inevitably, then, a state administrative agency of some
kind, removed from the separate institutions or campuses, will determine which programs are to be developed at each place and at
what levels of fiscal support. It will do so under the authority of
governor and legislators, who might in the past have made such
determinations themselves but much more spasmodically. This observation helps to state the point that ought to be stressed. The
state's input is becoming more regular and probably more effective,
as befits the scale of the enterprise. It means, among other things,
that the interest of the public—nonstudent and student taxpayers—
in undergraduate education will be systematically represented as
against any internal, largely professorial pressures to concentrate on
graduate training and research. However the state's authority is
developed for this purpose, be it under a coordinating council, a
multicampus superboard, a department of education, or a general
gubernatorial budget-management office, it seems certain to include
an administrative corps primarily responsible to the public's elected
representatives rather than to faculty power in campus constituencies.

These elected representatives, we can asume, will hear from
students among other constituents interested in universities. As I
suggested at the end of the previous chapter, students have plainly
legitimate as well as potentially effective roles to play as state citizens
in governing the university. The case is very different from that
made for student power on a campus. There the one-person-one-vote
principle means authority simply for the majority that happens to
be in residence, overriding both the special credentials of professors
and the general credentials of all of a state's noncampus citizens,
who are also consumers and potential consumers of the university.
As voting citizens themselves, however, students assert no privileged
claims to power, although their immediate interest may well com-

that recourse has an occasional advocate (Searle, 1971, pp. 112–113). As I granted in the earlier discussion of trusteeship, the conception may be shaky but it endures because of understandable fears that it would be succeeded by something worse. Enduring, however, does not exclude gradual transformation of the old independent and intermediary trusteeship, uncertain anyway in many states, into a more plainly state authority. Boards of regents may then remain as power holders but not in the traditional manner, having so much in common with trusteeship of private institutions. The alternative, it seems to me, is the transfer of a good deal of their power to other agencies of state government.

So far, this summary discussion has proceeded as though only state government, and the public it represents, had a basis for concern with higher education. From what we know about massive federal funding of university programs, another public concern does exist. But I believe, on the basis of the experience reviewed earlier in this volume, that federal expenditures do not lead to direct federal government management of either state or private universities. They do lead, of course, to substantial federal influence. Some influence flows naturally from large-scale funding for particular programs rather than for others, and some from general conditions attached to federal funding. These conditions include accounting requirements and affirmative-action employment criteria. No doubt, these conditions are irksome to universities as they are to other state and private recipients of federal money. And there may be new and more irksome conditions. For example, as suggested earlier, national authority, probably through the courts, could end the much higher nonresident tuition charges of state universities. Yet such assertions of national interest, whether or not they flow from federal funding, will not in themselves supersede state authority. They will limit its discretion in certain important respects and establish general parameters within which the state's authority can be exercised. But, short of a fundamental shift of the American system from a federal to a unitary one, the states will retain their governmental responsibility for institutions of higher education. After all, they assumed that responsibility a century ago even when the funds to start, or first build up, most of their new institutions came from the federal land-grant legislation. Even very large future federal subsidies for general university education need not mean the federal government's assumption of direct control. The states can become the agents for distributing the greater federal funds along with state tax moneys.

If I am wrong about this projection of national-state relations in the United States, the case for public input into university government remains substantially intact. It would merely have to be adapted to a new national form of control. I regard this form as frightening in its size, and undesirable for other reasons too, but still feasible according to the precedents of other nations. No matter whether we are contemplating state or national units, the crucial matter is to recognize the legitimacy of citizen concern with a major tax-supported public service, and to provide the means for that concern to be effectively expressed through a responsible public authority. I make the point less bluntly than does Dwight Waldo (1969, 1970), who treats universities as state agencies founded as utilities; and I am sensitive to the dangers of heavy-handed control of higher education by nonacademic administrators or legislators. Great universities, I grant, are those whose faculties and their administrators have freedom and independence in developing academic programs. I want to preserve this freedom and independence within very broad limits, but no state service should be directed entirely by its professional experts. A faculty is the university's most important element, but it is not the whole of the enterprise. Even if it were, the faculty and its leadership should remain accountable to the community that the enterprise is designed to serve.

In short, I reject the doctrine that any purely internal university bodies, such as faculties, with *their* administrators, should have all the power to determine state educational policy within the limits only of a total appropriation. That doctrine, while rarely stated in these terms, is often implicit in professorial discussion of university government. Its elitist assumptions are worth noting, partly because many of the doctrine's implicit believers like to think of themselves as opposed to elitism and are quick to castigate it wherever they perceive it outside a university. Professors do have good, more or less elitist claims to considerable power over the academic areas within their professional competence. Such areas consist of their own fields and closely related matters of curriculum.

Hence, I stress the preservation of professorial decision making at departmental and similar collegial levels. It follows also that specialized professionalism is entitled to highly influential consultative status at other levels and in other areas. With respect to deciding which programs to develop, professors should be more than advisors but less than final arbiters. I have cited as an example of this kind of decision the distribution of state expenditures as between graduate training and undergraduate instruction, and I can add questions of allocating programs and resources among campuses, or even the decision to start a new program about which most of the academic community may be unenthusiastic. These are matters of public policy in which professors and campus administrators are highly informed, interested parties; their concerns should weigh heavily without independently and authoritatively determining the outcome. The limitation on the reach of professorial power is consistent with the sharper line to be drawn between campus and extracampus administrative authorities. These authorities must deal with each other in various bargaining relationships, but it will be helpful if agents of the state have decision-making areas distinct from those of professors and campus administrators. Professorial power, remaining at its established departmental levels, should be expected to respond to students as their consumer-based influence is fortified by a buyer's market and by collective political influence in and especially out of the university.

On the other side, while holding that policies distributing the state's resources are for the state's representatives to decide, I expect these representatives to be significantly responsive to campus interests. Admittedly, governors and legislators and their staffs are tempted to exert their popularly based authority to override educational considerations for purposes that may not always be respectable, or to assume, with the best intentions, responsibility for university policies that they should leave to academic administrative specialists. Such dangers always accompany political power. We cannot be sure that state officials, any more than university leaders, will be consistently good and wise. But we do know that public officials, elected or appointed, have good reason to take into account the university's several participating constituencies: students and their parents, the less numerous but more intensively mobilized staff members, and the citizen groups devoted more generally to the maintenance of a quality university. These constituencies provide potentially formidable resistance to an educationally damaging perversion of the state's legitimate general policy-making authority. Universities do not have to rely solely on the good will of elected officials.

The political relationships are not simple. A campus governed in academic matters by its professors and their administrators cannot itself settle all its affairs. In areas like budgetary allotments, it will, as always, have to try to influence state authority, be it a superboard, a governmental department of administration, a governor, a legislature, or a combination of these. Complicating these relationships is the apparent growth of collective bargaining. Its likely consequence is a direct confrontation, in the state's political arena, between the economic interests of university staff members and the interests of students and taxpayers in holding down educational costs. This consequence strikes me as more important than the impact of collective bargaining on internal academic affairs (since I believe that professorial unionism is compatible with established faculty governing power in departments and at similar levels). I have therefore stressed the ways that collective bargaining fosters the general tendency for major financial decisions to be made by state rather than university authority. More broadly, too, collective bargaining is consistent with existing pressures for university compliance with certain state standards. The relevant employment-relations statutes and regulations themselves represent state authority. The dangers of subjecting a university to all the standards applied to other state services need not be reiterated, but many members of the academic community will welcome those standards that constitute requirements for orderly procedures, open to public scrutiny and designed to protect staff and students from arbitrary administrative actions.

Looking back at my effort to reconcile the several conceptions of university government, I believe that *pluralism* best describes the proper ordering of university government. The term has many meanings, including one that is now a much criticized empirical description of the American political order. But I use pluralism here mainly in the straightforward prescriptive sense of acknowledging that numerous interests in and out of a large state university have legitimate claims to share in decision-making power or influence. Pluralism, as I understand it, rejects the exclusionary claims of any one set of interests, whether asserted by a majority or by a specialized minority, and it stands for the reordering of any governing arrangements that allow exclusionary claims to be successfully maintained while other interests are ignored or readily overridden. In accord with such principles, which are not always observed in universities, I submit my modest restatement and attempted clarification of existing governing arrangements. The modesty is consistent with a framework intended to fit the practical possibilities for governing a large and diverse state university. More fundamentally, however, it is also consistent with the values and purposes of this kind of multifunctional institution.

Here, it seems to me, is the point of the consciously political inquiry that I have undertaken. I make no claim that my intellectual discipline, as I understand it, offers scientifically established precepts for governing a university or anything else. Rather, what I try to offer is a way of looking at governmental problems that derives from experience and a body of thought developed from studies of other political institutions. Not every political scientist would derive the same outlook from the discipline's experience and body of thought. In particular, not every political scientist shares the pluralist theory, even in the broad sense of my definition. Majoritarians believe that according legitimacy to several diverse interests leads to an unfortunate frustration of the popular will in a political community. Applied to the multiversity, this perspective could support either a majority of state citizens or an internal university community, of faculty and/or students, as rightful holders of all important policy-making power. Or it could lead to separate institutions, each governed by a given majoritarian interest.

Pluralism implies no such clear-cut solutions. Certainly, from my viewpoint, it recognizes in so substantial a degree the legitimacy of the several diverse interests within a large university that it limits the powers of all external and internal majorities. And, while attempting to draw new and sharper lines between authorities than are now apparent, I acknowledge that boundaries are not definitively established. By its nature, pluralism leaves room for continuous adjustment of power relationships as interests develop and as functions change.

Bibliography

ABBOTT, F. C. "Organization of Higher Education Coordination: The Alternatives." *Compact*, June 1969, *3*, 9–11.

ADAMS, T. W., AND MURPHY, T. P. "NASA's University Research Programs: Dilemmas and Problems on the Government-Academic Interface." *Public Administration Review*, March 1967, *27*, 10–17.

ALBORNOZ, O. "Academic Freedom and Higher Education in Latin America." *Comparative Education Review*, June 1966, *10*, 250–257.

ALTBACH, P. "Japanese Students and Japanese Politics." *Comparative Education Review*, Oct. 1963, *7*, 181–187.

American Association of University Professors. "Statement on Government of Colleges and Universities." *AAUP Bulletin*, December 1966, *52*, 375–379.

American Association of University Professors. "Joint Statement on Rights and Freedoms of Students." *AAUP Bulletin*, Dec. 1967, *53*, 365–368.

American Association of University Professors. "Report of Committee T." *AAUP Bulletin*, June 1969, *55*, 183.

233

American Association of University Professors. *Freedom and Responsibility*. Washington, D.C.: Council of the AAUP, October 1970.

American Association of University Professors. "Statement on Collective Bargaining." *AAUP Bulletin,* December 1972, *58,* 423.

Antioch College. *Antioch Community Handbook*. Yellow Springs, Ohio: Antioch College, 1969.

ARON, R. "Student Rebellion: Vision of the Future or Echo of the Past?" *Political Science Quarterly,* June 1969, *84,* 289–310.

ASHBY, E. *Any Person, Any Study*. New York: McGraw-Hill, 1971.

ASHBY, E., AND ANDERSON, M. *The Rise of the Student Estate in Britain*. Cambridge, Mass.: Harvard University Press, 1970.

Assembly on University Goals and Governance. *A First Report*. Cambridge, Mass.: American Academy of Arts and Sciences, Jan. 1971.

AVORN, J. L. *Up Against the Ivy Wall*. New York: Atheneum, 1969.

AXELROD, J., FREEDMAN, M. B., HATCH, W. R., KATZ, J., AND SANFORD, N. *Search for Relevance*. San Francisco: Jossey-Bass, 1969.

BACHRACH, P. *The Theory of Democratic Elitism: A Critique*. Boston: Little, Brown, 1967.

BALDRIDGE, J. V. *Power and Conflict in the University*. New York: Wiley, 1971.

BARLOW, W. G. "Management and Collective Bargaining on the Campus."*Association of Governing Boards Reports,* Nov. 1970, *13,* 8–16.

BARZUN, J. *The American University: How It Runs, Where It Is Going*. New York: Harper, 1968.

BECK, R. P. *Men Who Control Our Universities*. New York: King's Crown Press, 1947.

BECKER, C. L. *Cornell University: Founders and Founding*. Ithaca, N.Y.: Cornell University Press, 1943.

BECKER, H. S. *Campus Power Struggle*. New York: Aldine, 1970.

BEN-DAVID, J., AND ZLOCZOWER, A. "Universities and Academic Systems in Modern Societies." *European Journal of Sociology,* 1962, *3,* 45–84.

BERDAHL, R. O. *British Universities and the State*. Berkeley: University of California Press, 1959.

BERDAHL, R. O. "Private Higher Education and State Governments." *Educational Record,* Summer 1970, *51,* 285–295.

BERDAHL, R. O. *Statewide Coordination of Higher Education*. Washington, D.C.: American Council on Education, 1971.

BETTELHEIM, B. "Obsolete Youth." *Encounter,* Sept. 1969, *33,* 29–42.

Board of Public Affairs. *Introduction to Report upon the Survey of the University of Wisconsin.* Madison: State of Wisconsin, 1914.

BOLTON, R. E. "The Economics and Public Financing of Higher Education: An Overview." *The Economics and Financing of Higher Education in the United States.* Joint Economic Committee, 91st Congress. Washington, D.C.: U.S. Government Printing Office, 1969.

BOWEN, W. G. *Economic Aspects of Education.* Princeton, N.J.: Industrial Relations Section, Princeton University, 1964.

BREWSTER, K. *The Report of the President.* New Haven, Conn.: Yale University, 1970.

BRUCE, P. A. *History of the University of Virginia, 1819–1919.* Vol. I. New York: Macmillan, 1920.

CAINE, S. *British Universities: Purposes and Prospects.* Toronto: University of Toronto Press, 1969.

CAPLOW, T., AND MC GEE, R. J. *The Academic Marketplace.* New York: Basic Books, 1958.

CARBONE, R. F. *Resident or Nonresident?* Denver: Education Commission of the States, 1970.

Carnegie Commission on Higher Education. *Quality and Equality: New Levels of Federal Responsibility for Higher Education.* New York: McGraw-Hill, 1968.

Carnegie Commission on Higher Education. *Quality and Equality: Revised Recommendations.* New York: McGraw-Hill, 1970.

Carnegie Commission on Higher Education. *The Capitol and the Campus.* New York: McGraw-Hill, 1971.

Carnegie Commission on Higher Education. *Institutional Aid: Federal Support to Colleges and Universities.* New York: McGraw-Hill, 1972.

Carnegie Commission on Higher Education. *Governance of Higher Education.* New York: McGraw-Hill, 1973.

CARR, R. K., AND VAN EYCK, D. K. *Collective Bargaining Comes to the Campus.* Washington, D.C.: American Council on Education, 1973.

CARTTER, A. M. "The Economics of Higher Education." In N. W. Chamberlain (Ed.), *Contemporary Economic Issues.* Homewood, Ill.: Irwin, 1969.

CATTELL, J. M., *University Control.* New York: Science Press, 1913.

CHAMBERS, M. M. *Higher Education: Who Pays? Who Governs?* Danville, Ill.: Interstate Printers and Publishers, 1968.

CHEIT, E. F. *The New Depression in Higher Education.* New York: McGraw-Hill, 1971.

CLARK, B. R. "Faculty Authority." *AAUP Bulletin,* Dec. 1961, *47,* 293–302.

CLARK, B. R., AND TROW, M. "The Organizational Context." In T. M. Newcomb and E. K. Wilson (Eds.), *College Peer Groups, Problems and Prospects for Research.* Chicago: University of Chicago Press, 1966.

COHEN, M. D., AND MARCH, J. G. *Leadership and Ambiguity.* New York: McGraw-Hill, 1973.

COLE, S. *The Unionization of Teachers.* New York: Praeger, 1969.

Columbia University. *Proposal for a University Senate.* New York: Columbia Faculty Executive Committee, 1969.

Congressional Quarterly. *Education for a Nation.* Washington, D.C.: Congressional Quarterly, 1972.

CORSON, J. J. *Governance of Colleges and Universities.* New York: McGraw-Hill, 1960.

Cox Commission. *Crisis at Columbia.* New York: Random House, 1968.

CREMIN, L. A. *The Transformation of the School: Progressivism in American Education, 1876–1937.* New York: Knopf, 1962.

CURTI, M., AND CARSTENSEN, V. *The Universtiy of Wisconsin, 1848–1925.* Madison: University of Wisconsin Press, 1949.

DAHL, R. A. *After the Revolution?* New Haven, Conn.: Yale University Press, 1970.

DAVIS, N. P. *Lawrence and Oppenheimer.* New York: Fawcett, 1968.

DEMERATH, N. J., STEPHENS, R. W., AND TAYLOR, R. R. *Power, Presidents, and Professors.* New York: Basic Books, 1967.

DE WITT, N. *Soviet Professional Manpower.* Washington, D.C.: National Science Foundation, 1955.

DE WITT, N. "Reorganization of Science and Research in the U.S.S.R." *Science,* June 23, 1961, *133,* 1981–1991.

DONOGHUE, J. R., AND SHANNON, T. J. *The Training of Future Academic Administrators.* Madison: University of Wisconsin–Extension, 1972.

DRESSEL, P. L., JOHNSON, F. C., AND MARCUS, P. M. *The Confidence Crisis.* San Francisco: Jossey-Bass, 1970.

DUBIN, R., AND BEISSE, F. "The Assistant: Academic Subaltern." In C. E. Kruytbosch and S. L. Messinger (Eds.), *The State of the University.* Beverly Hills: Sage Publications, 1970.

DUSTER, T. "Student Interests, Student Power, and the Swedish Experience." *American Behavioral Scientist,* May–June 1968, *11,* 21–27.

EPSTEIN, L. *Citizens and Their State University.* Madison: University of Wisconsin Institute of Governmental Affairs, 1971.

ERIKSON, E. H. "Reflections on the Dissent of Contemporary Youth." *Daedalus,* Winter 1970, *99,* 154–176.

ETZIONI, A. *Toward Higher Education in an Active Society: Three Policy Guidelines.* New York and Washington, D.C.: Center for Policy Research, 1970.

EULAU, H., AND QUINLEY, H. *American State Officials and Higher Education.* New York: McGraw-Hill, 1970.

FEUER, L. S. *The Conflict of Generations.* New York: Basic Books, 1969.

FISK, T. "The Nature and Causes of Student Unrest." *Political Quarterly,* Oct.–Dec. 1969, *40,* 419–425.

FLACKS, R. "The Liberated Generation: An Exploration of the Roots of Student Protest." In J. McEvoy and A. Miller (Eds.), *Black Power and Student Rebellion.* Belmont, Cal.: Wadsworth, 1969.

FLEXNER, A. *Universities: American, English, German.* New York: Oxford University Press, 1930.

FRIEDENBERG, E. Z. "The University Community in an Open Society." *Daedalus,* Winter 1970, *99,* 56–74.

GALBRAITH, J. K. *The New Industrial State.* Boston: Houghton Mifflin, 1967.

GALLANT, J. A., AND PROTHERO, J. W. "Weight-Watching at the University: The Consequences of Growth." *Science,* Jan. 28, 1972, *175,* 381–388.

GERZON, M. *The Whole World Is Watching.* New York: Paperback Library, 1970.

GLENNY, L. J. *Autonomy of Public Colleges: The Challenge of Coordination.* New York: McGraw-Hill, 1959.

GOODMAN, P. *Growing Up Absurd.* New York: Vintage, 1960.

GOODMAN, P. *The Community of Scholars.* New York: Random House, 1962.

GRAUBARD, S. T. Preface to "The Embattled University." *Daedalus,* Winter 1970, *99,* v–xvi.

GRODZINS, M. "Centralization and Decentralization in the American Federal System." In R. A. Goldwin (Ed.), *A Nation of States.* Chicago: Rand McNally, 1963.

GROSS, E. "Universities as Organizations: A Research Approach." *American Sociological Review,* Aug. 1968, *33,* 518–543.

GUSFIELD, J. R. "Student Protest and University Response." *Annals of the American Academy of Political and Social Science,* May 1971, *395,* 26–38.

HALPERIN, S. *A University in the Web of Politics.* New Brunswick, N.J.: Eagleton Institute of Politics, Rutgers University, 1960.

HALSEY, A. H. "British Universities." *European Journal of Sociology,* 1962, *3,* 85–101.

HALSEY, A. H., AND TROW, M. A. *The British Academics.* Cambridge, Mass.: Harvard University Press, 1971.

HANDLIN, O., AND HANDLIN, M. *The American College and American Culture.* New York: McGraw-Hill, 1970.

HANSEN, W. L., AND WEISBROD, B. A. *Benefits, Costs, and Finance of Higher Education.* Chicago: Markham, 1969.

HANSEN, W. L., AND WEISBROD, B. *A New Approach to Higher Education Finance.* Madison: Institute for Research on Poverty, University of Wisconsin, Feb. 1970.

HANSEN, W. L., AND WEISBROD, B. "On the Distribution of Costs and Benefits of Public Higher Education." *Journal of Human Resources,* 1971a, *6,* 363–376.

HANSEN, W. L., AND WEISBROD, B. *On the Distribution of Costs and Benefits of Public Higher Education: Reply.* Madison: Institute for Research on Poverty, University of Wisconsin, 1971b.

HARRIS, S. E. *A Statistical Portrait of Higher Education.* New York: McGraw-Hill, 1972.

HARTNETT, R. T. "College and University Trustees." In C. E. Kruytbosch and S. L. Messinger (Eds.), *The State of the University.* Beverly Hills: Sage Publications, 1970.

HARTNETT, R. T. *College and University Trustees.* Princeton, N.J.: Educational Testing Service, 1969.

HEFFERLIN, JB L. *Dynamics of Academic Reform.* San Francisco: Jossey-Bass, 1969.

HODGKINSON, H. L. *Institutions in Transition.* Berkeley: Carnegie Commission on Higher Education, 1970.

HODGKINSON, H. L. "Broadly-Based Senates: A First Report." *Research Reporter,* 1973, *8,* 5–8.

HOFSTADTER, R. *Academic Freedom in the Age of the College.* New York: Columbia University Press, 1964.

HOOK, S. *Academic Freedom and Academic Anarchy.* New York: Cowles Book Co., 1969.

HUITT, R. K. "Governance in the 1970's." In H. L. Hodgkinson and L. R. Meeth (Eds.), *Power and Authority*. San Francisco: Jossey-Bass, 1971.

JASTROW, J. "The Administrative Peril in Education." In J. M. Cattell (Ed.), *University Control*. New York: Science Press, 1913.

JENCKS, C., AND RIESMAN, D. *The Academic Revolution*. Garden City, N.Y.: Doubleday, 1968.

JOHNSON, H. G. "The Economics of the 'Brain Drain': The Canadian Case." *Minerva*, Spring 1965, *3*, 299–311.

JOUGHIN, L. (Ed.) *Academic Freedom and Tenure: A Handbook of the American Association of University Professors*. Madison: University of Wisconsin Press, 1967.

KAMMERER, G. H. "The State University as a Political System." *Journal of Politics*. May 1969, *31*, 289–310.

KAYSEN, C. *The Higher Learning, The Universities and the Public*. Princeton, N.J.: Princeton University Press, 1969.

KELLEY, G. L. "The Politics of Higher Educational Coordination in Wisconsin, 1965–1969." Unpublished doctoral dissertation, University of Wisconsin, 1972.

KENISTON, K., AND LERNER, M. "Campus Characteristics and Campus Unrest." *Annals of the American Academy of Political and Social Science*, May 1971, *395*, 39–53.

KENNAN, G. *Democracy and the Student Left*. New York: Bantam Books, 1968.

KERR, C. *The Uses of the University*. New York: Harper, 1966.

KERR, C. "Governance of the Universities." *Daedalus*, Fall 1969, *98*, 1104.

KERR, C. "Presidential Discontent." In D. Nichols (Ed.), *Perspectives on Campus Tensions*. Washington, D.C.: American Council on Education, 1970.

KIDD, H. *The Trouble at L.S.E.* London: Oxford University Press, 1969.

KIRK, R. *Academic Freedom*. Chicago: Regnery, 1955.

KRUYTBOSCH, C. E., AND MESSINGER, S. L. "Unequal Peers: The Situation of Researchers." *American Behavioral Scientist*, May–June 1968, *11*, 33–43.

KUGLER, I. "The Union Speaks for Itself." *Educational Record*, Fall 1968, *49*, 414–418.

KUGLER, I. "Collective Bargaining for the Faculty." *Liberal Education*, March 1970, *56*, 78–85.

LAKOFF, S. (Ed.) *Private Government*. Glenview, Ill.: Scott, Foresman, 1973.

LAZARSFELD, P. "The Sociology of Empirical Social Research." *American Sociological Review*, Dec. 1962, *27*, 757–767.

LAZARSFELD, P., AND THIELENS, W. *The Academic Mind*. New York: Free Press, 1958.

LEE, E. C., AND BOWEN, F. M. *The Multicampus University*. New York: McGraw-Hill, 1971.

LEVI, E. *Plenary Sessions of the Conference on Negro Colleges*. Boston: American Academy of Arts and Sciences, March 1969.

LIEBERMAN, M. "Representational Systems in Higher Education." Is S. Elam and R. H. Moskow (Eds.), *Employment Relations in Higher Education*. Bloomington, Ind.: Phi Delta Kappa, 1969.

LIEBERMAN, M. "Professors, Unite!" *Harper's*, Oct. 1971, *243*, 61–70.

LIPSET, S. M. *Rebellion in the University*. Boston: Little, Brown, 1972.

LITT, E. *The Public Vocational University*. New York: Holt, 1969.

LUNSFORD, T. F. "Authority and Ideology in the Administered University." *American Behavioral Scientist*, May–June 1968, *11*, 5–14.

MASON, H. L. *College and University Government: A Handbook of Principle and Practice*. New Orleans: Department of Political Science, Tulane University, 1972.

MCCONNELL, G. "The Spirit of Private Government." *American Political Science Review*, Sept. 1958, *52*, 754–770.

MCCONNELL, T. R. "Faculty Government." In H. L. Hodgkinson and L. R. Meeth (Eds.), *Power and Authority*. San Francisco: Jossey-Bass, 1971a.

MCONNELL, T. R. *The Redistribution of Power in Higher Education*. Berkeley: Center for Research and Development in Higher Education, University of California, 1971b.

MCCONNELL, T. R., AND MORTIMER, K. P. *The Faculty in University Governance*. Berkeley: Center for Research and Development in Higher Education, University of California, 1971.

MCGRATH, E. J. *Should Students Share the Power?* Philadelphia: Temple University Press, 1970.

METZGER, W. P. *Academic Freedom in the Age of the University*. New York: Columbia University Press, 1964.

MILLETT, J. D. *The Academic Community*. New York: McGraw-Hill, 1962.

MILLETT, J. D. "State Administration of Higher Education." *Public Administration Review*, March/April 1970, *30*, 101–106.

MINOGUE, K. R. *Student Militancy at the London School of Economics.* London: London School of Economics, April 1969. Mimeographed memorandum.

MOONEY, R. L. "The Problem of Leadership in the University." In O. Milton and E. J. Shobe, Jr. (Eds.), *Learning and the Professors.* Athens, Ohio: Ohio University Press, 1968.

MOOS, M., AND ROURKE, F. E. *The Campus and the State.* Baltimore: Johns Hopkins Press, 1959.

MOSHER, F. C. *Democracy and the Public Service.* New York: Oxford University Press, 1968.

MUSHKIN, S. J. "Public Financing of Higher Education." In L. Wilson (Ed.), *Universal Higher Education.* Washington, D.C.: American Council on Education, 1972.

National Science Foundation. *Federal Support to Universities and Colleges, Fiscal Year 1967.* Washington, D.C.: U.S. Government Printing Office, 1968.

NEWCOMB, T. "University, Heal Thyself." *Political Science Quarterly,* June 1969, *84,* 351–366.

NISBET, R. "The Future of the University." *Commentary,* Feb. 1971, *51,* 62–71.

NOVAK, M. *A Theology for Radical Politics.* New York: Herder and Herder, 1969.

OBERER, W. E. "Faculty Participation in Academic Decision Making." In S. Elam and R. H. Moskow (Eds.), *Employment Relations in Higher Education.* Bloomington, Ind.: Phi Delta Kappa, 1969.

ORLANS, H. *The Effects of Federal Programs on Higher Education.* Washington, D.C.: Brookings Institution, 1962.

ORLANS, H. (Ed.) *Science Policy and the University.* Washington, D.C.: Brookings Institution, 1968.

OSTROM, V. "Education and Politics." In N. B. Henry (Ed.), *Social Forces Influencing American Education.* Chicago: University of Chicago Press, 1961.

PALOLA, E. G., LEHMANN, T., AND BLISCHKE, W. R. *Higher Education by Design: The Sociology of Planning.* Berkeley: Center for Research and Development in Higher Education, University of California, 1970.

PECHMAN, J. "The Distributional Effects of Public Higher Education in California." *Journal of Human Resources,* Summer 1970, *5,* 361–370.

PETERSEN, W. "What Is Left at Berkeley." In S. M. Lipset and S.

Wolin (Eds.), *The Berkeley Student Revolt.* Garden City, N.Y.: Doubleday, 1965.

PLATT, G. M., AND PARSONS, T. "Decision-Making in the Academic System: Influence and Power Exchange." In C. E. Kruytbosch and S. L. Messinger (Eds.), *The State of the University.* Beverly Hills: Sage Publications, 1968.

PRESTHUS, R. *The Organizational Society.* New York: Knopf, 1962.

RAUH, M. A. *The Trusteeship of Colleges and Universities.* New York: McGraw-Hill, 1969.

REAGEN, M. D. *Science and the Federal Patron.* New York: Oxford University Press, 1969.

RIESMAN, D. "Universities on Collision Course." *Trans-Action,* Sept. 1969, *6,* 3–4.

ROOSE, K. J., AND ANDERSEN, C. J. *A Rating of Graduate Programs.* Washington, D.C.: American Council on Education, 1970.

ROSZAK, T. *The Making of a Counter Culture.* Garden City, N.Y.: Doubleday, 1969.

ROURKE, F. E., AND BROOKS, G. E. *The Managerial Revolution in Higher Education.* Baltimore: Johns Hopkins Press, 1966.

RUDOLPH, F. *The American College and University.* New York: Random House, 1962.

RUML, B. *Memo to a College Trustee.* New York: McGraw-Hill, 1959.

SAGEN, H. B., AND HARCLEROAD, F. F. "The Developing State Colleges and Universities: Innovation or Imitation?" *North Central Association Quarterly,* Spring 1970, *44,* 345–351.

SCHNEIDER, J. "The Impact of Federal Funding on the Operation and Structure of the University Department." Unpublished doctoral dissertation, University of Wisconsin, 1971.

SCHOENBAUM, D. "The Free University of Berlin, or, How Free Can a University Be?" *AAUP Bulletin,* Spring 1973, *59,* 5–9.

SCHULTZ, T. W. "Education and Economic Growth." In N. B. Henry (Ed.), *Social Forces Influencing American Education.* Chicago: University of Chicago Press, 1961.

SCHULTZ, T. W. *The Economic Value of Education.* New York: Columbia University Press, 1963.

SCHULTZ, T. W. "Resources for Higher Education: An Economist's View." *Journal of Political Economy,* May/June 1968, *76,* 327–347.

Scranton Commission. *The Report of the President's Commission on Campus Unrest.* Washington, D.C.: U.S. Government Printing Office, 1970.

SEARLE, J. R. *The Campus War*. New York: World Publishing Co., 1971.

SHARKANSKY, I. "Communications." *Journal of Human Resources,* Spring 1970, *5,* 230–236.

SIEGFRIED, J. J., AND WHITE, K. J. *Financial Rewards to Research and Teaching: A Case Study of Academic Economists.* Madison: Social Systems Research Institute, University of Wisconsin, 1972.

SINGLETARY, O. A. (Ed.) *American Universities and Colleges.* Washington, D.C.: American Council on Education, 1968.

SKOLNICK, J. H. *The Politics of Protest*. New York: Ballantine Books, 1969.

SPENDER, S. *The Year of the Young People.* New York: Random House, 1968.

STINCHCOMBE, A. L. "Social Structure and Organization." In J. G. March (Ed.), *Handbook of Organizations.* Chicago: Rand McNally, 1965.

STROUP, H. *Bureaucracy in Higher Education.* New York: Free Press, 1966.

Study Commission on University Governance. *The Culture of the University: Governance and Education.* Berkeley: University of California, 1968.

SUMMERSKILL, J. *President Seven.* New York: World Publishing Co., 1971.

TROW, M. "The Democratization of Higher Education in America." *European Journal of Sociology,* 1962, *3,* 231–262.

TROW, M. "Reflections on the Transition from Mass to Higher Education." *Daedalus,* Winter 1970, *99,* 1–42.

TROW, M. *The Expansion and Transformation of Higher Education.* New York: General Learning Press, 1972.

U.S. Bureau of the Census. *School Enrollment in the United States: 1972.* Washington, D.C.: U.S. Government Printing Office, 1973.

U.S. Department of Health, Education, and Welfare. *Report on Higher Education.* Washington, D.C.: U.S. Government Printing Office, 1971.

University of Kansas. *Senate Code.* Lawrence: University of Kansas, 1969.

USDAN, M. D., MINAR, D. W., AND HURWITZ, E. *Education and State Politics.* New York: Teachers College Press, Columbia University, 1969.

VEBLEN, T. *The Higher Learning in America.* New York: Hill and Wang, 1957. Original publication 1918.

VEYSEY, L. R. *The Emergence of the American University.* Chicago: University of Chicago Press, 1965.

VICINICH, A. *The Soviet Academy of Sciences.* Stanford: Stanford University Press, 1956.

WALDO, D. "The University as Power Center." *Educational Record,* Summer 1969, *50,* 279–285.

WALDO, D. "The University in Relation to the Governmental-Political." *Public Administration Review,* March/April 1970, *30,* 106–113.

WALLERSTEIN, I. *University in Turmoil.* New York: Atheneum, 1969.

WATSON, R. A., AND DOWNING, R. G. *The Politics of the Bench and Bar.* New York: Wiley, 1969.

WEBER, M. *The Theory of Social and Economic Organization.* A. H. Henderson and T. Parsons (Trans.) New York: Free Press, 1947.

WEST, E. D., AND ANDERSEN, C. J. "Changing Public/Private Ratios in Higher Education." *Educational Record,* Fall 1970, *51,* 347–350.

WILSON, L. *The Academic Man.* New York: Oxford University Press, 1942.

WOLFF, R. P. *The Idea of the University.* Boston: Beacon Press, 1969.

WOLFLE, D. *The Home of Science: The Role of the University.* New York: McGraw-Hill, 1972.

WOODRING, P. *The Higher Learning in America: A Reassessment.* New York: McGraw-Hill, 1968.

WRIGHT, C. A. "The Constitution on the Campus." *Vanderbilt Law Review,* Oct. 1969, *22,* 1027–1088.

ZINN, H. *Disobedience and Democracy.* New York: Random House, 1968.

Index

A

ABBOTT, F. C., 60

Academic, as student type, 171-172, 174, 214-215

Academic cities, 219-220

Academic freedom: administration related to, 113; in pluralistic system, 222-223; and professorialism, 119-123; and state government, 38; and student protests, 187

Accountability, 141-142, 222

Accreditation, 164

ADAMS, T. W., 51

Administration and administrators: academic, 105-106; adequacy of, 113-114; budgeting authority of, 106-109; and collective bargaining, 144, 156-158; collegial, 102-106; as community of power, 101, 102; detached, 114, 151, 158; hierarchical, 99-101, 103, 106-107, 110-113; and managerialism, 99-114; and organized student power, 188-189; in pluralistic system, 215, 224; power of restricted, 108-109, 112-113; professorialism related to, 139; and regents, 77, 82, 89, 93-94; scholarly study of, 110-111; and teacher-scholars, 103-104, 157

Agriculture, regent representatives of, 81, 85

ALBORNOZ, O., 209

ALTBACH, P., 184

American Association of University Professors, 76-77, 117, 119-121, 125, 138, 149, 153, 158, 195